Dinner Made Simple

Dinner Made Simple

35 Everyday Ingredients, 350 Easy Recipes

by the Editors of REALSIMPLE

Oxmoor HOUSE.

REAL SIMPLE

EXECUTIVE EDITOR: Sarah Collins
DESIGN DIRECTOR: Abbey Kuster-Prokell
FOOD DIRECTOR: Sarah Copeland
DEPUTY PHOTO EDITOR: Kelly Clark
ART DIRECTOR: Alyce Jones
FOOD ASSISTANT: Heath Goldman
COPY CHIEF: Nancy Negovetich
EDITORIAL PRODUCTION MANAGER:
Albert Young

TIME INC. BOOKS

SENIOR EDITOR: Betty Wong
EDITORIAL ASSISTANT: Nicole Fisher
ASSISTANT PROJECT EDITOR: Lacie Pinyan
DESIGNERS: Michele Outland, Allison Chi
SENIOR PRODUCTION MANAGER:
Greg A. Amason
ASSISTANT PRODUCTION DIRECTOR:
Sue Chodakiewicz
COPY EDITORS: Adrienne Davis,
Jasmine Hodges
INDEXER: Mary Ann Laurens
FELLOWS: Natalie Schumann,
Mallory Short

Photographs by Johnny Miller,
Food Styling by Rebecca Jurkevich,
Prop Styling by Amy Wilson:
pages 1-11, 16-17, 298-299, 352

For additional credits, see page 341.

ISBN-13: 978-0-8487-4689-6
ISBN-10: 0-8487-4689-9

Library of Congress Control
Number: 2015958963

First Edition 2016

Printed in the United States
of America

10 9 8 7 6 5 4 3 2 1

Time Inc. Books products may
be purchased for business or
promotional use. For information
on bulk purchases, please contact
Christi Crowley in the Special Sales
Department at 845-895-9858.

We welcome your comments and
suggestions about Time Inc. Books.
Visit timeincbooks.com

For busy cooks everywhere

Contents

Introduction

When my then boyfriend and I were in graduate school and had no money but a lot of time, we used to cook regularly from Mollie Katzen's *The Enchanted Broccoli Forest* cookbook. We were quasi-vegetarians, and Katzen offered many recipes that featured the ingredients that we loved. The recipe we made most was a complicated "Greek pizza," which involved not pizza dough but phyllo, for reasons I was never able to explain.

That boyfriend is now my husband, and while we have more money now, we also have a lot less time. Although I remember that Greek pizza fondly, I also remember that making it involved carefully brushing melted butter over sheets and sheets and sheets of phyllo and stacking them—neatly, precisely—on a baking pan. Of course, the phyllo dough, being phyllo dough, sometimes ripped, which made me mad. But what's a little ripped phyllo when you're young and in love?

Having gained a couple of decades of wisdom, I've come to understand that I should avoid situations that make me mad in the kitchen, and so I have broken up with phyllo. Regular pizza dough, however, survived my transition to full-blown adulthood. When you fall in love with an ingredient, as with a man, you sometimes get lucky and you stay in love.

The genius thing about this, the latest cookbook by *Real Simple*, is that you can head straight for the ingredients you love and skip the ones that make you mad. Whether your favorite thing is apples or zucchini, you will find 10 recipes that celebrate the diversity of that thing. And if your favorite ingredient is pizza dough, just know that you haven't lived until you've eaten it fried, with chocolate sauce on the side (page 175). I'd like to see phyllo dough try that.

Kristin van Ogtrop

The Ingredients

Each of the recipes in this book starts with an everyday ingredient. Put these ingredients in heavy rotation on your grocery list and you'll have the makings for an endless number of satisfying, no-brainer meals.

APPLES

For baking (or just plain snacking), opt for sweet, crisp varieties—like Fuji, Braeburn, Empire, Gala, and Pink Lady. Tart apples (Granny Smith, we're looking at you) are best in savory dishes. Avoid apples with bruises, which usually signal mealy flesh underneath. To check for ripeness, flick an apple near its stem: Listen for a dull thud, which indicates you've found a ripe one. (A hollow sound means the apple is a bit too ripe.) Store apples in the vegetable drawer of the refrigerator for up to three weeks—cold maintains crispness.

AVOCADOS

Pebbly-skinned Hass avocados are more flavorful than smooth-skinned Fuertes. Choose avocados that are firm but give slightly, then ripen them at home. When selecting, don't squeeze too hard. Instead, cup the avocado in your hand and feel it gently with your fingers. To ripen avocados, store them on a countertop at room temperature. Extend the life of a ripe one by keeping it in the refrigerator, unbagged, for about three days. Avocados can be frozen as a puree (with a few drops of lemon juice) for up to two months for later use.

BAKED HAM

The most popular variety is city ham, which is wet-cured, or injected with a brine made of salt, sugar, and seasonings. Bone-in city hams tend to be more moist and flavorful than the boneless variety, but both come ready to eat. The shank end is easier to carve than the butt (or sirloin end) and is also juicier, with a higher ratio of fat. Look for a presliced spiral-cut ham for easy serving. Shrink-wrapped baked ham will last, unopened, for two weeks in the refrigerator and for three to five days after opening.

BASS

There's a wide variety of bass available on the market. Striped bass, white sea bass, bronzino, and barramundi are all members of the bass family, boasting mild, sweet white flesh. Ask your fishmonger for the most sustainable option. Aim for fish delivered that day or the day before at the latest. A strong fishy smell means it's not fresh. Leave the fish in its original packaging and, if possible, place on a bowl of ice in the refrigerator for up to two days.

BEANS

Nutritional powerhouses that deliver tons of fiber and protein for pennies, canned beans make a filling addition to salads and soups. Unopened, undented cans last about two years in the pantry. Leftover beans will keep in a sealed container for up to five days.

BROCCOLI

Look for heads that have firm stalks and tight, dark green clusters of buds. Yellowing florets and woody stalks with holes at the base are signs that a head is past its prime. Refrigerate unwashed broccoli in a plastic bag in the vegetable drawer for up to five days.

BUTTERNUT SQUASH

A hearty addition to stews, soups, and pastas, whole butternut squash will stay fresh for up to three months in your pantry. (Keep the stem on to retain moisture.) Look for squash with a hard, tough rind—a tender rind means that the squash isn't ripe. After it is cut open or cooked, butternut squash keeps for up to five days in the refrigerator, wrapped in plastic or stored in an airtight container.

CARROTS

Choose bright orange carrots that are firm, without cracks. Try to buy carrots without greens, which can leach moisture and nutrients. Place carrots in a resealable plastic bag in the crisper drawer for up to two weeks. If you want sticks for snacking, peel, wash, and slice the carrots, then store them in a container filled with ¼ cup water.

CHICKEN CUTLETS

Store-bought chicken cutlets can also be labeled as "thin-cut breast." Store in the original packaging in the refrigerator for up to two days or in the freezer for up to six months. If the pieces aren't shrink-wrapped, wrap them individually before slipping them into a freezer bag to avoid freezer burn.

CHICKEN THIGHS

Chicken is the most perishable type of meat, so make sure it's not close to its sell-by date. Steer clear of dry-looking meat (thighs should look plump), and sniff before buying. Put back any package that smells off. Store in the refrigerator in the original packaging for two days or in the freezer for up to six months.

CORN

Look for grassy green, tightly wrapped husks. The silk should be glossy and pale yellow; the stem, moist. Squeeze the ear to feel whether the kernels are closely spaced, firm, and round. Refrigerate ears unshucked in a bag. Corn is best within 24 hours of purchasing (afterward the sugar turns to starch), but it will last for three days.

EGGS

It's worth paying more for organic eggs if they are an option. Omega-3–enriched eggs are an especially good choice for vegetarians, because they can contain up to 10 times more omega-3s than standard eggs do. Other common designations, like "free-range" and "pasture-raised," are not clear-cut, because they're not regulated by the federal government, and certification is voluntary. In the refrigerator, eggs do best where the temperature is most consistent—on the middle shelf. Store in the original cartons. (Don't transfer to the refrigerator's egg holder.) Raw, unshelled eggs last for up to five weeks.

FLANK STEAK

This long, flat cut from the belly muscle has a distinctive vertical grain. Look for a piece that has a uniform thickness so that it cooks as evenly as possible. (When overcooked, it can get tough and stringy.) Store wrapped in the refrigerator for up to three days.

GROUND BEEF

When you can, opt for ground chuck, which is typically 80 or 85 percent lean. A lot of the extra fat drains off as the meat cooks, which loosens the interior structure of the meat, so you end up with a juicy, less dense, more tender burger. Ground meat lasts for two days in the refrigerator; in the freezer, double-wrapped in film and foil, it lasts for four months.

GROUND TURKEY

Look for organic ground turkey and skip the lean varieties for the juiciest, most flavorful results. When checking out at the grocery store, make sure that the turkey is put in its own plastic bag so it can't contaminate produce if it leaks. Store in your refrigerator for up to two days or in the freezer, double-wrapped in film and foil, for four months.

ITALIAN SAUSAGE

These links come in hot and sweet blends. Made with coarsely ground fresh pork, they're flavored with garlic and fennel seed. Store in the refrigerator for two days or in the freezer, double-wrapped in film and foil, for up to two months.

KALE

Tuscan kale, also called lacinato or dinosaur, is the most tender variety, but you can use curly kale interchangeably. Choose bunches with stems shorter than 12 inches. Look for deep green, evenly colored leaves with no dried-out yellow patches. Store in the refrigerator, in a plastic bag, for up to three days.

MOZZARELLA

Balls of fresh mozzarella (buffalo mozzarella) should smell fresh and milky and, ideally, come packed in salt water or whey. Alternative varieties include bocconcini (small balls of fresh mozzarella) and burrata (fresh mozzarella that's filled with cream and pieces of mozzarella). Store in the refrigerator for about three days. Shrink-wrapped mozzarella will keep, unopened, for a week.

OATMEAL

For oatmeal that takes just minutes to cook, look for quick-cooking (also referred to as instant) oatmeal or old-fashioned rolled oats. Steel-cut oats, which look similar to rice, take longer to cook and maintain their chewy, granular texture. Store opened oats in an airtight container in the pantry for one month or in the freezer for six months.

PIZZA DOUGH

Balls of refrigerated pizza dough can be found in the cheese, dairy, or produce aisle. Some stores also carry frozen dough in one-pound balls, which are a great option because they keep for three months, versus three days for the refrigerated kind. If you come up empty-handed, ask your local pizza parlor if it will sell you its dough by the pound.

PORK TENDERLOIN

This lean, tender cut from the end of the loin is pale pink and has a fine grain. Long, narrow, and tapering at one end, it cooks quickly and is a good choice for weeknight dinners. Store in the refrigerator for three days or in the freezer, double-wrapped in film and foil, for six months.

POTATOES

Spuds can be divided into three basic categories: starchy, medium-starch, and waxy. Starchy potatoes, like russets, absorb other flavors well and are great for frying and baking. Waxy potatoes, like Red Bliss, are better for soups and salads, because they hold their shape when cooked. Select potatoes that are firm, smooth, and free of sprouts, eyes, and soft patches. Refrigeration adversely affects their flavor, so store in a cool, dry place (like the pantry) in paper bags. (Plastic bags trap moisture and speed decay.) Most varieties should last three weeks.

QUINOA

Tasty in breakfast bowls, soups, and salads, this small, gluten-free seed can be used like a whole grain and is available in red, white, or black varieties. Give it a good wash before cooking to remove the naturally bitter coating. Store in an airtight container in the pantry for one month or in the freezer for six months. Store cooked quinoa in the refrigerator for up to five days.

RICOTTA

This ultra-soft cheese is made from fresh whole or skimmed milk and acid. It should taste sweet and creamy, like fresh dairy—never sour or funky. The texture varies from slightly granular to smooth, depending on how it's made. After opening, store in the refrigerator for up to one week.

ROTISSERIE CHICKEN

A plump, golden brown chicken is usually a juicy one. If the skin is shriveled and looks dry, the meat probably is, too. For the same reason, avoid a chicken that's very dark—it may have been in the oven too long. Use the chicken while it's still fresh and warm if you can, or store it, well wrapped, in the refrigerator for up to three days.

SALAD GREENS

Purchase loose bunches of greens or greens packed in clamshells, not plastic bags. The greens should be fresh and perky. Avoid any that look damp or slimy—a telltale sign that bacteria is starting to develop. To store, transfer the greens to an airtight container or line the clamshell with paper towels, which will absorb excess moisture. Salad greens stay fresh for three to five days. (Be sure to follow the sell-by date.)

SALMON FILLETS

Pick salmon fillets that appear deep orange, glossy, and moist. Salmon should smell slightly salty, like the ocean, but never fishy. Common varieties include king, sockeye, coho, pink, and chum. If you're deciding between wild and farmed, choose wild Alaskan salmon when possible. Leave the fish in its original packaging and place on a bowl or rimmed plate with ice in the refrigerator for up to two days.

SHRIMP

The shiny, plump shrimp at the seafood counter may seem like your best bet, but frozen shrimp in packaging printed with the letters IQF (individually quick frozen) are preferable. Almost all shrimp are frozen to keep them fresh during shipping. Shrimp labeled "fresh" are usually thawed frozen shrimp marked up at a premium. To cut down on prep time, buy frozen shrimp that are peeled and deveined. Store in the freezer for up to six months.

SIRLOIN

Look for pieces that are a light cherry color (never dark red), with white marbling throughout. Store in the refrigerator for three days or in the freezer, double-wrapped in film and foil, for six months.

SMOKED SALMON

Smoked salmon comes cold smoked and hot smoked (and is not to be confused with lox, which is cured in salt). Cold smoked is exposed to smoke but is not cooked through, so it looks silky and translucent pink. Hot smoked is cooked all the way through and has a firm, flaky texture. (Most recipes call for cold smoked.) Unopened, smoked salmon will last for about two weeks in the refrigerator; opened, for about one week. Store in the freezer, double-wrapped in film and foil, for up to two months.

SPAGHETTI

Made of little more than semolina flour, water, and salt, dried pasta can be stored at room temperature for years. Most shapes double in size when cooked. Fresh pasta differs from dried because it contains eggs and additional water. Try it for a special treat. It is tender, takes half the time to cook, and lasts for about two days in the refrigerator or two weeks in the freezer.

TILAPIA

Because tilapia is usually farmed and harvested year-round, it's often one of the freshest fish in the market. Buy tilapia from the United States or Latin America rather than Asia, which has looser regulations. Ask your fishmonger to remove the bitter-tasting skin from fillets. To store, leave the fish in its original packaging and, if possible, place on a bowl or rimmed plate with ice in the refrigerator for up to two days.

TOMATOES

Look for a rich red skin that is smooth, firm, and blemish-free; skip any tomatoes with soft spots. Tomatoes should be stored at room temperature on a counter, stem-side up. Keep them out of direct sun, and never put them in the refrigerator, which will ruin their flavor and texture. Tomatoes will last two to five days, depending on their ripeness when purchased.

TORTILLAS

Whether they're made of corn, whole wheat, or flour, tortillas will last about two weeks in the refrigerator or three months (well wrapped) in the freezer. Bend the package in the store to make sure they're flexible, not brittle. You want them to stretch around as many ingredients as possible without breaking.

ZUCCHINI

Select zucchini less than eight inches long; these squash can become bitter the larger they grow. Make sure they are firm, particularly at the stems, and have bright skins. Refrigerate, unwashed, in a plastic bag in the vegetable drawer for three to five days.

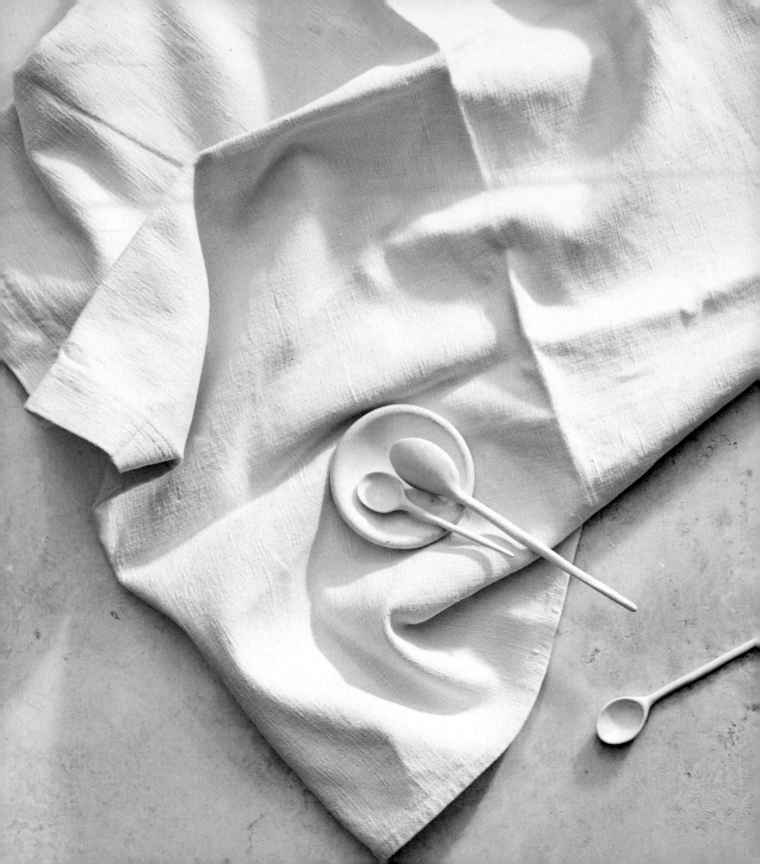

The Recipes

TIP
A melon baller makes coring and stemming apples quick and neat. Leave the skins on for extra color and fiber.

CRUNCHY DINNER
SALAD WITH
PROSCIUTTO, APPLE,
AND HAZELNUT
PAGE 25

Apples

Let's be honest: An apple a day is kind of boring. But an apple and sausage monkey bread one day and an apple-Cheddar tartine the next? Now we're talking.

1
Sautéed Cauliflower and Apples with Pecans

HANDS-ON: **30 MINUTES** TOTAL: **30 MINUTES** SERVES **4**

¼ cup pecans

1 small shallot, chopped

2 tablespoons olive oil

1 small head cauliflower (about 1½ pounds), cut into florets (about 5 cups)

Kosher salt and black pepper

1 red apple (such as Fuji or Braeburn), thinly sliced

1 teaspoon fresh thyme leaves or ½ teaspoon dried thyme

2 tablespoons unsalted butter

TOAST the pecans on a rimmed baking sheet at 350°F, tossing occasionally, until fragrant, 6 to 8 minutes. Chop roughly.

COOK the shallot in the oil in a large skillet over medium-high heat, stirring frequently, until softened, 3 to 4 minutes. Add the cauliflower and ¼ teaspoon each salt and pepper; cook until golden, 4 to 6 minutes.

ADD the apple, thyme, and ½ cup water. Cover and cook until the cauliflower is tender, 8 to 10 minutes more.

STIR in the butter and sprinkle with the pecans.

2
Apple Vichyssoise

HANDS-ON: **15 MINUTES** TOTAL: **4 HOURS, 50 MINUTES** SERVES **4**

2 tablespoons butter, melted

3 leeks, thinly sliced (white and pale green parts only)

1 large russet potato, thinly sliced

1 large unpeeled Macoun or McIntosh apple, cored, quartered, and thinly sliced

Kosher salt and black pepper

3 cups chicken broth

1½ cups half-and-half

2 tablespoons chopped fresh dill or chives (optional)

Olive oil, for serving

COOK the butter, leeks, potato, apple, 1 teaspoon salt, and ¼ teaspoon pepper in a sauce-pan over medium-low heat for 5 minutes. Add the broth; bring to a boil over high heat.

SIMMER, partially covered, until the potato and apple are tender, about 30 minutes. Add the half-and-half.

PUREE in a blender, working in batches. Refrigerate for 4 hours or overnight to chill thoroughly. Serve topped with dill or chives (if desired) and a drizzle of olive oil.

3
Slow-Cooker Pork Shoulder with Apple Relish

HANDS-ON: **15 MINUTES** TOTAL: **5 TO 8 HOURS** SERVES **4**

2   pounds boneless pork shoulder
½   cup low-sodium chicken broth
⅓   cup apple cider
1   small onion, sliced
2   teaspoons dill seed
    Kosher salt and black pepper
1   cup fresh flat-leaf parsley, chopped
½   Granny Smith apple, finely chopped
2   tablespoons olive oil
1   teaspoon lemon zest plus 1 tablespoon lemon juice
¾   pound cooked wide egg noodles

COMBINE the pork, broth, cider, onion, dill seed, and ½ teaspoon each salt and pepper in a 4- to 6-quart slow cooker. Cook until the pork is tender, on low for 7 to 8 hours, or on high for 5 to 6 hours. Shred the pork.

COMBINE the parsley, apple, oil, lemon zest and juice, and ¼ teaspoon each salt and pepper in a small bowl.

SERVE the pork and its juices over the noodles; top with the apple relish.

4
Turkey Waldorf Salad

HANDS-ON: **10 MINUTES** TOTAL: **10 MINUTES** SERVES **4**

2   tablespoons sour cream
2   tablespoons mayonnaise
1   tablespoon white wine vinegar
1   cup shredded roasted turkey or chicken
1   celery stalk, sliced
1   green apple, cut into ½-inch pieces
2   tablespoons chopped toasted walnuts
    Kosher salt and black pepper
1   small head red leaf lettuce, torn into pieces

MIX the sour cream, mayonnaise, and vinegar. Add the turkey, celery, apple, and walnuts and toss to combine; season with ½ teaspoon salt and ¼ teaspoon pepper. Serve over the lettuce.

5

Caramelized Onion Tarts with Apples

HANDS-ON: **20 MINUTES**

TOTAL: **55 MINUTES** MAKES **2 TARTS**

2 medium onions, sliced

2 tablespoons olive oil

2 red apples (such as Braeburn or Gala), cut into small pieces

Kosher salt and black pepper

2 sheets frozen puff pastry (from a 17.3-ounce package), thawed

½ cup crème fraîche or sour cream

COOK the onions in the oil in a large skillet over medium heat, until soft and golden brown, 12 to 15 minutes. Add the apples, ½ teaspoon salt, and ¼ teaspoon pepper and cook until just tender, 2 minutes.

PLACE each sheet of pastry on a parchment-lined baking sheet and prick all over with a fork. Spread with the crème fraîche, leaving a ½-inch border. Top with the onion mixture and bake at 400°F until the pastry is crisp and browned, 30 to 35 minutes. Cut into pieces before serving.

6

Ravioli with Apples and Walnuts

HANDS-ON: **20 MINUTES** TOTAL: **20 MINUTES** SERVES **4**

1 pound cheese ravioli (fresh or frozen)

½ cup walnuts, roughly chopped

2 tablespoons olive oil

1 crisp apple (such as Braeburn or Gala), cut into matchsticks

½ cup chopped fresh flat-leaf parsley

Kosher salt and black pepper

¼ cup grated Parmesan (1 ounce)

COOK the ravioli according to the package directions.

COOK the walnuts in the oil in a skillet over medium heat, stirring often, until lightly toasted, 4 to 5 minutes.

ADD the apple, parsley, ½ teaspoon salt, and ¼ teaspoon pepper and toss to combine. Spoon over the ravioli and sprinkle with the Parmesan.

7

Apple and Cheddar Tartine

HANDS-ON: **10 MINUTES** TOTAL: **10 MINUTES** SERVES **2**

½ small baguette (5 ounces), split lengthwise,
   then crosswise
2 tablespoons apple butter
½ apple, thinly sliced
2 ounces white Cheddar, sliced

BROIL the baguette pieces until lightly toasted, 1 to
2 minutes.

TOP evenly with the apple butter, apple, and Cheddar.
Broil until the Cheddar has melted, 2 to 3 minutes.

8

Roasted Chicken, Apples, and Leeks

HANDS-ON: **10 MINUTES** TOTAL: **55 MINUTES** SERVES **4**

4 small crisp apples (such as Empire or
   Braeburn), quartered
2 leeks, halved crosswise and lengthwise
6 small sprigs fresh rosemary
2 tablespoons olive oil
   Kosher salt and black pepper
8 small chicken thighs and drumsticks (about
   2½ pounds)

TOSS the apples, leeks, rosemary, oil, ½ teaspoon salt,
and ¼ teaspoon pepper on a rimmed baking sheet or in a
roasting pan.

SEASON the chicken with ½ teaspoon each salt and
pepper. Nestle, skin-side up, among the apples and leeks.

ROAST at 400°F until the chicken is cooked through and
the apples and leeks are tender, 40 to 45 minutes.

9

Apple, Sausage, and Cheddar Monkey Bread

HANDS-ON: 15 MINUTES TOTAL: 40 MINUTES SERVES 12

- 8 ounces crumbled breakfast sausage
- 2 red apples, diced
- 1 16-ounce can biscuit dough, cut into 1-inch pieces
- 1½ cups grated Cheddar (6 ounces)

COOK the sausage in a 10-inch cast-iron skillet over medium heat until browned. Stir in the apples. Cook until the apples are soft; transfer mixture to a bowl. In the bowl, toss in the biscuit dough. Spread the mixture in the skillet and top with the Cheddar. Bake at 425°F until golden, 22 minutes.

10

Crunchy Dinner Salad with Prosciutto, Apple, and Hazelnut

HANDS-ON: 25 MINUTES TOTAL: 25 MINUTES SERVES 4

- ½ cup hazelnuts
- ¼ cup olive oil
- 1 tablespoon red wine vinegar
- 2 teaspoons Dijon mustard
  Kosher salt and black pepper
- 1 small head radicchio, torn (about 5 cups)
- 1 small head romaine, torn (about 6 cups)
- 3 ounces prosciutto, torn
- 3 scallions, chopped
- 1 apple (such as Pink Lady or Gala), chopped

TOAST the nuts on a rimmed baking sheet at 350°F, tossing occasionally, until fragrant, 10 to 12 minutes. Rub the warm nuts between clean towels to remove the skins.

WHISK together the oil, vinegar, mustard, and ½ teaspoon each salt and pepper. Add the radicchio, romaine, prosciutto, scallions, apple, and nuts and toss to combine.

TOFU AND
AVOCADO
RICE BOWL
PAGE 33

TIP
Avocados are harvested when rock-hard and ripen after they're picked. Buy them slightly firm, then let them ripen on a counter. They're ready to use when you can press your thumb gently into the stem end.

Avocados

You can do a lot with avocados. Delicious with everything from salmon to sweet potatoes, this versatlle fruit is also high in healthy monounsaturated fat and packed with fiber, folate, magnesium, vitamin E, and lutein.

1
Glazed Chicken with Citrus Salad

HANDS-ON: **20 MINUTES** TOTAL: **30 MINUTES** SERVES **4**

3 **tablespoons honey**
1 **teaspoon fresh orange juice**
  Kosher salt and black pepper
4 **chicken legs (about 2½ pounds total)**
2 **oranges, peeled and sliced**
2 **avocados, sliced**
1 **tablespoon olive oil**
1 **tablespoon red wine vinegar**
  Fresh mint leaves, for serving

COMBINE the honey, orange juice, and ½ teaspoon each salt and pepper.

PLACE the chicken on a foil-lined rimmed baking sheet and brush with the glaze. Roast on the top rack at 475°F, basting twice, until cooked through, 18 to 22 minutes.

COMBINE the oranges, avocados, oil, vinegar, and ¼ teaspoon each salt and pepper.

TOP with mint. Serve with the chicken.

2

Salmon, Green Beans, and Avocado

HANDS-ON: 15 MINUTES **TOTAL: 25 MINUTES** **SERVES 4**

1 pound green beans

3 tablespoons olive oil
   Kosher salt and black pepper

4 6-ounce pieces boneless, skinless salmon

1 teaspoon ground coriander

2 avocados, chopped

1 tablespoon white wine vinegar

1 tablespoon chopped fresh dill

TOSS the green beans with 2 tablespoons of the oil and ¼ teaspoon each salt and pepper. Season the fish with the coriander and ¼ teaspoon each salt and pepper. Nestle the fish among the green beans on a rimmed baking sheet and broil until the fish is just opaque throughout, 6 to 8 minutes.

COMBINE the avocados, vinegar, dill, the remaining tablespoon of oil, and ¼ teaspoon salt. Serve on top of the fish and green beans.

3

Shrimp and
Avocado Nachos

HANDS-ON: **15 MINUTES** TOTAL: **20 MINUTES** SERVES **4**

12 ounces peeled and deveined medium shrimp
½   teaspoon cayenne pepper
    Kosher salt
2   tablespoons canola oil
6   ounces tortilla chips
6   ounces Cheddar, grated (about 1½ cups)
¼   red onion, sliced
2   avocados, chopped
2   radishes, sliced
    Fresh cilantro leaves and sour cream, for serving

COOK the shrimp, cayenne, and ½ teaspoon salt in the
oil in a large skillet over high heat, tossing, until opaque,
2 to 3 minutes.

LAYER the tortilla chips, Cheddar, and onion on a foil-
lined baking sheet. Bake at 450°F until the cheese is
melted, 4 to 5 minutes. Top with the shrimp, avocados,
radishes, cilantro, and sour cream.

4

Loaded Baked Sweet Potato

HANDS-ON: **10 MINUTES** TOTAL: **1 HOUR** SERVES **4**

4   large sweet potatoes (about 3 pounds total)
2   tablespoons canola oil
    Kosher salt and black pepper
2   tablespoons olive oil
1   avocado, sliced
¼   cup chopped pecans, toasted
¼   cup chopped fresh flat-leaf parsley
4   ounces fresh goat cheese, crumbled (about 1 cup)
    Green salad, for serving

RUB the sweet potatoes with the canola oil and ¼ teaspoon salt. Bake on a rimmed baking sheet at 400°F
until tender, 40 to 50 minutes.

SPLIT the sweet potatoes open lengthwise. Drizzle with
the olive oil and season with salt and pepper. Top with
the avocado, pecans, parsley, and cheese. Serve with a
green salad.

5

Chopped Salad with Avocado Dressing

HANDS-ON: **20 MINUTES** TOTAL: **20 MINUTES** SERVES **4**

- ½ **avocado**
- 1 **ounce Parmesan, grated (about ¼ cup), plus more for serving**
- ¼ **cup plain yogurt**
- ¼ **cup fresh lemon juice**
- ¼ **cup fresh flat-leaf parsley, chopped**
- 2 **tablespoons olive oil**
   Kosher salt and black pepper
- 1 **head romaine, chopped (about 8 cups)**
- 2 **cups rotisserie chicken, shredded**
- 1 **15.5-ounce can chickpeas, rinsed**
- 2 **cups grape tomatoes, halved**
   Pita chips, for serving

BLEND the avocado, Parmesan, yogurt, lemon juice, parsley, oil, ⅓ cup water, and ½ teaspoon each salt and pepper until creamy.

TOSS the romaine, chicken, chickpeas, tomatoes, ½ teaspoon each salt and pepper, and the dressing. Serve topped with pita chips and additional Parmesan.

6

Avocado Caprese Burgers

HANDS-ON: **20 MINUTES** TOTAL: **20 MINUTES** SERVES **4**

- 1 **avocado, mashed**
- 2 **tablespoons chopped fresh basil**
   Kosher salt and black pepper
- 1¼ **pounds ground beef chuck**
   Canola oil, for the grill
- 4 **slices fresh mozzarella**
- 4 **potato buns**
   Sliced tomato, for serving

COMBINE the avocado, basil, and ¼ teaspoon each salt and pepper.

SEASON the beef with ½ teaspoon each salt and pepper. Form into four ¾-inch-thick patties.

GRILL, covered, on an oiled grill rack over medium-high heat until medium-rare, 3 to 4 minutes per side.

TOP with the cheese and grill, covered, until the cheese melts, 30 to 60 seconds. Divide among the buns. Top with sliced tomato and the avocado mixture.

7

Beet, Potato, and Avocado Salad

HANDS-ON: **20 MINUTES** TOTAL: **45 MINUTES** SERVES **4**

- 1 pound beets, peeled and cut into ¾-inch pieces
- 1 pound fingerling potatoes, halved
- ¼ cup olive oil
- 2 teaspoons crushed fennel seeds
  Kosher salt and black pepper
- 5 ounces greens (such as mâche; about 6 cups)
- 2 avocados, chopped
- ⅓ cup cornichons, halved
- 2 tablespoons lemon juice
  Brie and bread, for serving

TOSS the beets and potatoes with 2 tablespoons of the oil, the fennel seeds, and ½ teaspoon salt. Roast on a baking sheet at 400°F, tossing once, until tender, 24 to 28 minutes; let cool.

TOSS with the greens, avocados, cornichons, the remaining 2 tablespoons of oil, the lemon juice, and ½ teaspoon each salt and pepper. Serve with Brie and bread.

8

Avocado, Prosciutto, and Egg Open-Faced Sandwich

HANDS-ON: **15 MINUTES** TOTAL: **15 MINUTES** SERVES **4**

- 4 large eggs
- 2 tablespoons olive oil, plus more for serving
  Kosher salt and black pepper
- 4 large slices country bread, toasted
- 1 avocado, sliced
- 2 ounces prosciutto, sliced

COOK the eggs in the oil in a large nonstick skillet, covered, over medium heat, 2 to 4 minutes for slightly runny yolks. Season with ¼ teaspoon each salt and pepper.

TOP the bread slices with the avocado, prosciutto, and eggs. Drizzle with oil. Season with pepper.

9

Bacon, Avocado, and Egg Salad

HANDS-ON: **25 MINUTES**   TOTAL: **25 MINUTES**   SERVES **4**

- 4 slices thick-cut bacon
- 8 hard-cooked eggs, chopped
- 2 avocados, chopped
- ¼ cup chopped fresh chives
- 2 tablespoons olive oil
- 2 tablespoons fresh lemon juice
- 1 tablespoon mayonnaise
   Kosher salt and black pepper
   Lettuce, for serving

COOK the bacon in a large skillet over medium-high heat, turning once, until browned, 6 to 8 minutes; crumble.

COMBINE the bacon with the eggs, avocados, chives, oil, lemon juice, mayonnaise, and ½ teaspoon each salt and pepper. Serve over lettuce.

10

Tofu and Avocado Rice Bowl

HANDS-ON: **20 MINUTES**   TOTAL: **50 MINUTES**   SERVES **4**

- 1 cup brown rice
- 14 ounces extra-firm tofu, cut into 1-inch pieces
- ¼ cup canola oil
   Kosher salt
- 2 tablespoons rice vinegar
- 2 tablespoons low-sodium soy sauce
- 2 tablespoons white miso (soybean paste, found in the refrigerated section of the supermarket)
- 1 15.5-ounce can pinto beans, rinsed
- 1 avocado, sliced
   Sliced scallions and sliced red chilies, for serving

COOK the rice according to the package directions.

COOK the tofu in 2 tablespoons of the oil in a nonstick skillet over medium-high heat, tossing occasionally, until golden, 12 to 15 minutes. Season with ½ teaspoon salt.

COMBINE the vinegar, soy sauce, miso, and the remaining 2 tablespoons of oil. Drizzle over the tofu, rice, beans, and avocado. Serve topped with scallions and red chilies.

TIP
No leftover baked ham? These recipes are also delicious made with sliced deli ham.

**CAULIFLOWER
AND HAM HASH**
PAGE 41

Baked Ham

Talk about no-fuss. This ready-to-eat, kid-approved protein soups up breakfast, lunch, and dinner. Go hog wild.

1
Ham Sandwich with Fennel Slaw

HANDS-ON: **10 MINUTES** TOTAL: **15 MINUTES** SERVES **4**

¼ cup mayonnaise

2 tablespoons cider vinegar
  Kosher salt and black pepper

¼ cup raisins

1 fennel bulb (10 ounces), thinly
  sliced (3 cups)

1 stalk celery, sliced (½ cup)

1 shallot, thinly sliced (½ cup)

8 slices dark rye bread

½ pound baked or deli ham,
  sliced
  Potato chips, for serving

WHISK together the mayonnaise,
vinegar, ½ teaspoon salt, and
¼ teaspoon pepper. Add the
raisins, fennel, celery, and shallot.

FORM sandwiches with the bread,
slaw, and ham. Serve with potato
chips.

2

Ham and Asparagus Quiche

HANDS-ON: **15 MINUTES** TOTAL: **1 HOUR, 15 MINUTES** SERVES **4**

- 4 large eggs
- ¾ cup half-and-half
  Kosher salt and black pepper
- ¼ pound baked or deli ham,
  chopped (1 cup)
- 1 bunch asparagus (14 ounces),
  chopped
- 4 ounces Gruyère, grated (1 cup)
- 1 store-bought 9-inch piecrust
- 2 tablespoons olive oil
- 1 tablespoon white wine
  vinegar
- 6 cups mixed greens
- 1 cup grape tomatoes,
  quartered

BEAT together the eggs and half-and-half; season with ¾ teaspoon salt and ¼ teaspoon pepper. Mix in the ham, asparagus, and Gruyère. Pour into the piecrust and bake at 325°F until set, 50 to 60 minutes.

WHISK together the oil, vinegar, ½ teaspoon salt, and ¼ teaspoon pepper. Add the greens and tomatoes. Serve with the quiche.

3
Tropical Pizza

HANDS-ON: **10 MINUTES** TOTAL: **30 MINUTES** SERVES **4**

- 1 **pound pizza dough, at room temperature**
  Canola oil for the baking sheet
- 8 **ounces mozzarella, grated (2 cups)**
- 1 **14.5-ounce can diced tomatoes, drained**
- 1 **8-ounce can pineapple chunks, drained**
- ¼ **pound baked or deli ham, thinly sliced (1 cup)**
- 1 **jalapeño, sliced**

SHAPE the dough into a large oval on an oiled baking sheet. Top with the mozzarella, tomatoes, pineapple, and ham.

BAKE at 425°F until the crust is golden and the cheese is melted, 15 to 20 minutes. Top with the sliced jalapeño.

4
Crispy Ham and Arugula Salad

HANDS-ON: **15 MINUTES** TOTAL: **20 MINUTES** SERVES **4**

- ½ **pound baked or deli ham, sliced and cut into 2-inch pieces**
- ¼ **cup plus 1 tablespoon olive oil**
- 1 **orange, segmented, with its juice**
- 2 **tablespoons red wine vinegar**
  Kosher salt and black pepper
- 2 **bunches arugula, thick stems removed (about 8 cups)**
- 1 **small red onion, thinly sliced**

COOK the ham in 1 tablespoon of the oil in a large skillet until crisp, 5 to 7 minutes.

TOSS together the orange segments with juice, vinegar, and the remaining oil; season with ¾ teaspoon salt and ¼ teaspoon pepper. Add the arugula, onion, and ham and toss to coat.

5
Asian Ham Salad

HANDS-ON: **10 MINUTES** TOTAL: **45 MINUTES** SERVES **4**

- 1 cup brown rice
- 1 cup frozen shelled edamame
- 2 tablespoons rice vinegar
- 2 tablespoons vegetable oil
- 1 teaspoon sesame oil
- ¼ teaspoon crushed red pepper
  Kosher salt and black pepper
- ¼ pound baked or deli ham, chopped (1 cup)
- 6 radishes, sliced
- 4 scallions, sliced
- 2 tablespoons roasted, salted peanuts, chopped

COOK the rice according to the package directions. Cook the edamame.

WHISK together the vinegar, oils, red pepper, and ¼ teaspoon each salt and black pepper. Toss with the rice, edamame, ham, radishes, and scallions. Top with the peanuts.

6
Ham and Corn Turnovers

HANDS-ON: **25 MINUTES** TOTAL: **1 HOUR** SERVES **4**

- ½ pound russet potatoes (about 2; peeled if desired), boiled
- 3 tablespoons unsalted butter
- ¼ pound baked or deli ham, chopped (1 cup)
- ½ medium onion, chopped
- ½ cup frozen corn
- 1 tablespoon fresh chives, chopped
  Kosher salt and black pepper
- 2 sheets frozen puff pastry (one 17.25-ounce package), thawed and halved
  Chutney, for serving

MASH the boiled potatoes with the butter, ham, onion, corn, and chives; season with ¾ teaspoon salt and ¼ teaspoon pepper.

TOP the 4 puff-pastry halves with the ham mixture; fold over and seal. Bake at 425°F until golden, 25 to 30 minutes. Serve with chutney.

7
Pasta with Ham and Green Beans

HANDS-ON: **25 MINUTES** TOTAL: **25 MINUTES** SERVES **4**

¾ pound spaghetti
2 leeks, thinly sliced
2 tablespoons unsalted butter
6 ounces baked or deli ham, sliced and cut into strips
1 cup green beans, sliced
    Kosher salt and black pepper
2 teaspoons lemon zest

COOK the pasta according to the package directions; drain, reserving ½ cup of the cooking water.

COOK the leeks in the butter in a large skillet over medium heat until tender, 4 to 6 minutes. Add the ham, green beans, and reserved cooking water; season with ¾ teaspoon salt and ¼ teaspoon pepper. Cook until the green beans are just tender.

TOSS with the pasta and lemon zest.

8
Split Pea Soup with Ham

HANDS-ON: **10 MINUTES**
TOTAL: **1 HOUR, 20 MINUTES** SERVES **4**

1 medium onion, chopped (1½ cups)
1 carrot, chopped (⅓ cup)
1 stalk celery, chopped (⅓ cup)
2 tablespoons olive oil
6 cups low-sodium chicken broth
½ pound baked or deli ham, chopped (2 cups)
½ pound dried split peas (1 cup)
1 tablespoon fresh thyme, chopped
    Kosher salt and black pepper
    Croutons, for serving

COOK the onion, carrot, and celery in the oil in a large saucepan over medium-high heat until tender.

ADD the broth, ham, split peas, and thyme; season with ¾ teaspoon salt and ¼ teaspoon pepper. Simmer until the peas are tender, 55 to 65 minutes. Top with croutons.

9
Quesadillas with Ham and Peppers

HANDS-ON: **10 MINUTES** TOTAL: **15 MINUTES** SERVES **4**

- 4 8-inch flour tortillas
- 8 ounces pepper Jack, grated (2 cups)
- ¼ pound baked or deli ham, chopped (1 cup)
- 1 small bell pepper, sliced
- 1 tablespoon olive oil
  Sour cream and salsa, for serving

TOP the tortillas with the pepper Jack, ham, and bell pepper; fold each in half.

BRUSH the tortillas with the oil and broil on a baking sheet until the pepper Jack is melted and the tortillas are crisp, 2 to 3 minutes per side. Serve with sour cream and salsa.

10
Cauliflower and Ham Hash

HANDS-ON: **35 MINUTES** TOTAL: **35 MINUTES** SERVES **4**

- 1 head cauliflower, cut into florets (5 cups)
- 1 medium onion, chopped
- 4 tablespoons olive oil
- ½ pound baked or deli ham, chopped (2 cups)
- 1 teaspoon paprika
  Kosher salt and black pepper
- 4 large eggs
- 1 tablespoon fresh parsley, chopped

COOK the cauliflower and onion in 3 tablespoons of the oil in a large skillet over medium-high heat until browned, 10 to 12 minutes. Add the ham and paprika; season with ¾ teaspoon salt and ¼ teaspoon pepper. Cook, tossing, until tender, 10 to 15 minutes; transfer to a plate.

FRY the eggs in the remaining tablespoon of oil to the desired doneness, 2 to 3 minutes for slightly runny yolks. Serve on the hash, sprinkled with the parsley.

TIP
Cooking bass in a skillet is a quick way to achieve flavorful fillets. To prevent sticking, start with a nonstick pan, then make sure to heat the oil until it simmers before adding the fish.

**SMOKY BASS,
FENNEL, AND
CHORIZO SOUP**
PAGE 49

Bass

No more excuses. For every complaint about fish, there's a delicious answer. Use this flaky white catch in dishes that are family-friendly or fancy.

1
Warm Bass Niçoise Salad

HANDS-ON: **25 MINUTES** TOTAL: **25 MINUTES** SERVES **4**

4 6-ounce boneless, skinless bass fillets
Kosher salt and black pepper
⅓ cup plus 2 tablespoons olive oil
¼ cup fresh lemon juice
3 tablespoons Dijon mustard
4 soft-cooked eggs, halved
¼ cup pitted olives (such as kalamata)
4 anchovy fillets
8 steamed new potatoes, halved
1 cup steamed green beans

SEASON the fish with ½ teaspoon salt and ¼ teaspoon pepper. Cook in 2 tablespoons of the oil in a large nonstick skillet over medium-high heat until opaque, 2 to 3 minutes per side; break into pieces.

COMBINE the lemon juice, mustard, the remaining ⅓ cup of oil, ½ teaspoon salt, and ¼ teaspoon pepper.

SERVE the fish with the eggs, olives, anchovies, potatoes, and green beans. Drizzle with the dressing.

<u>2</u>
Open-Faced Bass Sandwich

HANDS-ON: **20 MINUTES** TOTAL: **20 MINUTES** SERVES **4**

¼ small red onion, sliced

3 tablespoons red wine vinegar

1 pound boneless, skinless bass fillets

1 teaspoon crushed fennel seeds

Kosher salt and black pepper

1 tablespoon olive oil

½ cup plain yogurt

2 tablespoons prepared horseradish

2 tablespoons capers, chopped

4 slices rye bread

Fresh dill, for serving

TOSS the onion with the vinegar.

SEASON the fish with the fennel seeds and ¾ teaspoon each salt and pepper. Cook the fish in the oil in a large nonstick skillet over medium-high heat until opaque, 2 to 3 minutes per side; break into pieces.

COMBINE the yogurt, horseradish, and capers.

TOP the bread slices with the yogurt mixture, fish, onion, and dill.

3

Poached Bass over Frisée
with Mustard Dressing

HANDS-ON: 15 MINUTES TOTAL: **30 MINUTES** SERVES **4**

½ cup plus 3 tablespoons olive oil
1 shallot, sliced
6 sprigs fresh thyme
6 sprigs fresh parsley
1 tablespoon mustard seeds
   Kosher salt and black pepper
4 6-ounce boneless, skinless bass fillets
1 head frisée
1 tablespoon white wine vinegar
   Toasted bread, for serving

BRING ½ cup of the oil, the shallot, thyme, parsley, mustard seeds, 1 cup water, ½ teaspoon salt, and ½ teaspoon pepper to a low simmer in a large skillet.

ADD the fish and cook, covered, until opaque, 10 to 12 minutes.

TOSS the frisée with the remaining 3 tablespoons of oil, the white wine vinegar, ½ teaspoon salt, and ¼ teaspoon pepper. Serve the fish and shallots over the frisée with toasted bread.

4

Bass Tacos with
Grapefruit Salsa

HANDS-ON: 20 MINUTES TOTAL: **20 MINUTES** SERVES **4**

4 6-ounce boneless, skinless bass fillets
¾ teaspoon ground coriander
   Kosher salt and black pepper
3 tablespoons olive oil
1 grapefruit, peeled and chopped
1 avocado, chopped
8 corn tortillas, warmed
   Chopped fresh chives, for serving

SEASON the fish with the coriander, ½ teaspoon salt, and ¼ teaspoon pepper.

COOK in 2 tablespoons of the oil in a large nonstick skillet over medium-high heat until opaque, 2 to 3 minutes per side; break into pieces.

COMBINE the grapefruit, avocado, and the remaining tablespoon of oil; season with ½ teaspoon salt and ¼ teaspoon pepper.

DIVIDE the fish and grapefruit salsa among the tortillas. Serve with chives.

5

Provençal Bass in Tomato Broth

HANDS-ON: **20 MINUTES** TOTAL: **30 MINUTES** SERVES **4**

4 cloves garlic, smashed

3 tablespoons olive oil

2 small bunches Swiss chard, stems discarded and leaves torn

2 28-ounce cans diced tomatoes
Kosher salt and black pepper

4 6-ounce boneless, skinless bass fillets
Olive tapenade, for serving

COOK the garlic in the oil in a large saucepan over medium heat until fragrant, 1 to 2 minutes.

ADD the chard and tomatoes (and their juices); season with 1 teaspoon each salt and pepper. Cook, stirring often, until the chard is tender, 8 to 10 minutes.

NESTLE the fish in the chard mixture. Cover and cook until the fish is opaque, 10 to 12 minutes. Serve with the tapenade.

6

Bass with Potato-Cauliflower Puree

HANDS-ON: **20 MINUTES** TOTAL: **30 MINUTES** SERVES **4**

2 russet potatoes (about 1 pound), chopped

2 small heads cauliflower (about 1 pound), chopped
Kosher salt and black pepper

4 6-ounce boneless, skinless bass fillets

¼ cup olive oil

¼ cup chopped pecans, toasted

2 tablespoons chopped fresh tarragon

1 tablespoon fresh lemon juice

STEAM the potatoes and cauliflower until soft, 18 to 22 minutes. Puree with 1 teaspoon salt and ½ teaspoon pepper.

COOK the fish in 2 tablespoons of the oil in a nonstick skillet over medium-high heat until opaque, 2 to 3 minutes per side.

COMBINE the pecans, tarragon, lemon juice, the remaining 2 tablespoons of oil, and ¼ teaspoon each salt and pepper. Serve the fish over the potato-cauliflower puree, topped with the pecan sauce.

7
Coconut Bass over Rice Noodles

HANDS-ON: **25 MINUTES** TOTAL: **25 MINUTES** SERVES **4**

- 4 scallions, chopped
- 2 tablespoons Thai red curry paste
- 2 tablespoons canola oil
- 1 15-ounce can coconut milk
- 2 tablespoons Asian fish sauce
- 1 pound boneless, skinless bass fillets, cut into 2-inch pieces
- 8 ounces rice noodles, cooked
- 3 cups Napa cabbage, shredded
  Sliced red chilies and lime wedges, for serving

COOK the scallions and curry paste in the oil in a large saucepan over medium heat, stirring often, until tender, 6 to 8 minutes. Add the coconut milk, 2 cups water, and the fish sauce; bring to a boil.

ADD the fish; simmer until opaque, 2 to 4 minutes. Serve with the cooked rice noodles, cabbage, sliced red chilies, and lime wedges.

8
Roasted Bass and Carrots over Quinoa

HANDS-ON: **15 MINUTES** TOTAL: **30 MINUTES** SERVES **4**

- 1 pound carrots, sliced
- 1 onion, sliced
- ¼ cup olive oil
  Kosher salt and black pepper
- 4 6-ounce boneless, skinless bass fillets
- ¾ teaspoon paprika
- 1 cup quinoa, cooked
  Chopped fresh flat-leaf parsley and lemon wedges, for serving

TOSS the carrots and onion with 2 tablespoons of the oil, ½ teaspoon salt, and ¼ teaspoon pepper.

ROAST the carrot mixture on a rimmed baking sheet at 375°F until beginning to soften, 13 to 15 minutes. Season the fish with the remaining 2 tablespoons of oil, the paprika, and ¼ teaspoon each salt and pepper.

NESTLE the fish in the carrot mixture; roast until opaque, 10 to 12 minutes more. Serve over the cooked quinoa, topped with parsley and lemon wedges.

9

Bass, Bacon, and Arugula Sandwich

HANDS-ON: **20 MINUTES** TOTAL: **25 MINUTES** SERVES **4**

- 4 slices bacon
- 2 6-ounce boneless, skinless bass fillets, halved lengthwise through the center into 4 thin fillets
  Kosher salt and black pepper
- ⅓ cup mayonnaise
- ¼ cup prepared pesto
- 1 bunch arugula, thick stems removed
- 8 slices white sandwich bread, toasted

COOK the bacon in a large nonstick skillet over medium heat until crisp, 6 to 8 minutes; remove.

SEASON the fish with ¼ teaspoon each salt and pepper. Cook in the bacon drippings until opaque, 1 to 2 minutes per side.

COMBINE the mayonnaise and pesto.

DIVIDE the pesto mayonnaise, bacon, fish, and arugula among the bread slices to make sandwiches.

10

Smoky Bass, Fennel, and Chorizo Soup

HANDS-ON: **20 MINUTES** TOTAL: **25 MINUTES** SERVES **4**

- 2 small bulbs fennel, roughly chopped
- 4 ounces chorizo, chopped
- 2 tablespoons olive oil
- 6 cups low-sodium chicken broth
  Kosher salt and black pepper
- 1 pound boneless, skinless bass fillets, cut into 2-inch pieces
- 1 15-ounce can hominy, rinsed
  Chopped fresh cilantro and lime wedges, for serving

COOK the fennel and chorizo in oil in a large saucepan over medium heat, stirring occasionally, until the fennel is tender, 8 to 10 minutes.

ADD the broth and ½ teaspoon each salt and pepper; bring to a boil.

ADD the fish and hominy. Simmer until the fish is opaque, 2 to 4 minutes. Serve with cilantro and lime wedges.

TIP
Dried beans are lower in sodium, but rinsing and draining canned beans reduces their salt content significantly. Or look for low-sodium canned beans.

GREENS AND BEAN SALAD WITH GRAPES
PAGE 57

Beans

Inexpensive, filling, and virtually interchangeable, depending on your tastes, beans add a healthy boost of protein to any weekday dish. Stock them liberally in your pantry.

1
Red Bean Chili

HANDS-ON: **20 MINUTES** TOTAL: **45 MINUTES** SERVES **6 TO 8**

2 to 2¼ pounds lean ground beef

1 large onion, chopped (about 1½ cups)

5 cloves garlic, finely chopped

2 14.5-ounce cans beef broth

⅓ cup chili powder

2 teaspoons ground cumin

1 14.5-ounce can diced tomatoes

2 15.5-ounce cans kidney beans, drained

1 teaspoon kosher salt

1 tablespoon cider vinegar

Grated Cheddar, sour cream, and chopped jalapeños, for topping (optional)

BROWN the beef in a large saucepan over medium-high heat. Add the onion and cook until translucent. Add the garlic. Gradually add the broth, scraping up any browned bits; bring to a boil. Add the chili powder, cumin, and tomatoes; simmer, covered, for 10 minutes.

ADD the beans, salt, and vinegar. Simmer, uncovered, for 10 minutes more. Serve topped with Cheddar, sour cream, and chopped jalapeños (if desired).

2

Lemony Shrimp with White Beans and Couscous

HANDS-ON: **20 MINUTES** TOTAL: **20 MINUTES** SERVES **4**

- 1 10-ounce box couscous (1½ cups)
- 2 cloves garlic, chopped
- 4 scallions, chopped
- 3 tablespoons unsalted butter
- 1 pound medium shrimp, peeled and deveined
- 1 15.5-ounce can cannellini beans, rinsed
- ½ cup chopped fresh flat loaf parsley
- 2 tablespoons fresh lemon juice
  Kosher salt and black pepper

COOK the couscous according to the package directions.

COOK the garlic and scallions in 1 tablespoon of the butter in a large skillet over medium-high heat for 30 seconds. Add the shrimp and cook, stirring, until they begin to turn pink, about 3 minutes.

ADD the beans, parsley, lemon juice, the remaining 2 tablespoons of butter, 1 teaspoon salt, and ¼ teaspoon pepper. Cook until heated through, 2 to 3 minutes. Serve with the couscous.

3
—
Sausage and
White Bean Casserole

HANDS-ON: **15 MINUTES** TOTAL: **45 MINUTES** SERVES **4**

 1 pound Italian sausage links
 1 tablespoon plus 1 teaspoon olive oil
 2 carrots, cut into ½-inch pieces
 2 cloves garlic, chopped
 2 bunches Swiss chard, leaves cut into
    2-inch strips (about 12 cups)
 2 15.5-ounce cans cannellini beans, rinsed
    Kosher salt and black pepper
 2 tablespoons bread crumbs

BROWN the sausage in 1 tablespoon of the oil in a large ovenproof skillet over medium-high heat, turning, until cooked through, 5 to 6 minutes. Transfer to a plate.

ADD the carrots and garlic to the skillet and cook for 1 minute. Add the chard; cook until wilted, 1 to 2 minutes. Add the beans, ½ cup water, and ¼ teaspoon each salt and pepper; bring to a boil. Nestle in the sausages.

COMBINE the bread crumbs and remaining teaspoon of oil. Sprinkle over the sausage mixture. Transfer skillet to oven and bake at 400°F until golden, 20 to 30 minutes.

4
—
Lemon-Spinach Chickpeas

HANDS-ON: **15 MINUTES** TOTAL: **15 MINUTES** SERVES **4**

 1 15-ounce can chickpeas, drained
 ¼ cup olive oil
 1 10-ounce bag fresh spinach, washed
    Juice of 1 lemon
    Kosher salt
 1 bag pita bread, toasted

COOK the chickpeas in the oil in a large skillet over medium heat for 2 minutes. Add the spinach in batches, stirring until just wilted.

SPRINKLE the lemon juice and 1 teaspoon salt over the spinach mixture and stir. Serve warm with the toasted pita.

5
Bean Salad with Bacon and Chives

HANDS-ON: **25 MINUTES** TOTAL: **25 MINUTES** SERVES **8**

- 6 slices bacon
- 3 15.5-ounce cans cannellini beans, rinsed
- 3 tablespoons cider vinegar
- 3 tablespoons olive oil
- 3 tablespoons whole-grain mustard
  Kosher salt and black pepper
- 3 tablespoons chopped fresh chives

COOK the bacon in a large skillet over medium heat until crisp, 12 to 15 minutes; crumble and set aside.

TOSS the beans with the vinegar, oil, and mustard. Season with ½ teaspoon each salt and pepper.

ADD the chives and bacon just before serving.

6
White Bean and Escarole Soup with Chicken Sausage

HANDS-ON: **10 MINUTES** TOTAL: **25 MINUTES** SERVES **4**

- ½ pound fully cooked chicken sausage links, sliced
- 2 tablespoons olive oil
- 2 cloves garlic, sliced
- 6 cups low-sodium chicken broth
- 1 15.5-ounce can cannellini beans, rinsed and slightly mashed
- 1 small head escarole, torn
  Kosher salt and black pepper

BROWN the sausages in the oil in a large saucepan over medium-high heat, 3 to 5 minutes. Add the garlic and cook, stirring, for 1 minute.

ADD the broth, beans, escarole, ½ teaspoon salt, and ¼ teaspoon pepper. Simmer until escarole is tender, 8 to 10 minutes.

7

Beef and Bean Enchiladas with Sautéed Zucchini

HANDS-ON: **30 MINUTES** TOTAL: **40 MINUTES** SERVES **4**

- 1 medium onion, chopped
- 2 tablespoons canola oil
- ½ pound ground beef
- 1 15.5-ounce can pinto beans, rinsed
- 2 cups grated Cheddar (about 8 ounces)
- 2 cups enchilada sauce
- 8 6-inch corn tortillas
- 2 medium zucchini (about 1 pound), thinly sliced
  Kosher salt
  Sour cream, salsa, and cilantro, for serving

COOK the onion in 1 tablespoon of the oil in a skillet over medium heat, 3 to 5 minutes. Add the beef; cook until browned. Add the beans and 1 cup of the Cheddar.

SPREAD 1 cup of sauce in a 9-by-13-inch baking dish. Roll the beef mixture in the tortillas; place in dish. Top with remaining sauce and cheese. Bake at 400°F for 10 to 15 minutes.

COOK the zucchini and ¼ teaspoon salt in the remaining tablespoon of oil in a skillet until tender. Serve with the enchiladas, topped with sour cream, salsa, and cilantro.

8

Chickpea, Vegetable, and Pesto Soup

HANDS-ON: **15 MINUTES** TOTAL: **35 MINUTES** SERVES **4**

- 2 stalks celery, sliced
- 2 carrots, sliced
- 1 onion, chopped
  Kosher salt and black pepper
- 2 tablespoons olive oil
- 2 tablespoons tomato paste
- 6 cups low-sodium vegetable broth
- ½ pound green beans, halved
- 1 15.5-ounce can chickpeas, rinsed
- 1 cup frozen peas
- ¼ cup prepared pesto

COOK the celery, carrots, onion, ½ teaspoon salt, and ¼ teaspoon pepper in the oil in a large saucepan over medium heat, stirring, until softened, 5 to 7 minutes. Add the tomato paste and cook, stirring, for 1 minute.

ADD the broth, green beans, chickpeas, and peas. Simmer until the vegetables are tender, 15 to 20 minutes. Top with the pesto.

9
Mexican Pinto Bean Salad

HANDS-ON: **15 MINUTES** TOTAL: **15 MINUTES** SERVES **8**

- 2 15.5-ounce cans pinto beans, rinsed
- 1 bell pepper, chopped
- 4 scallions, chopped
- 1 cup fresh salsa (or pico de gallo)
- 4 ounce crumbled Cotija or ricotta salata (about 1 cup)
- ¼ cup olive oil
- 2 tablespoons lime juice
  Kosher salt and black pepper

COMBINE the beans, bell pepper, scallions, salsa, Cotija, oil, and lime juice. Season with 1 teaspoon salt and ½ teaspoon black pepper. Serve chilled or at room temperature.

10
Greens and Bean Salad with Grapes

HANDS-ON: **20 MINUTES** TOTAL: **20 MINUTES** SERVES **8**

- ¾ cup nuts (such as pecans, pistachios, or pine nuts)
- 3 tablespoons olive oil
- 2 tablespoons lemon juice
  Kosher salt and black pepper
- 6 cups (5 ounces) mizuna or arugula
- 1 15.5-ounce can cannellini beans, drained
- 1½ cups halved seedless red grapes

TOAST the nuts on a rimmed baking sheet at 350°F, tossing occasionally, until fragrant, 4 to 6 minutes. Let cool, then coarsely chop.

WHISK together the oil, lemon juice, and ½ teaspoon each salt and pepper. Add the mizuna, beans, grapes, and nuts and toss to combine.

TIP
To wash a head of broccoli thoroughly, fill a basin with cool water and dunk the vegetable head-first several times.

BROCCOLI,
ORANGE, AND
OLIVE SALAD
PAGE 65

Broccoli

You'll have no trouble getting the kids to eat their vegetables with these delicious ideas. Broccoli stalks are sweet and tender—too tasty to waste. Peel and slice them to use along with the florets in these recipes.

1
Curried Broccoli Couscous

HANDS-ON: **15 MINUTES** TOTAL: **20 MINUTES** SERVES **4**

¼ bunch broccoli, finely chopped (1½ cups)

2 tablespoons olive oil

1 cup canned chickpeas, rinsed

⅓ cup golden raisins

1 teaspoon curry powder
 Kosher salt

¾ cup couscous

COOK the broccoli in oil in a large saucepan over medium-high heat, tossing, until tender, 2 to 3 minutes.

ADD the chickpeas, raisins, curry powder, 1 cup water, and ½ teaspoon salt and bring to a boil.

STIR in the couscous, cover, remove from heat, and let steam for 5 minutes. Fluff with a fork.

2

Broccoli and
Blue Cheese Salad

HANDS-ON: **10 MINUTES** TOTAL: **15 MINUTES** SERVES **4**

- 1 **bunch broccoli, cut into florets (6 cups)**
- ¼ **cup buttermilk**
- 2 **tablespoons sour cream**
- 2 **ounces blue cheese, crumbled (about ½ cup)**
- 1 **scallion, sliced**
- ½ **teaspoon red wine vinegar**
  Kosher salt and black pepper
- ½ **cup chopped walnuts, toasted**

STEAM the broccoli until tender, 5 to 7 minutes; rinse with cold water to cool.

COMBINE the buttermilk, sour cream, blue cheese, scallion, and red wine vinegar; season with ½ teaspoon salt and ¼ teaspoon pepper.

TOP the broccoli with the buttermilk dressing and toasted walnuts.

3

Broccoli and Pepper Stir-Fry

HANDS-ON: **15 MINUTES** TOTAL: **15 MINUTES** SERVES **4**

- 1 bell pepper, chopped
- 1 bunch broccoli, cut into florets (6 cups)
- 1 bunch scallions, sliced
- 1 tablespoon grated fresh ginger
- 1 tablespoon canola oil
- ¼ cup hoisin sauce
- 1 tablespoon toasted sesame seeds

COOK the bell pepper, broccoli, scallions, and ginger in the oil in a large skillet over medium-high heat, tossing often, until the broccoli is crisp-tender, 3 to 5 minutes.

ADD the hoisin sauce and ¼ cup water and cook, tossing, until tender, 2 to 3 minutes. Sprinkle with toasted sesame seeds.

4

Parmesan-Roasted Broccoli and Onions

HANDS-ON: **10 MINUTES** TOTAL: **30 MINUTES** SERVES **4**

- 1 bunch broccoli, cut into florets (6 cups)
- 1 small red onion, cut into wedges
- 2 tablespoons olive oil
- ½ cup grated Parmesan (2 ounces)
   Kosher salt and black pepper

TOSS the broccoli and onion with the oil and Parmesan on a rimmed baking sheet; season with ½ teaspoon each salt and pepper. Roast at 425°F, tossing once, until tender, 20 to 25 minutes.

5

Sautéed Broccoli, Tomatoes, and Bacon

HANDS-ON: **25 MINUTES** TOTAL: **25 MINUTES** SERVES **4**

- 4 slices bacon, cut into 1-inch pieces
- 1 bunch broccoli, cut into florets (6 cups)
- 1 cup cherry tomatoes, halved
  Kosher salt and black pepper

COOK the bacon in a large skillet over medium heat, stirring often, until crisp, 6 to 8 minutes; transfer to a plate.

COOK the broccoli and tomatoes in the bacon drippings, tossing often, until the broccoli is tender, 8 to 10 minutes. Season with salt and pepper and sprinkle with the bacon.

6

Broccoli Gratin with Crispy Onions

HANDS-ON: **25 MINUTES** TOTAL: **30 MINUTES** SERVES **4**

- 2 tablespoons butter
- 2 tablespoons all-purpose flour
- 2 cups whole milk
- 1 bunch broccoli, chopped (6 cups)
  Kosher salt and black pepper
- 2 cups grated fontina (8 ounces)
- 1 cup French-fried onions

COOK the butter and flour in a large saucepan over medium heat, whisking, for 1 minute. Whisk in the milk.

ADD the broccoli; season with ½ teaspoon salt and ¼ teaspoon pepper. Simmer until tender, 8 to 12 minutes.

ADD the fontina, transfer to a baking dish, and top with the French-fried onions. Bake at 350°F until browned, 5 to 7 minutes.

7

Mashed Potatoes
and Broccoli

HANDS-ON: **15 MINUTES** TOTAL: **20 MINUTES** SERVES **4**

½   bunch broccoli, finely chopped (3 cups)
1   pound Yukon gold potatoes, peeled and cut
    into ½-inch pieces
¼   cup sour cream
4   tablespoons butter, softened
    Kosher salt and black pepper

STEAM the broccoli and potatoes until very tender,
10 to 12 minutes.

DRAIN well and mash with the sour cream and butter;
season with ½ teaspoon salt and ¼ teaspoon pepper.

8

Grilled Broccoli
and Lemons

HANDS-ON: **20 MINUTES** TOTAL: **20 MINUTES** SERVES **4**

1   bunch broccoli, cut into 8 large spears
2   lemons, quartered
2   tablespoons olive oil, plus more for drizzling
    Kosher salt and black pepper

TOSS the broccoli and lemons with the oil; season with
½ teaspoon salt and ¼ teaspoon pepper. Grill the broccoli
and lemons over medium heat, turning occasionally, until
tender and lightly charred, 10 to 15 minutes.

SQUEEZE the lemons over the broccoli and drizzle with oil.

9

Creamy Broccoli
and Apple Slaw

HANDS-ON: **15 MINUTES** TOTAL: **15 MINUTES** SERVES **4**

- ½ cup plain low-fat yogurt
- ¼ cup mayonnaise
- 1 tablespoon cider vinegar
- 1 small shallot, chopped
  Kosher salt and black pepper
- ½ bunch broccoli, finely chopped (3 cups)
- ½ apple, finely chopped
- ¼ cup dried cranberries
- 2 tablespoons pine nuts, toasted

COMBINE the yogurt, mayonnaise, vinegar, shallot, ¾ teaspoon salt, and ½ teaspoon pepper. Add the broccoli, apple, cranberries, and pine nuts and toss to combine.

10

Broccoli, Orange,
and Olive Salad

HANDS-ON: **10 MINUTES** TOTAL: **15 MINUTES** SERVES **4**

- 1 bunch broccoli, cut into florets (6 cups)
- ¼ cup pitted kalamata olives, chopped
- 2 tablespoons olive oil
- 1 orange, segmented, plus 1 tablespoon finely grated orange zest
  Kosher salt and black pepper

STEAM the broccoli until tender, 5 to 7 minutes; rinse with cold water to cool.

TOSS the broccoli with the olives, oil, orange segments and zest (squeeze in any juice remaining in the orange membranes); season with ½ teaspoon salt and ¼ teaspoon pepper.

BUTTERNUT
SQUASH AND
BEAN TACOS
PAGE 73

TIP
To easily (and safely)
trim a squash: Cut
off both ends, halve
lengthwise, and
scoop out the seeds.
Peel and slice or
chop, as desired.

Butternut Squash

Think it's good only for Thanksgiving? Squash any preconceived notions and see how versatile butternut can be. Puree it, roast it, or toss it into rice or pasta.

1

Roasted Squash and Eggplant with Crispy Soba Noodles

HANDS-ON: **25 MINUTES** TOTAL: **25 MINUTES** SERVES **4**

8 ounces soba noodles

1 butternut squash (about 1½ pounds), cut into ¾-inch pieces

1 eggplant, cut into ¾-inch pieces

5 tablespoons canola oil

¼ small head red cabbage, sliced

¼ cup low-sodium soy sauce

¼ cup rice vinegar

1 tablespoon sesame oil

1 teaspoon brown sugar
   Fresh mint leaves, for serving

COOK the noodles according to the package directions.

TOSS the squash and eggplant with 3 tablespoons of the canola oil on 2 rimmed baking sheets. Roast at 450°F, tossing once, until tender, 16 to 20 minutes.

TOSS the noodles, vegetables, and cabbage with the soy sauce, vinegar, sesame oil, brown sugar, and the remaining 2 tablespoons of canola oil. Serve topped with mint leaves.

2

Butternut Squash and Chickpea Stew

HANDS-ON: **20 MINUTES** TOTAL: **35 MINUTES** SERVES **4**

1 **large onion, chopped**

2 **tablespoons olive oil**

2 **medium zucchini (about 1 pound total), cut into ½-inch pieces**

1 **butternut squash (about 1½ pounds), cut into ½-inch pieces**

1 **15.5-ounce can diced tomatoes**

1 **15.5-ounce can chickpeas, rinsed**

1 **teaspoon ground ginger**

1 **teaspoon ground coriander**
  Kosher salt and black pepper

1 **cup couscous**
  Fresh cilantro leaves, for serving

COOK the onion in oil in a large saucepan over medium heat until tender, 6 to 8 minutes. Add the zucchini and cook until crisp-tender, 3 to 5 minutes. Add the squash, tomatoes, chickpeas, ginger, coriander, and ¼ teaspoon each salt and pepper. Cook, covered, until the squash is tender, 15 to 18 minutes.

COOK the couscous according to the package directions. Serve topped with the stew and cilantro.

3

Seared Pork Chops and Pesto with Mashed Squash

HANDS-ON: 25 MINUTES **TOTAL: 25 MINUTES** SERVES **4**

1 butternut squash (about 1½ pounds),
   cut into 1-inch pieces

2 tablespoons unsalted butter
   Kosher salt and black pepper

4 bone-in pork chops (1 inch thick;
   about 2½ pounds total)

1 teaspoon ground coriander

2 tablespoons olive oil
   Prepared pesto, for serving

STEAM the squash until tender, 12 to 15 minutes; mash with the butter. Season with ¼ teaspoon each salt and pepper.

SEASON the pork chops with the coriander, ½ teaspoon salt, and ¼ teaspoon pepper. Cook in the oil in a large skillet over medium-high heat for 6 to 8 minutes per side.

SERVE with the squash and pesto.

4

Creamy Butternut Squash and Parsnip Soup

HANDS-ON: 25 MINUTES **TOTAL: 25 MINUTES** SERVES **4**

1 onion, chopped

2 tablespoons olive oil

1 butternut squash (about 1½ pounds),
   cut into 1-inch pieces

2 parsnips, chopped

4 cups low-sodium chicken broth
   Kosher salt and black pepper

2 tablespoons fresh lime juice
   Plain yogurt and lime zest, for serving

COOK the onion in the oil in a medium saucepan over medium heat until tender, 6 to 8 minutes. Add the squash, parsnips, broth, and 1 cup water; season with ½ teaspoon salt and ¼ teaspoon pepper. Simmer until the squash is tender, 12 to 15 minutes. Puree in a blender, working in batches. Stir in lime juice. Serve topped with yogurt, lime zest, and additional pepper.

5

Bacon-and-Egg
Butternut Squash

HANDS-ON: **20 MINUTES** TOTAL: **50 MINUTES** SERVES **4**

1 **butternut squash (about 1½ pounds), unpeeled
   and cut into quarters lengthwise**
2 **tablespoons olive oil**
  Kosher salt and black pepper
4 **slices bacon**
4 **large eggs**
1 **avocado, chopped**

TOSS the squash with the oil; season with ¼ teaspoon
each salt and pepper. Roast on a rimmed baking sheet at
400°F until tender, 35 to 45 minutes.

COOK the bacon in a large nonstick skillet over medium
heat until browned, 6 to 8 minutes; remove and crumble.

ADD the eggs to the skillet and cook, covered, for 2 to
4 minutes for slightly runny yolks; season with pepper.
Serve the squash with the eggs, bacon, and avocado.

6

Squash and Ricotta
Toasts

HANDS-ON: **25 MINUTES** TOTAL: **25 MINUTES** SERVES **4**

1 **butternut squash (about 1½ pounds),
   cut into ½-inch pieces**
2 **tablespoons olive oil**
  Kosher salt and black pepper
½ **cup balsamic vinegar**
1 **tablespoon honey**
4 **slices country bread, toasted**
½ **cup ricotta**

TOSS the squash with the oil; season with ½ teaspoon
salt and ¼ teaspoon pepper. Roast on a rimmed baking
sheet at 450°F, tossing once, until tender, 16 to 18
minutes.

COOK the vinegar and honey in a small saucepan over
medium heat, stirring occasionally, until syrupy, 8 to
10 minutes; let cool.

TOP the bread slices with the ricotta and squash. Drizzle
with the syrup.

7

Butternut Squash Galette

HANDS-ON: **30 MINUTES**

TOTAL: **1 HOUR, 25 MINUTES** SERVES **4**

- 1 onion, sliced
- 1 butternut squash (about 1½ pounds),
  cut into ⅛-inch-thick slices
- 3 tablespoons unsalted butter
  Kosher salt and black pepper
- 2 teaspoons chopped fresh sage leaves
- 1 refrigerated piecrust
- 1 tablespoon heavy cream
- ½ cup crumbled blue cheese (2 ounces)
  Green salad, for serving

COOK the onion and squash in the butter in a large skillet over medium heat for 8 to 12 minutes. Season with ½ teaspoon salt and ¼ teaspoon pepper. Stir in the sage.

ROLL the piecrust into a 12-inch circle; place on a baking sheet lined with parchment. Top with the squash and onion, leaving a 2-inch border. Fold the dough inward, overlapping slightly; brush with the cream. Bake at 350°F until golden, 45 to 55 minutes. Top with the blue cheese. Serve with a green salad.

8

Butternut Squash and Kale Lasagna

HANDS-ON: **25 MINUTES**

TOTAL: **1 HOUR, 35 MINUTES** SERVES **4**

- 6 tablespoons unsalted butter, plus more for the foil
- 6 tablespoons all-purpose flour
- 4 cups whole milk
  Kosher salt and black pepper
- 6 no-cook lasagna noodles
- 1 butternut squash (about 1½ pounds), thinly sliced
- 4 cups torn kale leaves (from 1 small bunch)
- 1½ cups grated Gruyère (6 ounces)

MELT the butter in a large saucepan over medium heat. Whisk in the flour and cook until foamy, 30 seconds. Whisk in the milk, ½ teaspoon salt, and ¼ teaspoon pepper. Simmer, stirring, until thickened, 8 to 10 minutes.

LAYER the lasagna noodles, sauce, squash, and kale in an 8-inch baking dish. Top with the Gruyère.

BAKE, covered with buttered foil, at 350°F until tender, 1 hour. Let cool for 10 minutes before serving.

9
Butternut Squash and Barley Risotto

HANDS-ON: **25 MINUTES**

TOTAL: **1 HOUR, 25 MINUTES** SERVES **4**

- 1 onion, chopped
- 2 tablespoons unsalted butter
- ½ cup dry white wine
- 6 cups low-sodium vegetable broth
- 1 cup pearl barley
  Kosher salt and black pepper
- 1 butternut squash (about 1½ pounds),
  cut into ½-inch pieces
- ½ cup grated Parmesan (2 ounces),
  plus more, shaved, for serving

COOK the onion in the butter in a large saucepan over medium heat until tender, 6 to 8 minutes. Add the wine; cook until syrupy, 5 to 7 minutes.

ADD the broth and barley. Season with salt and pepper. Simmer, stirring occasionally, until almost tender, 25 minutes. Add the squash and cook, stirring occasionally, until soft, 25 to 35 minutes. Stir in the grated Parmesan.

SERVE topped with shaved Parmesan.

10
Butternut Squash and Bean Tacos

HANDS-ON: **25 MINUTES** TOTAL: **25 MINUTES** SERVES **4**

- 1 butternut squash (about 1½ pounds),
  cut into ½-inch pieces
- ½ teaspoon ground cumin
- 2 tablespoons olive oil
  Kosher salt and black pepper
- 1 15.5-ounce can black beans, rinsed
- ½ small red onion, sliced
- 1 cup crumbled goat cheese (4 ounces)
- 8 corn tortillas, warmed
- ¼ cup torn fresh flat-leaf parsley leaves
  Lime wedges, for serving (optional)

COOK the squash and cumin in the oil in a large skillet over medium heat until almost tender, 11 to 13 minutes; season with ½ teaspoon salt and ¼ teaspoon pepper. Add the beans and ¼ cup water and cook until warm, 1 to 2 minutes.

DIVIDE the squash mixture, onion, and goat cheese among the tortillas. Serve with the parsley and lime wedges (if desired).

TIP
These recipes assume you are using peeled carrots, but the skins on tender, young baby carrots (like those you find at a farmers' market) are edible. No peeling is required. Just scrub well and proceed.

CARROT, BEAN, AND
RADICCHIO SALAD
PAGE 81

Carrots

Nutrient-dense and great raw or cooked, the carrot deserves better than a tub of hummus. Unearth some surprising ideas for this popular root vegetable.

1
Spiced Carrot Soup

HANDS-ON: **30 MINUTES** TOTAL: **50 MINUTES** SERVES **4**

2 **onions, chopped**
2 **pounds carrots, sliced**
1 **tablespoon fresh thyme leaves**
1 **tablespoon paprika**
3 **tablespoons olive oil, plus
   more for serving
   Kosher salt and black pepper**
4 **cups low-sodium vegetable
   broth**
2 **tablespoons lemon juice
   Plain yogurt, for serving**

COOK the onions, carrots, thyme, and paprika in oil in a large saucepan over medium-high heat, stirring often, until the onions are tender, 10 to 12 minutes. Season with ½ teaspoon each salt and pepper. Add the broth and 2 cups water. Simmer until the carrots are soft, 12 to 15 minutes.

PUREE in a blender. Stir in the lemon juice. Top with yogurt, plus additional oil and black pepper.

2
Creamy Carrot Dip with Crudités

HANDS-ON: **20 MINUTES** TOTAL: **45 MINUTES** SERVES **4**

- 1 tablespoon ground coriander
- ¼ cup olive oil, plus more for serving
- 1½ pounds carrots, sliced
  Kosher salt and black pepper
- ¼ cup fresh cilantro leaves
- 3 ounces fresh goat cheese, crumbled (about ¾ cup)
  Flatbread, endive leaves, snap peas, and radishes, for serving

HEAT the coriander in oil in a large skillet over medium heat until fragrant, 1 to 2 minutes. Add the carrots and ¾ cup water. Season with 1 teaspoon salt and ¼ teaspoon pepper. Cook, covered, stirring often, until the carrots are soft, 15 to 20 minutes; puree in a food processor until smooth.

TOP with the cilantro, goat cheese, and additional oil. Serve with flatbread, endive leaves, snap peas, and radishes.

3

Mexican Pork Loin and Carrots

HANDS-ON: **15 MINUTES** TOTAL: **40 MINUTES** SERVES **4**

- 1 pound carrots, peeled
- 2 tablespoons olive oil
- 1½ pounds boneless pork loin
- 1 teaspoon ground cumin
  Kosher salt
- 1 avocado, mashed
- 3 tablespoons plain yogurt
- 3 tablespoons fresh lime juice
  Pepitas and lime wedges, for serving

TOSS the carrots with the oil on a rimmed baking sheet. Season the pork with the cumin and ½ teaspoon salt; nestle among the carrots.

ROAST at 450°F until the internal temperature of the pork registers 145°F, 20 to 25 minutes. Let rest for 10 minutes; slice.

COMBINE the avocado, yogurt, and lime juice. Season with ¼ teaspoon salt. Serve with the pork and carrots. Top with pepitas; serve with lime wedges.

4

Cod and Spinach with Carrot-Almond Dressing

HANDS-ON: **20 MINUTES** TOTAL: **30 MINUTES** SERVES **4**

- 4 6-ounce pieces boneless, skinless cod
  Kosher salt and black pepper
- 6 tablespoons olive oil
- ¼ cup grated carrots
- ¼ cup chopped roasted almonds
- 1 tablespoon white wine vinegar
- 1 teaspoon orange zest
  Wilted baby spinach, for serving

SEASON the fish with ¼ teaspoon each salt and pepper. Cook in batches in 2 tablespoons of the oil in a large nonstick skillet over medium-high heat until opaque throughout, 2 to 3 minutes per side.

COMBINE the carrots, almonds, vinegar, orange zest, and the remaining ¼ cup of oil. Season with ¼ teaspoon each salt and pepper. Serve the dressing over the fish and wilted baby spinach.

5

Roasted Chicken, Carrots, and Shallots

HANDS-ON: 15 MINUTES TOTAL: 45 MINUTES SERVES 4

- 8 bone-in, skin-on chicken thighs (2½ pounds total)
- 1½ pounds carrots, chopped
- 6 shallots, quartered
- 3 tablespoons olive oil
  Kosher salt and black pepper
- ¼ cup chopped fresh chives
- 2 tablespoons white wine vinegar

TOSS the chicken, carrots, and shallots with 1 tablespoon of the oil and ½ teaspoon each salt and pepper.

ROAST on a rimmed baking sheet on the top rack at 450°F until the chicken is cooked through, 25 to 30 minutes.

COMBINE the chives, vinegar, and the remaining 2 tablespoons of oil. Season with ½ teaspoon salt. Serve over the chicken and vegetables.

6

Raisin-and-Carrot Chicken Salad

HANDS-ON: 20 MINUTES TOTAL: 30 MINUTES SERVES 4

- 6 boneless, skinless chicken thighs (about 1 pound total)
  Kosher salt and black pepper
- ½ cup grated carrots
- ½ cup chopped pecans, toasted
- ¼ cup mayonnaise
- ¼ cup golden raisins
- ¼ cup chopped fresh flat-leaf parsley leaves
- 1 tablespoon fresh lemon juice
  Lettuce and buttered toast, for serving

SEASON the chicken with ¼ teaspoon pepper. Simmer, covered, in a large saucepan of salted water until cooked through, 8 to 10 minutes. Shred the chicken.

TOSS the chicken with the carrots, pecans, mayonnaise, raisins, parsley, and lemon juice. Season with ¾ teaspoon salt and ¼ teaspoon pepper.

SERVE over lettuce with buttered toast.

7

Slow-Cooker Carrot and Beef Stew

HANDS-ON: **20 MINUTES**

TOTAL: **8 HOURS, 20 MINUTES** SERVES **6**

1½ pounds beef chuck, cut into 2 pieces
3 cups low-sodium chicken broth
1 pound carrots, sliced
¼ small cabbage, sliced (about 6 cups)
2 onions, chopped
½ cup red wine
¼ cup tomato paste
2 tablespoons all-purpose flour
2 teaspoons fresh thyme leaves
   Kosher salt and black pepper

COMBINE the beef, broth, carrots, cabbage, onions, wine, tomato paste, flour, thyme, 1½ teaspoons salt and ½ teaspoon pepper in a 4- to 6-quart slow cooker.

COVER and cook until the beef is tender, on low for 7 to 8 hours or on high for 4 to 5 hours.

CUT the meat into chunks and return to the stew before serving.

8

Orecchiette with Rosemary Carrots

HANDS-ON: **20 MINUTES** TOTAL: **25 MINUTES** SERVES **4**

1 pound carrots, cut into 1-inch pieces
1 tablespoon finely chopped fresh rosemary leaves
4 tablespoons unsalted butter
   Kosher salt and black pepper
¾ pound orecchiette or other short pasta
1 tablespoon fresh lemon juice
   Grated Parmesan, for serving

COOK the carrots and rosemary in 2 tablespoons of the butter in a large skillet over medium heat, stirring often, until tender, 12 to 15 minutes. Season with ¾ teaspoon each salt and pepper.

COOK the pasta according to the package directions. Toss with the carrots, lemon juice, and the remaining 2 tablespoons of butter. Serve topped with grated Parmesan.

9
Lamb with Carrot–Red Pepper Puree

HANDS-ON: 20 MINUTES TOTAL: 30 MINUTES SERVES 4

- 1½ pounds carrots, chopped
- ½ cup roasted red peppers
- 2 tablespoons olive oil
- 2 tablespoons fresh lemon juice
  Pinch cayenne pepper
  Kosher salt and black pepper
- 4 lamb loin chops (1½ inches thick; about 2½ pounds total)
  Chopped roasted almonds and fresh cilantro leaves, for serving

STEAM the carrots until soft, 10 to 12 minutes. Puree with the roasted red peppers, oil, lemon juice, and cayenne in a food processor until smooth, 2 to 3 minutes. Season with ½ teaspoon salt.

SEASON the lamb with ¼ teaspoon each salt and black pepper. Cook, covered, in a grill pan over medium-high heat, 3 to 5 minutes per side for medium-rare.

SERVE the lamb over the puree, topped with almonds and cilantro.

10
Carrot, Bean, and Radicchio Salad

HANDS-ON: 20 MINUTES TOTAL: 20 MINUTES SERVES 4

- ¼ small red onion, very thinly sliced
- 3 tablespoons olive oil
- 3 tablespoons red wine vinegar
  Kosher salt and black pepper
- 1 pound carrots, chopped
- 1 15.5-ounce can cannellini beans, rinsed
- 1 head radicchio, torn
- ¼ cup chopped fresh flat-leaf parsley leaves
- 3 ounces blue cheese, crumbled (about ¾ cup)

COMBINE the onion, oil, vinegar, 1 teaspoon salt, and ½ teaspoon pepper.

STEAM the carrots until tender, 10 to 12 minutes; let cool.

ADD the carrots, beans, radicchio, and parsley to the onion. Toss to combine. Serve topped with the cheese.

TIP
Save money by making your own cutlets. Cut a boneless, skinless chicken breast in half cross-wise, then gently press to flatten with your hands or a heavy-bottomed skillet.

SPICY CHICKEN
AND RANCH
SANDWICH
WITH CRUDITÉS
PAGE 89

Chicken Cutlets

In the pecking order of weeknight staples, this family-friendly cut comes out on top. Turn it into a super-fast supper tonight with one of these easy recipes.

1
Grilled Chicken and Spring Vegetables

HANDS-ON: **30 MINUTES** TOTAL: **30 MINUTES** SERVES **4**

1½ pounds new potatoes
    (about 15), quartered

 1 bunch asparagus (about
    1 pound), trimmed

 2 tablespoons olive oil

 2 tablespoons red wine vinegar

 2 tablespoons whole-grain
    mustard
    Kosher salt and black pepper

 8 chicken cutlets (about
    1½ pounds total)

 1 teaspoon ground coriander

STEAM the potatoes until tender,
12 to 14 minutes, adding the
asparagus during the last 3 minutes.
Toss with the oil, vinegar, and
mustard. Season with ¼ teaspoon
each salt and pepper.

SEASON the chicken with the
coriander and ½ teaspoon each salt
and pepper. Grill over medium heat
until cooked through, 2 to 4 minutes
per side. Serve with the vegetables.

2
Chicken and Chorizo Tacos with Slaw

HANDS-ON: **25 MINUTES** TOTAL: **25 MINUTES** SERVES **4**

4 **ounces cured chorizo, sliced**
1 **teaspoon plus 1 tablespoon olive oil**
4 **chicken cutlets (about ¾ pound total), sliced**
¼ **jicama, sliced**
2 **radishes, sliced**
1 **tablespoon fresh lime juice**
Kosher salt
8 **corn tortillas, warmed**
½ **cup guacamole, for serving**

BROWN the chorizo in 1 teaspoon of the oil in a large skillet over medium heat, 3 to 4 minutes. Add the chicken and cook, tossing, until cooked through, 3 to 4 minutes.

TOSS the jicama, radishes, lime juice, the remaining tablespoon of oil, and ½ teaspoon salt. Divide the chorizo, chicken, and slaw among the tortillas. Serve with guacamole.

3

Chicken and Ricotta Pizza

HANDS-ON: **20 MINUTES** TOTAL: **40 MINUTES** SERVES **4**

- 4 chicken cutlets (about ¾ pound total)
  Kosher salt and black pepper
- 1 tablespoon olive oil, plus more for the baking sheets
- 1 pound pizza dough, at room temperature
- 1 cup marinara sauce
- 1 cup ricotta
- 1 ounce shaved Parmesan (about ¼ cup)
- 1 tablespoon fresh oregano leaves

SEASON the chicken with ¼ teaspoon each salt and pepper. Cook in oil in a large skillet over medium heat until cooked through, 2 to 4 minutes per side; slice.

SHAPE the pizza dough into 4 rounds and place on 2 oiled baking sheets. Top with the chicken, marinara sauce, and ricotta, dividing evenly. Bake at 450°F until golden, 16 to 18 minutes. Top the pizzas with the Parmesan and oregano.

4

Chicken, Cheddar, and Bacon Salad

HANDS-ON: **30 MINUTES** TOTAL: **30 MINUTES** SERVES **4**

- 5 slices bacon
- 1 tablespoon olive oil
- 4 chicken cutlets (about ¾ pound total)
  Kosher salt and black pepper
- 1 small head romaine, chopped
- 4 ounces Cheddar, cubed (about 1 cup)
- ¼ small red onion, thinly sliced
- 6 tablespoons of your favorite vinaigrette

COOK the bacon in a large skillet over medium heat until crisp, 6 to 8 minutes; remove and crumble. Add the oil to the skillet.

SEASON the chicken with ¼ teaspoon each salt and pepper and cook until cooked through, 2 to 4 minutes per side; slice.

TOSS with the bacon, romaine, Cheddar, red onion, and vinaigrette.

5

Jerk Chicken with Seared Pineapple

HANDS-ON: **30 MINUTES** TOTAL: **45 MINUTES** SERVES **4**

- 1 cup jasmine rice
- ½ pineapple, cut into spears
- 3 tablespoons canola oil
- 8 chicken cutlets (about 1½ pounds total)
- 1 tablespoon jerk seasoning or rub
- ¼ cup fresh cilantro leaves

COOK the rice according to the package directions. Cook the pineapple in 1 tablespoon of the oil in a large skillet over medium heat, turning occasionally, until golden, 12 to 14 minutes; remove.

ADD the remaining 2 tablespoons of oil to the skillet. Rub the chicken with the jerk seasoning. Cook in batches until cooked through, 2 to 4 minutes per side. Serve with the rice and pineapple and top with cilantro.

6

Chicken Salad with Celery and Shallot

HANDS-ON: **25 MINUTES** TOTAL: **25 MINUTES** SERVES **4**

- 6 chicken cutlets (about 1 pound total)
- ¼ lemon, sliced
- 3 stalks celery, 1 halved and 2 chopped, plus 2 tablespoons chopped celery leaves
  Kosher salt and black pepper
- 1 small shallot, chopped
- ⅔ cup mayonnaise
- ¼ cup chopped roasted almonds
- ¼ cup raisins
  Lettuce leaves and toasted baguette, for serving

SIMMER the chicken, lemon, halved celery stalk, and ½ teaspoon pepper in a large saucepan of salted water until cooked through, 4 to 5 minutes. Shred the chicken.

TOSS the chicken with the chopped celery, celery leaves, shallot, mayonnaise, almonds, and raisins; season with ¼ teaspoon pepper. Serve over lettuce with the baguette.

7

Prosciutto Chicken
with Broccolini

HANDS-ON: 25 MINUTES TOTAL: **25 MINUTES** SERVES **4**

- 8 chicken cutlets (about 1½ pounds total)
  Kosher salt and black pepper
- 8 slices prosciutto (about 4 ounces)
- 2 bunches broccolini, trimmed
- 2 tablespoons olive oil
  Lemon wedges, for serving

PLACE the chicken on a baking sheet; season with ¼ teaspoon each salt and pepper. Place the prosciutto on a second baking sheet. Roast at 450°F until the chicken is cooked through and the prosciutto is darkened, 6 to 8 minutes.

STEAM the broccolini until tender, 3 to 5 minutes. Toss with the oil; season with ¼ teaspoon each salt and pepper.

TOP the chicken with the prosciutto. Serve with the broccolini and lemon wedges.

8

Lemony Chicken and
Olive Pasta

HANDS-ON: 25 MINUTES TOTAL: **25 MINUTES** SERVES **4**

- ¾ pound gemelli or penne
- 4 chicken cutlets (about ¾ pound total)
- ¼ lemon, sliced, plus 1 tablespoon lemon zest and
  1 tablespoon lemon juice
  Kosher salt and black pepper
- ⅓ cup chopped fresh flat-leaf parsley
- ⅓ cup grated pecorino (about 1½ ounces)
- ¼ cup pitted kalamata olives, sliced
- 3 tablespoons olive oil
- ½ clove garlic, finely chopped

COOK the pasta according to the package directions; drain.

SIMMER the chicken, lemon, and ¼ teaspoon pepper in a large saucepan of salted water until cooked through, 4 to 5 minutes. Shred the chicken. Discard the lemon.

TOSS the parsley, pecorino, olives, oil, lemon zest, lemon juice, garlic, pasta, and shredded chicken. Season with ¾ teaspoon salt and ½ teaspoon pepper.

9
Crispy Chicken with Corn Salad

HANDS-ON: **30 MINUTES** TOTAL: **30 MINUTES** SERVES **4**

8 chicken cutlets (about 1½ pounds total)
   Kosher salt and black pepper
2 large eggs, lightly beaten
2 cups crushed corn flakes
5 tablespoons canola oil
1 cup fresh corn kernels (from 1 to 2 ears)
1 pint cherry tomatoes, halved
2 tablespoons olive oil
1 tablespoon fresh lime juice
1 tablespoon chopped fresh chives

SEASON the chicken with ½ teaspoon salt and ¼ teaspoon pepper. Dip the chicken in the eggs (letting the excess drip off), then the corn flakes.

FRY in batches in the canola oil in a large nonstick skillet over medium heat until golden, 2 to 4 minutes per side.

TOSS the corn, tomatoes, olive oil, lime juice, and chives. Season with ¼ teaspoon each salt and pepper. Serve with the chicken.

10
Spicy Chicken and Ranch Sandwich with Crudités

HANDS-ON: **25 MINUTES** TOTAL: **25 MINUTES** SERVES **4**

4 chicken cutlets (about ¾ pound total)
¼ teaspoon cayenne pepper
   Kosher salt
1 tablespoon olive oil
½ cup ranch dressing
8 slices bread, toasted
½ cup sliced dill pickles
4 lettuce leaves
   Crudités, for serving

SEASON the chicken with the cayenne and ¼ teaspoon salt. Cook in the oil in a large skillet over medium heat until cooked through, 2 to 4 minutes per side.

SPREAD the ranch dressing, dividing evenly, on the bread. Top with the chicken, pickles, and lettuce. Serve with crudités.

TIP
Since chicken thighs
are dark meat, they
can still look a bit pink
when fully cooked.
Use an instant-read
thermometer to con-
firm they reach 165°F.

**ROASTED
CHICKEN WITH
ASPARAGUS**
PAGE 97

Chicken Thighs

Juicy thighs deliver the flavor of a whole roasted chicken in half the time. They have a slightly higher fat content than chicken breasts, which helps them to stay moist no matter how they're cooked—breaded, shredded, or served whole.

1
Crispy Chicken with Coleslaw

HANDS-ON: **20 MINUTES** TOTAL: **20 MINUTES** SERVES **4**

⅓ cup sour cream

1 tablespoon red wine vinegar
  Kosher salt and black pepper

½ small head red cabbage,
  thinly sliced (about 2 cups)

2 carrots, grated

8 boneless, skinless chicken
  thighs (1½ pounds)

½ cup all-purpose flour

2 large eggs, beaten

1 cup bread crumbs

½ cup canola oil
  Lemon wedges, for serving

WHISK together the sour cream, vinegar, ½ teaspoon salt, and ¼ teaspoon pepper. Add the cabbage and carrots and toss to combine.

POUND the chicken between 2 sheets of plastic wrap until ½ inch thick; season with ¾ teaspoon salt and ¼ teaspoon pepper. Dredge in the flour, dip in the eggs, then coat with the bread crumbs.

COOK the chicken in batches in the oil in a large skillet over medium heat until golden brown and cooked through, 4 to 5 minutes per side. Season with ¼ teaspoon each salt and pepper. Serve with the coleslaw and lemon wedges.

2
Chicken Cobb Salad

HANDS-ON: **30 MINUTES** TOTAL: **30 MINUTES** SERVES **4**

4 **boneless, skinless chicken thighs (¾ pound)**
3 **tablespoons olive oil**
   Kosher salt and black pepper
1 **head romaine, chopped**
2 **tablespoons red wine vinegar**
4 **hard-cooked eggs, chopped**
1 **avocado, chopped**
4 **slices cooked bacon, crumbled**
4 **ounces blue cheese, crumbled (1 cup)**

RUB the chicken with 1 tablespoon of the oil, ½ teaspoon salt, and ¼ teaspoon pepper. Roast on a rimmed baking sheet at 400°F until cooked through, 20 to 25 minutes. Shred the chicken.

TOSS the romaine with the vinegar and the remaining 2 tablespoons of oil; season with ¼ teaspoon each salt and pepper. Top with the eggs, avocado, bacon, blue cheese, and chicken.

3

Chicken with Mushroom Sauce

HANDS-ON: **25 MINUTES** TOTAL: **40 MINUTES** SERVES **4**

- 8 **boneless, skinless chicken thighs (1½ pounds)**
  Kosher salt and black pepper
- ½ **cup all-purpose flour**
- 2 **tablespoons olive oil**
- 8 **ounces cremini mushrooms, halved**
- ½ **cup white wine**
- ½ **cup chicken broth**
- 1 **pound green beans, trimmed and cooked**
  Fresh chives, chopped, for serving

SEASON the chicken with ½ teaspoon salt and ¼ teaspoon pepper; dredge in the flour. Brown in the oil in a large skillet over medium-high heat, 4 to 5 minutes per side; remove.

ADD the mushrooms to the skillet and cook, tossing, until browned, 4 to 6 minutes. Add the chicken, wine, and broth; simmer until cooked through, 8 to 10 minutes.

SERVE with the green beans and top with chives.

4

Spiced Chicken Kebabs

HANDS-ON: **25 MINUTES** TOTAL: **45 MINUTES** SERVES **4**

- 8 **boneless, skinless chicken thighs (1½ pounds),**
  cut into 1-inch pieces
- 1 **tablespoon paprika**
- 1 **tablespoon ground cumin**
- 1 **bell pepper, cut into 1-inch pieces**
- 1 **zucchini, cut into 1-inch pieces**
- 2 **tablespoons olive oil**
  Kosher salt and black pepper
- 1 **10-ounce box couscous (1½ cups)**
  Fresh mint, torn, for serving

SEASON the chicken with the paprika and cumin. Thread onto skewers with the bell pepper and zucchini. Drizzle with the oil; season with ½ teaspoon salt and ¼ teaspoon black pepper. Broil the kebabs on a rimmed baking sheet, turning once, until the chicken is cooked through, 15 to 18 minutes.

COOK the couscous according to the package directions. Serve with the kebabs and sprinkle with mint.

5

Teriyaki Chicken with Bok Choy

HANDS-ON: **10 MINUTES** TOTAL: **1 HOUR, 5 MINUTES** SERVES **4**

- 1 clove garlic, chopped
- ¼ cup plus ⅓ cup teriyaki sauce
- 8 bone-in chicken thighs (2½ pounds)
- 1 cup long-grain white rice
- 2 bunches baby bok choy, quartered

COMBINE the garlic and ¼ cup of the teriyaki sauce. Add the chicken and marinate for 30 minutes.

COOK the rice according to the package directions.

ROAST the chicken on a foil-lined rimmed baking sheet at 450°F, basting with the remaining ⅓ cup of teriyaki sauce, until cooked through, 25 to 30 minutes. Add the bok choy 10 minutes before the chicken is done. Serve over rice.

6

Chicken Philly Cheesesteaks

HANDS-ON: **30 MINUTES** TOTAL: **30 MINUTES** SERVES **4**

- 4 cups frozen French fries
- 8 boneless, skinless chicken thighs (1½ pounds), cut into strips
- 1 onion, sliced
- 1 bell pepper, sliced
- 2 tablespoons olive oil
  Kosher salt and black pepper
- 4 hoagie rolls, split
- 8 slices provolone (4 ounces)

COOK the French fries according to the package directions.

BROWN the chicken, onion, and bell pepper in oil in a large skillet over medium-high heat, 10 to 12 minutes; season with ½ teaspoon salt and ¼ teaspoon pepper.

FILL the rolls with the chicken mixture and the provolone, dividing evenly. Broil the cheesesteaks on a rimmed baking sheet until the provolone has melted, 2 to 3 minutes. Serve with the French fries.

7

Lemon and Garlic Grilled Chicken

HANDS-ON: **10 MINUTES**

TOTAL: **1 HOUR, 25 MINUTES** SERVES **4**

- 2 tablespoons lemon zest plus 2 tablespoons fresh lemon juice
- 1 tablespoon chopped garlic
- 1 tablespoon chopped fresh oregano
- 5 tablespoons olive oil
  Kosher salt and black pepper
- 8 bone-in chicken thighs (2½ pounds)
- 2 cups frozen lima beans, cooked
- 2 ounces Feta, crumbled (½ cup)
- 1 shallot, sliced

COMBINE the lemon zest and juice, garlic, oregano, 2 tablespoons of the oil, ½ teaspoon salt, and ¼ teaspoon pepper. Add the chicken and marinate for 30 minutes.

GRILL the chicken over medium heat until cooked through, 25 to 35 minutes.

TOSS the lima beans with the Feta, the remaining 3 tablespoons of oil, the shallot, and ¼ teaspoon each salt and pepper. Serve with the chicken.

8

Pesto Chicken Pasta Salad

HANDS-ON: **10 MINUTES** TOTAL: **30 MINUTES** SERVES **4**

- ¾ pound rigatoni
- 4 boneless, skinless chicken thighs (¾ pound)
- 1 tablespoon olive oil
  Kosher salt and black pepper
- ¾ cup prepared pesto
- ½ cup chopped pitted kalamata olives
- 1 cup halved bocconcini (fresh mozzarella balls)

COOK the pasta according to the package directions. Drain and let cool.

RUB the chicken with the oil, ½ teaspoon salt, and ¼ teaspoon pepper. Roast the chicken on a rimmed baking sheet at 400°F until cooked through, 20 to 25 minutes; shred the chicken.

TOSS the pasta, shredded chicken, pesto, olives, bocconcini, and ¼ teaspoon each salt and pepper.

9
Prosciutto-Wrapped Chicken

HANDS-ON: 10 MINUTES **TOTAL: 30 MINUTES** SERVES **4**

- 8 slices prosciutto
- 8 boneless, skinless chicken thighs (1½ pounds)
- 2 tablespoons butter, at room temperature
- 2 cloves garlic, chopped, plus 1 clove, sliced
   Kosher salt and black pepper
- 2 tablespoons olive oil
- 1 10-ounce package baby spinach

TOP the prosciutto with the chicken, dividing evenly, on a rimmed baking sheet. Top with the butter mixed with the chopped garlic. Season the chicken with ½ teaspoon salt and ¼ teaspoon pepper. Roll up the chicken in the prosciutto. Drizzle with 1 tablespoon of the oil. Roast at 400°F until cooked through, 25 to 30 minutes.

COOK the sliced garlic in the remaining tablespoon of oil in a large skillet over medium heat. Add the spinach and ¼ teaspoon each salt and pepper; cook until the spinach begins to wilt. Serve with the chicken.

10
Roasted Chicken with Asparagus

HANDS-ON: 10 MINUTES **TOTAL: 45 MINUTES** SERVES **4**

- 8 bone-in chicken thighs (2½ pounds)
   Kosher salt and black pepper
- 1 tablespoon olive oil
- 1 bunch asparagus, trimmed
- 1 pint grape tomatoes
- 1 tablespoon fresh thyme, plus more for serving

SEASON the chicken with ½ teaspoon salt and ¼ teaspoon pepper. Cook in batches in the oil in a large ovenproof skillet, skin-side down, until browned and crisp, 8 to 10 minutes; remove.

ADD the asparagus, tomatoes, and thyme to the skillet. Top with the chicken and roast at 400°F until the chicken is cooked through, 20 to 25 minutes. Serve sprinkled with more thyme.

TIP
A medium ear will give you about ½ cup of kernels, or you can substitute frozen corn in any of these recipes. Thaw, then pat dry before using.

SAUTÉED CORN WITH
COCONUT MILK,
CHILI, AND BASIL
PAGE 105

Corn

Will kernels get stuck in your teeth? Probably. But it'll be worth it. Here's how to enjoy the cream of summer's crop. (Come fall, you can switch to frozen—also delicious!)

1
Corn Polenta with Shrimp

HANDS-ON: **40 MINUTES** TOTAL: **1 HOUR** SERVES **4**

1 cup polenta

1 quart low-sodium chicken broth

1 cup fresh or frozen corn kernels

1 onion, chopped

1 poblano pepper, chopped

1 clove garlic, chopped

2 tablespoons olive oil

¾ pound shrimp, peeled and deveined

Kosher salt and black pepper

Hot sauce, for serving

COOK the polenta in simmering broth in a large saucepan over medium heat, whisking until creamy, 25 to 35 minutes. Stir in the corn.

COOK the onion, poblano pepper, and garlic in the oil in a skillet over medium heat until soft, 8 to 10 minutes. Stir in the shrimp; season with salt and black pepper. Cook until opaque, 5 to 6 minutes. Serve over the polenta with hot sauce.

2

Charred-Corn Succotash

HANDS-ON: **30 MINUTES** TOTAL: **30 MINUTES** SERVES **4**

1 **pound fresh fava beans,
   shelled (1 cup)**

4 **cups fresh or frozen corn
   kernels**

1 **small onion, finely chopped**

2 **small cloves garlic, finely
   chopped**

2 **tablespoons olive oil
   Kosher salt**

½ **red bell pepper, thinly sliced**

1 **scallion, thinly sliced**

BOIL the fava beans for 2 minutes;
drain and rinse under cold water to
stop the cooking. Remove the skins.

COOK the corn, onion, and garlic in
the oil in a large skillet over medium
heat until the vegetables are slightly
charred and golden, 6 to 7 minutes.
Season with 1 teaspoon salt. Add
the bell pepper and beans and cook
for 2 minutes.

REMOVE from heat, add the
scallion, and toss. Serve warm or
at room temperature.

3
Smoky Corn Chowder

HANDS-ON: 20 MINUTES TOTAL: 40 MINUTES SERVES 6

- 8 ounces sliced bacon, cut into ½-inch pieces
- 1 large sweet onion, chopped
- 2 cloves garlic, finely chopped
- ½ teaspoon smoked paprika
- ¼ teaspoon crushed red pepper
- 2½ cups fresh or frozen corn kernels
- 3 cups low-sodium chicken or vegetable broth
- 1 cup half-and-half
  Kosher salt and black pepper
- 4 scallions, thinly sliced

COOK the bacon in a large saucepan over medium heat until crisp. Discard all but 2 tablespoons of the drippings. Add the onion and cook, stirring occasionally, until soft, 5 to 7 minutes.

ADD the garlic, paprika, and red pepper and cook for 2 minutes. Add the corn, broth, and half-and-half; bring to a boil. Reduce heat and simmer for 15 minutes.

PUREE half the soup in a blender and return to the pan. Season with ½ teaspoon each salt and black pepper. Top with the scallions and bacon.

4
Green Curry with Halibut and Corn

HANDS-ON: 20 MINUTES TOTAL: 30 MINUTES SERVES 4

- 2 shallots, thinly sliced
- 3 tablespoons green curry paste
- 2 tablespoons canola oil
- 1 15-ounce can unsweetened coconut milk
- ¾ cup low-sodium chicken broth
- 2 cups fresh or frozen corn kernels
- 1½ pounds boneless, skinless halibut, cut into 1½-inch pieces
  Cooked rice
- 1 jalapeño, thinly sliced
  Fresh basil leaves and lime wedges, for serving

COOK the shallots and green curry paste in the oil in a large saucepan over medium-high heat until the shallots are soft, 2 to 3 minutes. Add the coconut milk and chicken broth and bring to a simmer.

STIR in the corn and halibut. Simmer, covered, over medium heat until the fish is opaque throughout, 6 to 8 minutes. Serve over the rice. Top with the jalapeño, basil, and a squeeze of lime.

5
Parmesan Corn Pudding

HANDS-ON: **15 MINUTES** TOTAL: **50 MINUTES** SERVES **4**

- 2 large eggs
- ½ cup milk
- 2 ounces Parmesan, grated (½ cup)
- 3 tablespoons cornmeal
- 2 cups fresh or frozen corn kernels
- 2 scallions, chopped, plus 1 scallion, sliced, for serving
- 2 tablespoons unsalted butter

PUREE the eggs, milk, Parmesan, cornmeal, and 1 cup of the corn kernels in a blender. Stir in the remaining cup of corn kernels and the chopped scallions.

MELT the butter in a small ovenproof skillet over medium heat. Pour in the corn mixture and bake at 350°F until set, 30 to 35 minutes. Top with the sliced scallion.

6
Corn Salad with Parmesan and Chilies

HANDS-ON: **15 MINUTES** TOTAL: **15 MINUTES** SERVES **8**

- 4 cups fresh or frozen corn kernels
- ¼ cup olive oil
- 2 tablespoons fresh lemon juice
- 2 red chili peppers, sliced
- 2 ounces shaved Parmesan
  Kosher salt and black pepper
- 2 tablespoons fresh oregano leaves

TOSS the corn with the oil, lemon juice, chilies, and Parmesan; season with 1 teaspoon salt and ½ teaspoon pepper. Set aside at room temperature for up to 8 hours. Toss with the oregano just before serving.

7

Corn and Tomato Salad with Cumin-Lime Dressing

HANDS-ON: 15 MINUTES TOTAL: **15 MINUTES** SERVES **4**

- 3 tablespoons olive oil
- 2 tablespoons lime juice
- ¾ teaspoon cumin seeds
  Kosher salt and black pepper
- 1 pita bread, toasted
- 1 cup fresh or frozen corn kernels
- 1 cup halved cherry tomatoes
- 4 radishes, quartered
- 2 small cucumbers, sliced
  Torn fresh mint, for serving

COMBINE 2 tablespoons of the oil, the lime juice, and cumin seeds; season with ½ teaspoon each salt and pepper.

BRUSH the pita with the remaining tablespoon of oil. Tear into pieces and toss with the corn, tomatoes, radishes, cucumbers, and the dressing. Top with mint.

8

Grilled Corn with Harissa Yogurt

HANDS-ON: 20 MINUTES TOTAL: **20 MINUTES** SERVES **4**

- ½ cup plain Greek yogurt
- 1 tablespoon fresh lemon juice
- 1 tablespoon harissa or hot sauce
  Kosher salt and black pepper
- 4 ears fresh corn, halved
- 2 teaspoons canola oil

COMBINE the yogurt, lemon juice, and harissa. Season with ½ teaspoon each salt and pepper.

BRUSH the corn with the oil. Season with ½ teaspoon each salt and pepper.

GRILL the corn over medium heat, turning occasionally, until browned and crisp-tender, 6 to 8 minutes. Serve with the yogurt for dipping or spreading.

9

Nachos with
Corn Salsa

HANDS-ON: 10 MINUTES TOTAL: **15 MINUTES** SERVES **4**

- 1 **cup fresh or frozen corn kernels**
- ½ **red onion, chopped**
- 3 **tablespoons lime juice**
- 1 **jalapeño, chopped**
  Kosher salt and black pepper
- 8 **ounces corn tortilla chips**
- 1 **cup grated Cheddar (4 ounces)**
  Fresh cilantro, sour cream, and chopped avocado, for serving

COMBINE the corn, onion, lime juice, and jalapeño. Season with salt and pepper.

SPREAD the tortilla chips on a foil-lined baking sheet. Top with the Cheddar. Bake at 400°F until the cheese melts, 5 to 6 minutes. Serve topped with the corn salsa, cilantro, sour cream, and avocado.

10

Sautéed Corn
with Coconut Milk,
Chili, and Basil

HANDS-ON: 15 MINUTES TOTAL: **15 MINUTES** SERVES **4**

- 2 **shallots, chopped**
- 1 **red chili pepper, sliced**
- 1 **tablespoon chopped fresh ginger**
- 2 **tablespoons canola oil**
- 2 **cups fresh or frozen corn kernels**
  Kosher salt
- ½ **cup coconut milk**
  Fresh basil, for serving

COOK the shallots, chili pepper, and ginger in the oil in a skillet over medium-high heat until fragrant, 1 minute. Add the corn. Cook, tossing, until the corn is crisp-tender, 3 to 5 minutes. Season with ¾ teaspoon salt. Serve drizzled with coconut milk and topped with basil.

**EGG-IN-A-HOLE WITH
SMOKED SALMON**
PAGE 113

TIP
To tell if an egg is
fresh, toss it gently
into a bowl of water.
If the egg sinks to
the bottom and lies
on its side, it's fresh.
If it sinks and stands
large-end up, get
crackin', since it's on
the verge of going
bad. If it floats, toss it.

Eggs

Beat the weekday scramble with one of these speedy, protein-packed plates. Crack eggs on a flat surface rather than on the edge of a bowl to avoid getting bits of shell in your food.

1

Frisée with Bacon and Soft-Cooked Eggs

HANDS-ON: **25 MINUTES** TOTAL: **25 MINUTES** SERVES **4**

8 large eggs

4 slices bacon

3 tablespoons red wine vinegar

1 tablespoon olive oil

4 cups frisée, torn

4 cups radicchio, torn

Black pepper

COOK the eggs in a saucepan of boiling water for 6 minutes; rinse and peel.

COOK the bacon in a large skillet over medium heat until crisp, 7 to 9 minutes; remove and crumble. Add the vinegar and oil to the drippings; stir to combine.

TOSS the frisée and radicchio with the dressing. Top with the eggs and bacon; season with ¼ teaspoon pepper.

2

Spaghetti with Herbs, Chilies, and Eggs

HANDS-ON: **10 MINUTES** TOTAL: **20 MINUTES** SERVES **4**

¾ **pound spaghetti**

4 **tablespoons olive oil**

2 **cloves garlic, sliced**

1 **red chili pepper, sliced**

½ **cup chopped fresh herbs**

4 **large eggs**

¼ **cup shaved Parmesan (1 ounce)**

COOK the pasta according to the package directions.

WARM 3 tablespoons of the oil, the garlic, and the chili pepper in a small saucepan. Toss with the pasta and herbs.

FRY the eggs in the remaining tablespoon of oil in a large nonstick skillet over medium heat. Cook until the whites are set, 2 to 3 minutes; serve on the pasta with the Parmesan.

3
Baked Eggs with Cream and Herbs

HANDS-ON: **5 MINUTES** TOTAL: **20 MINUTES** SERVES **4**

- 1 tablespoon unsalted butter, softened
- 8 tablespoons heavy cream
- 8 large eggs
  Kosher salt and black pepper
- 1 tablespoon chopped fresh herbs (such as parsley and dill)
  Toast, for serving

COAT four 4-ounce ramekins with the butter. Place 2 tablespoons cream in each ramekin. Crack 2 eggs into each ramekin; season with ½ teaspoon salt and ¼ teaspoon pepper.

BAKE at 425°F until the whites are set, 10 to 12 minutes. Sprinkle with the herbs and serve with toast.

4
Huevos Rancheros

HANDS-ON: **10 MINUTES** TOTAL: **20 MINUTES** SERVES **4**

- 1 15.5-ounce can black beans, rinsed
- 1 tablespoon fresh lime juice
- ½ teaspoon ground cumin
- 3 tablespoons olive oil
- 4 small corn tortillas
- 4 large eggs
- 1 cup salsa
- 4 ounces queso fresco or Feta, crumbled (1 cup)
- 1 avocado, sliced
- ¼ cup fresh cilantro leaves

COMBINE the beans, lime juice, cumin, and 1 tablespoon of the oil.

BRUSH the tortillas on both sides with 1 tablespoon oil; bake at 400°F until crisp, 8 to 10 minutes.

FRY the eggs in the remaining tablespoon of oil in a large nonstick skillet over medium heat. Cook until the whites are set, 2 to 3 minutes. Serve on the tortillas with the beans, salsa, cheese, avocado, and cilantro.

5

Curried Egg Salad Sandwich

HANDS-ON: 10 MINUTES TOTAL: **20 MINUTES** SERVES **4**

- 8 large eggs
- ⅓ cup mayonnaise
- 1 teaspoon curry powder
- 1 tablespoon chopped fresh chives
  Kosher salt and black pepper
- 4 slices pumpernickel bread
- 4 large leaves Bibb lettuce
  Potato chips, for serving

PLACE the eggs in a saucepan and add enough water to cover. Bring to a boil, cover, remove from heat, and let sit for 12 minutes. Rinse, peel, and coarsely chop the eggs.

COMBINE the mayonnaise and curry powder. Fold in the eggs and chives; season with ½ teaspoon salt and ¼ teaspoon pepper. Top each slice of bread with lettuce, then egg salad, dividing evenly. Serve with potato chips.

6

Spinach, Feta, and Sun-Dried Tomato Omelet

HANDS-ON: 5 MINUTES TOTAL: **10 MINUTES** SERVES **1**

- 2 large eggs
  Kosher salt and black pepper
- ½ tablespoon unsalted butter
- ½ cup spinach, chopped
- 2 tablespoons oil-packed sun-dried tomatoes, chopped
- 2 tablespoons crumbled Feta
  Country bread, for serving

BEAT the eggs with a pinch each salt and pepper. Cook in butter in a medium nonstick skillet over medium heat, stirring and tilting the pan, until just set, 2 to 3 minutes. Sprinkle with the spinach, sun-dried tomatoes, and Feta; fold over the filling. Serve with country bread.

7

Swiss Chard and Cheddar Quiche

HANDS-ON: 15 MINUTES TOTAL: 1 HOUR SERVES 6

- 1 bunch Swiss chard, chopped
- 1 onion, chopped
- 3 tablespoons olive oil
- 3 large eggs
- ¾ cup half-and-half
  Kosher salt and black pepper
- 2 ounces Cheddar, grated (½ cup)
- 1 prebaked 9-inch piecrust
- 4 cups baby lettuce
- 1 tablespoon red wine vinegar

COOK the chard and onion in 1 tablespoon of the oil in a large skillet over medium-high heat until tender, 3 to 4 minutes. Beat the eggs with the half-and-half; season with 1 teaspoon salt and ¼ teaspoon pepper. Mix in the chard mixture and Cheddar. Pour into the piecrust and bake at 350°F until set, 40 to 45 minutes.

TOSS the lettuce with the vinegar, remaining oil, ½ teaspoon salt, and ¼ teaspoon pepper. Serve with the quiche.

8

Poached Eggs with Grits and Tomatoes

HANDS-ON: 10 MINUTES TOTAL: 25 MINUTES SERVES 4

- 1 pound cherry tomatoes
- 1 bunch scallions, cut into 2-inch lengths
- 1 tablespoon olive oil
  Kosher salt and black pepper
- 1 tablespoon white vinegar
- 8 large eggs
- 1 cup quick-cooking grits
- 2 tablespoons unsalted butter

TOSS the tomatoes and scallions with the oil on a rimmed baking sheet; season with ½ teaspoon salt and ¼ teaspoon pepper. Roast at 400°F until soft, 18 to 22 minutes.

ADD the vinegar to a large skillet of barely simmering water. Crack the eggs into the water in 2 batches and cook until the whites are set, 2 to 3 minutes.

COOK the grits according to the package directions. Stir in the butter. Serve the grits topped with the eggs and vegetables.

9
Scrambled Eggs with Chorizo and Onions

HANDS-ON: **10 MINUTES** TOTAL: **50 MINUTES** SERVES **4**

1½ pounds new potatoes, halved if large
2 tablespoons olive oil
   Kosher salt and black pepper
2 ounces cured chorizo, sliced
1 small onion, chopped
8 large eggs
1 teaspoon chopped fresh chives

TOSS the potatoes with the oil on a rimmed baking sheet; season with ½ teaspoon salt and ¼ teaspoon pepper. Roast at 425°F until tender, 40 to 45 minutes.

COOK the chorizo and onion in a large nonstick skillet over medium heat until the onion is soft, 5 to 6 minutes.

BEAT the eggs with ¼ teaspoon each salt and pepper, add to the skillet, and cook, stirring, until set but still soft, 2 to 3 minutes. Sprinkle with chives and serve with the potatoes.

10
Egg-in-a-Hole with Smoked Salmon

HANDS-ON: **10 MINUTES** TOTAL: **10 MINUTES** SERVES **2**

2 slices country bread
1 tablespoon unsalted butter
2 large eggs
¼ cup crème fraîche
4 ounces smoked salmon
1 tablespoon capers
½ small red onion, thinly sliced
   Black pepper

CUT a 3-inch hole in the center of each slice of bread. Melt the butter in a large nonstick skillet over medium heat. Place the bread slices in the skillet, crack an egg into the center of each, and cook until the bread is golden and the whites are set, 1 to 2 minutes per side.

TOP with the crème fraîche, smoked salmon, capers, and red onion; season with pepper.

STEAK WITH
CHIMICHURRI SAUCE
PAGE 121

TIP
To tenderize this meat,
try a marinade. And
always slice it thinly
against the grain.

Flank Steak

Solve the mystery of what to make on busy nights with this lean-but-juicy favorite. Let the steak rest for at least 5 minutes after cooking to allow the juices to redistribute.

1

Steak and Eggs with Seared Tomatoes

HANDS-ON: **15 MINUTES** TOTAL: **15 MINUTES** SERVES **4**

1 **pound flank steak**
  Kosher salt and black pepper
1 **tablespoon plus 1 teaspoon olive oil**
4 **medium tomatoes, halved**
1 **tablespoon chopped fresh oregano**
4 **large eggs**

SEASON the steak with ½ teaspoon salt and ¼ teaspoon pepper. Cook in 1 tablespoon of the oil in a skillet over medium-high heat, 4 to 5 minutes per side for medium-rare; remove and slice.

ADD the tomatoes to the skillet, cut-side down; cook until browned. Sprinkle with the oregano and ⅛ teaspoon each salt and pepper; set aside. Meanwhile, heat the remaining teaspoon of oil in a nonstick skillet over medium heat.

CRACK the eggs into the skillet and cook, covered, to the desired doneness. Serve with the tomatoes and steak.

2
Grilled Steak, Plums, and Bok Choy

HANDS-ON: **20 MINUTES** TOTAL: **50 MINUTES** SERVES **4**

1½ **pounds flank steak**
¼ **cup soy sauce**
4 **plums, sliced**
4 **baby bok choy, halved**
1 **tablespoon canola oil**
   Kosher salt and black pepper
2 **teaspoons sesame seeds**

MARINATE the steak in the soy sauce for 30 minutes.

TOSS the plums and bok choy with the oil, ½ teaspoon salt, and ¼ teaspoon pepper.

GRILL everything over medium-high heat, turning, until the steak is medium-rare and the plums and bok choy are tender, 4 to 6 minutes. Sprinkle with the sesame seeds.

3
Spinach-Stuffed Steak Roulades

HANDS-ON: **10 MINUTES** TOTAL: **30 MINUTES** SERVES **4**

½ **pound flank steak**
¼ **cup olive tapenade**
2 **cups spinach, thick stems removed**
   Kosher salt and black pepper
2 **tablespoons olive oil**
1 **tablespoon red wine vinegar**
1 **teaspoon Dijon mustard**
6 **cups mixed greens**

CUT the steak in half horizontally (don't cut all the way through) and open like a book. Top with the tapenade and spinach. Roll up and tie with twine. Season with ½ teaspoon salt and ¼ teaspoon pepper.

GRILL the steak, covered, over medium-high heat, turning occasionally, 15 to 18 minutes for medium-rare. Let rest before slicing.

COMBINE the oil, vinegar, mustard, and ¼ teaspoon each salt and pepper and toss with the greens. Serve with the steak.

4
Chopped Steak Salad

HANDS-ON: **15 MINUTES** TOTAL: **15 MINUTES** SERVES **4**

¾ **pound flank steak**
   Kosher salt and black pepper
1 **head romaine, chopped**
¼ **small head red cabbage, chopped (about 2 cups)**
1 **15.5-ounce can white beans, rinsed**
½ **cup chopped roasted red peppers**
¼ **cup chopped fresh parsley**
¼ **cup store-bought Italian dressing**

SEASON the steak with ½ teaspoon salt and ¼ teaspoon black pepper. Broil 4 to 5 minutes per side for medium-rare; chop into ½-inch pieces.

COMBINE the romaine, red cabbage, beans, red peppers, parsley, and steak. Toss with the dressing.

5

Sweet and Spicy
Beef Stir-Fry

HANDS-ON: **20 MINUTES** TOTAL: **20 MINUTES** SERVES **4**

8 ounces lo mein or other Asian noodles
1 pound flank steak, thinly sliced against the grain
  Kosher salt and black pepper
1 tablespoon canola oil
½ pound snow peas, halved lengthwise
2 medium carrots, thinly sliced
2 shallots, sliced
⅓ cup red pepper jelly

COOK the noodles according to the package directions.

SEASON the steak with ½ teaspoon salt and ¼ teaspoon pepper. Brown in the oil in a skillet over medium-high heat, 3 to 4 minutes; remove.

ADD the snow peas, carrots, and shallots to the skillet and cook, tossing, 4 minutes. Return the steak to the skillet and add the jelly; toss. Serve with the noodles.

6

Steak Sandwiches
with Brie

HANDS-ON: **15 MINUTES** TOTAL: **15 MINUTES** SERVES **4**

½ pound flank steak
  Kosher salt and black pepper
1 tablespoon olive oil
1 baguette, cut crosswise into 4 pieces
1 cup baby arugula
8 ounces sliced Brie
¼ small red onion, sliced

SEASON the steak with ½ teaspoon salt and ¼ teaspoon pepper. Cook in the oil in a skillet over medium-high heat 4 to 5 minutes per side for medium-rare; slice.

FORM sandwiches with the baguette pieces, arugula, steak, Brie, and onion.

7

Beef Skewers with Blue Cheese Sauce

HANDS-ON: 15 MINUTES **TOTAL: 25 MINUTES** **MAKES 16**

- ½ **pound flank steak**
- 2 **tablespoons balsamic vinegar**
  Kosher salt and black pepper
- ½ **cup blue cheese dressing**
- 2 **scallions, sliced**

FREEZE the flank steak for 10 minutes; slice very thinly. Thread onto skewers.

BRUSH the steak with the vinegar and season with ¼ teaspoon each salt and pepper.

GRILL over medium-high heat until cooked through, 1 to 2 minutes per side. Serve with the blue cheese dressing and sprinkle with the scallions.

8

Cuban Braised Beef

HANDS-ON: 15 MINUTES

TOTAL: 2 HOURS, 15 MINUTES **SERVES 4**

- 1 **28-ounce can diced tomatoes**
- 1½ **pounds flank steak, cut in half crosswise**
- 1 **large onion, cut into wedges**
- 1½ **teaspoons chili powder**
  Kosher salt and black pepper
  Cooked rice, for serving
- ½ **ripe mango, peeled, pitted, and cut into bite-size pieces**
- ¼ **cup fresh cilantro leaves**

COMBINE the tomatoes, steak, onion, chili powder, ½ teaspoon salt, and ¼ teaspoon pepper in a large saucepan. Simmer, covered, until fork-tender, about 2 hours.

SHRED the beef and serve with the rice. Top with the mango and cilantro.

9
Grilled Beef and Pepper Fajitas

HANDS-ON: 20 MINUTES TOTAL: 20 MINUTES SERVES 4

- 1 pound flank steak
- 1 teaspoon ground cumin
  Kosher salt and black pepper
- 2 bell peppers, sliced ½ inch thick
- 1 tablespoon olive oil
- 8 small tortillas
- 1 avocado, sliced
- ½ cup sour cream
  Hot sauce, for serving

SEASON the steak with the cumin, ½ teaspoon salt, and ¼ teaspoon black pepper.

TOSS the bell peppers with the oil and ¼ teaspoon each salt and pepper.

GRILL everything over medium-high heat, turning, until the steak is medium-rare and the peppers are tender, 8 to 12 minutes.

SLICE the steak. Serve the steak and peppers with the tortillas, avocado, sour cream, and hot sauce.

10
Steak with Chimichurri Sauce

HANDS-ON: 20 MINUTES TOTAL: 20 MINUTES SERVES 4

- 1½ pounds flank steak
  Kosher salt and black pepper
- ½ cup chopped fresh parsley
- 1 tablespoon red wine vinegar
- 1 clove garlic, chopped
- ¼ teaspoon crushed red pepper
- ⅓ cup olive oil
- 4 ears fresh corn, grilled

HEAT grill to medium-high.

SEASON the steak with ½ teaspoon salt and ¼ teaspoon black pepper. Grill the steak, 4 to 5 minutes per side for medium-rare.

COMBINE the parsley, vinegar, garlic, red pepper, oil, and ¼ teaspoon salt. Serve over the steak with the grilled corn.

TIP
Shaping ground beef can be a sticky business. To keep meat from glomming onto your hands, wet them in cold water first (repeat as needed). The moisture will create a barrier between your skin and the meat.

BURGER WITH RICOTTA SALATA AND PICKLED ZUCCHINI
PAGE 129

Ground Beef

Chuck your tried-and-true meat loaf and burger recipes—at least for now—and cook up one of these twists on the beloved wallet-friendly staple. (You can also substitute ground turkey, pork, or lamb.)

1
Easy Shepherd's Pie

HANDS-ON: **10 MINUTES** TOTAL: **20 MINUTES** SERVES **4**

1 pound ground beef

⅓ cup ketchup

1 teaspoon Worcestershire sauce

8 ounces frozen mixed vegetables (such as carrots, peas, and corn), thawed

¼ cup (1 ounce) grated Cheddar (optional)

1 16-ounce package mashed potatoes, refrigerated or frozen and thawed

COOK the beef in a large skillet over medium-high heat until no trace of pink remains, about 5 minutes. Spoon off any fat. Stir in the ketchup and Worcestershire. Add the vegetables and cook, stirring, 1 minute. Spoon into a baking dish.

MIX the cheese (if desired) with the potatoes. Spread over the beef and bake at 400°F until heated through, 10 minutes.

2

Beef and Mushroom Ragù with Pappardelle

HANDS-ON: **20 MINUTES** TOTAL: **25 MINUTES** SERVES **4**

½ pound pappardelle or fettuccine

10 ounces button mushrooms, quartered

½ medium onion, chopped

2 cloves garlic, chopped

Kosher salt and black pepper

2 tablespoons olive oil

⅛ pound ground beef

2 tablespoons tomato paste

¼ cup dry white wine

1 14.5-ounce can diced tomatoes

Grated Parmesan, for serving

COOK the pasta according to the package directions; drain.

COOK the mushrooms, onion, garlic, ½ teaspoon salt, and ¼ teaspoon pepper in the oil in a large skillet over medium-high heat until the onion is soft, 5 to 7 minutes. Add the beef and brown, 3 to 5 minutes.

ADD the tomato paste and wine; simmer until the wine is nearly evaporated. Add the tomatoes (and their juices) and simmer until thickened, 4 to 5 minutes.

TOSS with the pasta. Serve sprinkled with the Parmesan.

3
Quick Beef Tacos

HANDS-ON: **20 MINUTES** TOTAL: **20 MINUTES** SERVES **4**

1½ pounds ground beef
1 teaspoon ground cumin
1½ cups jarred salsa
   Kosher salt
8 taco shells
1 avocado, diced
½ cup sour cream
1 cup fresh cilantro

BROWN the beef in a large skillet over medium-high heat, breaking it up with a spoon, 6 to 8 minutes. Spoon off and discard any drippings. Stir in the cumin, 1 cup of the salsa, and ¾ teaspoon salt and cook, stirring occasionally, until heated through, 2 to 3 minutes.

FILL the taco shells with the beef mixture and top with the avocado, sour cream, cilantro, and the remaining ½ cup of salsa.

4
Glazed Meatballs

HANDS-ON: **30 MINUTES** TOTAL: **30 MINUTES** SERVES **4**

1 pound ground beef
½ small onion, finely chopped
½ cup bread crumbs
1 large egg
¼ teaspoon ground nutmeg
   Kosher salt and black pepper
1 cup currant jelly
   Smashed potatoes and chopped fresh dill,
   for serving

COMBINE the beef, onion, bread crumbs, egg, nutmeg, ½ tablespoon salt, and 1 teaspoon pepper. Shape into 1-inch balls.

BOIL the meatballs until cooked through, 5 to 6 minutes.

HEAT the jelly in a large skillet; add the meatballs and toss to coat. Serve the meatballs with smashed potatoes, sprinkled with dill.

5

Parmesan Meat Loaf

HANDS-ON: **10 MINUTES** TOTAL: **1 HOUR** SERVES **4**

1½ pounds ground beef
1 large egg
1 onion, grated
½ cup chopped fresh flat-leaf parsley
½ cup bread crumbs
½ cup grated Parmesan (2 ounces)
¼ cup tomato paste
   Kosher salt and black pepper
   Salad greens, for serving

COMBINE the beef, egg, onion, parsley, bread crumbs, Parmesan, and tomato paste; season with 1 teaspoon salt and 1 teaspoon pepper.

FORM the mixture into an 8-inch loaf on a foil-lined baking sheet. Bake at 400°F until cooked through, 40 to 50 minutes. Serve with a salad.

6

Lemony Meatball and Escarole Soup

HANDS-ON: **40 MINUTES** TOTAL: **50 MINUTES** SERVES **4**

1 pound ground beef
½ small onion, finely chopped
½ cup bread crumbs
1 large egg
¼ teaspoon ground nutmeg
   Kosher salt and black pepper
6 cups chicken broth
1 14.5-ounce can cannellini beans, rinsed
2 cloves garlic, thinly sliced
1 small head escarole, torn (about 8 cups)
1 tablespoon fresh lemon juice

COMBINE the beef, onion, bread crumbs, egg, nutmeg, ½ tablespoon salt, and 1 teaspoon pepper. Shape into 1-inch balls.

BOIL until cooked through, 5 to 6 minutes.

COMBINE the broth, beans, garlic, and meatballs in a saucepan; bring to a boil. Stir in the escarole; reduce heat and simmer until tender, 8 to 10 minutes. Add the lemon juice and season with ½ teaspoon each salt and pepper.

7

Burger with Cheddar, Avocado, and Sprouts

HANDS-ON: **25 MINUTES** TOTAL: **25 MINUTES** SERVES **4**

1¼ pounds ground chuck (85 percent lean or less)
    Kosher salt and black pepper
    Canola oil, for the grill
 4 ounces Cheddar, sliced
 8 slices multigrain bread
 ½ cup mayonnaise
 4 leaves red leaf lettuce
 1 avocado, sliced
 ½ cup alfalfa or radish sprouts

FORM the beef into four ¾-inch-thick patties; season with ½ teaspoon each salt and pepper. Oil the grill rack and grill, 4 to 5 minutes per side. During the last 3 minutes of cooking, top the burgers with the Cheddar.

SPREAD the bread slices with the mayonnaise.

FORM sandwiches with the bread, lettuce, burgers, 1 slice avocado, and sprouts.

8

Burger with Bacon and Egg

HANDS-ON: **20 MINUTES** TOTAL: **25 MINUTES** SERVES **4**

1¼ pounds ground chuck (85 percent lean or less)
 4 slices bacon, chopped
    Kosher salt and black pepper
 2 teaspoons canola oil, plus more for the grill
 4 English muffins, split
 4 large eggs
 1 large tomato, sliced

COMBINE the beef, bacon, and ½ teaspoon each salt and pepper.

FORM the beef into four ¾-inch-thick patties. Oil the grill rack and grill, 4 to 5 minutes per side. Grill the English muffins, split-side down, until toasted, 10 to 20 seconds.

COOK the eggs in oil, covered, in a large skillet over medium heat, 2 to 3 minutes for slightly runny yolks. Season with ¼ teaspoon each salt and pepper.

STACK the tomato, burgers, and eggs between the muffins.

9

Burger with Barbecue Sauce, Pepper Jack, and Jalapeños

HANDS-ON: **15 MINUTES** TOTAL: **15 MINUTES** SERVES **4**

- 1¼ pounds ground chuck (85 percent lean or less)
  Kosher salt and black pepper
  Canola oil, for the grill
- 4 ounces pepper Jack, sliced
- 4 Kaiser rolls, split
- ¼ cup barbecue sauce
- 4 leaves romaine
- 1 large tomato, sliced
- ½ cup sliced pickled jalapeños

FORM the beef into four ¾-inch-thick patties; season with ½ teaspoon each salt and pepper. Oil the grill rack and grill, 4 to 5 minutes per side. Top the burgers with the pepper Jack during the last 3 minutes of cooking.

GRILL the rolls until toasted, 1 to 2 minutes. Spread with the barbecue sauce. Form sandwiches with the rolls, romaine, burgers, tomato, and jalapeños.

10

Burger with Ricotta Salata and Pickled Zucchini

HANDS-ON: **25 MINUTES** TOTAL: **35 MINUTES** SERVES **4**

- ¼ cup distilled white vinegar
- 2 tablespoons sugar
- ½ teaspoon crushed red pepper
  Kosher salt and black pepper
- 2 zucchini
- 1¼ pounds ground chuck (85 percent lean or less)
  Canola oil, for the grill
- 4 brioche buns, split
- ¼ head radicchio
- 4 ounces ricotta salata or Feta, thinly sliced

COMBINE the vinegar and sugar with the red pepper and 1 teaspoon salt. Cut the zucchini into ribbons with a vegetable peeler; add to the vinegar mixture and let stand for 10 minutes.

FORM the beef into four ¾-inch-thick patties; season with ½ teaspoon each salt and black pepper. Oil the grill rack and grill, 4 to 5 minutes per side.

FORM sandwiches with the buns, radicchio, burgers, ricotta salata, and pickled zucchini.

TIP
Cook ground turkey
until it's no longer pink.
But don't leave it on
the heat too long—it
dries out more quickly
than ground beef does.

**THAI TURKEY
SALAD**
PAGE 137

Ground Turkey

This family favorite is leaner than beef, less pricey than lamb, and—as you'll see on these pages—fast-cooking and versatile, too. Gobble, gobble.

1
Turkey Meat Loaf

HANDS-ON: **20 MINUTES** TOTAL: **45 MINUTES** SERVES **4**

1½ **pounds ground turkey**

¼ **cup bread crumbs**

1 **large egg**

½ **medium onion, grated**

½ **cup plus 2 tablespoons whole milk**

¼ **cup plus 2 tablespoons ketchup**

Kosher salt and black pepper

1½ **pounds new potatoes, cut into 1-inch chunks**

¼ **cup (½ stick) unsalted butter**

1 **pound green beans, trimmed**

COMBINE the turkey, bread crumbs, egg, onion, and 2 tablespoons each of the milk and ketchup; season with ½ teaspoon each salt and pepper. Form into a loaf on a rimmed baking sheet and top with the remaining ¼ cup of ketchup. Bake at 450°F for 30 to 35 minutes.

BOIL the potatoes with 1 teaspoon salt in enough water to cover. Reduce heat and simmer until tender, 20 to 25 minutes; drain. Mash with the butter, the remaining ½ cup milk, and ¼ teaspoon pepper.

BOIL the green beans with 1 tablespoon salt until just tender, 4 to 5 minutes. Rinse to cool; drain. Serve with the meat loaf and potatoes.

2
Turkey Empanadas

HANDS-ON: **15 MINUTES** TOTAL: **40 MINUTES** SERVES **4**

¾ **pound ground turkey**
1 **onion, chopped**
1 **clove garlic, chopped**
1 **teaspoon cumin**
1 **tablespoon olive oil**
⅓ **cup raisins**
½ **cup pitted olives**
   Kosher salt and black pepper
2 **refrigerated piecrusts, halved**
   Mixed salad, for serving

BROWN the turkey with the onion, garlic, and cumin in oil in a large skillet over medium-high heat. Stir in the raisins and olives; season with ½ teaspoon salt and ¼ teaspoon pepper.

TOP the piecrust halves with the turkey mixture; fold in half and seal the edges. Bake at 375°F until golden, 20 to 25 minutes. Serve with a salad.

3

Eggs with Turkey Breakfast Sausage

HANDS-ON: **15 MINUTES** TOTAL: **15 MINUTES** SERVES **4**

- 1 pound ground turkey
- 1 teaspoon dried sage
- ½ teaspoon dried thyme
- 1 tablespoon pure maple syrup
  Kosher salt and black pepper
- 1 tablespoon canola oil
- 8 large eggs, beaten
- 1 tablespoon unsalted butter
  Fruit, for serving

COMBINE the turkey, sage, thyme, and maple syrup; season with ½ teaspoon salt and ¼ teaspoon pepper. Form into eight 2½-inch-thick patties and cook in the oil in a large skillet, turning once, until cooked through, 2 to 3 minutes per side.

SEASON the eggs with ¼ teaspoon each salt and pepper. Cook in the butter in a large skillet over medium heat, stirring, until set but still soft, 2 to 3 minutes. Serve with the sausage patties and fruit.

4

Turkey Sloppy Joes

HANDS-ON: **15 MINUTES** TOTAL: **15 MINUTES** SERVES **4**

- 1 pound ground turkey
- 1 onion, chopped
- 1 clove garlic, chopped
- 1 tablespoon canola oil
- 1 8-ounce can tomato sauce
- ¼ cup dark brown sugar
- ¼ cup barbecue sauce
- 1 tablespoon Worcestershire sauce
  Kosher salt and black pepper
- 4 hamburger buns
  Coleslaw, for serving

BROWN the turkey, onion, and garlic in the oil in a large skillet. Mix in the tomato sauce, brown sugar, barbecue sauce, and Worcestershire; season with ½ teaspoon salt and ¼ teaspoon pepper. Simmer until thickened, 3 to 5 minutes.

SERVE on the buns with coleslaw.

5
Turkey Fried Rice

HANDS-ON: **20 MINUTES** TOTAL: **40 MINUTES** SERVES **4**

¾ cup long-grain white rice
½ pound ground turkey
1 tablespoon chopped garlic
1 tablespoon chopped ginger
4 scallions, sliced
2 tablespoons canola oil
1 cup frozen peas
1 cup snow peas, halved
4 carrots, sliced
2 tablespoons hoisin sauce
2 tablespoons rice vinegar

COOK the rice according to the package directions.
BROWN the turkey, garlic, ginger, and half the scallions in the oil in a large skillet. Add the rice, peas, snow peas, carrots, hoisin sauce, and vinegar and cook until heated through, 2 to 3 minutes. Top with the remaining scallions.

6
Turkey-Chorizo Tacos

HANDS-ON: **15 MINUTES** TOTAL: **15 MINUTES** SERVES **4**

1 onion, chopped
4 ounces Spanish chorizo, chopped
1 tablespoon canola oil
½ pound ground turkey
Kosher salt and black pepper
8 corn tortillas, warmed
Sour cream, sliced avocado, salsa, fresh cilantro sprigs, and lime wedges, for serving

COOK the onion and chorizo in the oil in a large skillet over medium-high heat until crisp. Add the turkey, season with ½ teaspoon salt and ¼ teaspoon pepper, and cook until no longer pink, 3 to 5 minutes.
DIVIDE the mixture among the tortillas and top with sour cream, avocado, salsa, cilantro, and lime wedges.

7

Turkey and Feta Flatbread

HANDS-ON: **10 MINUTES** TOTAL: **40 MINUTES** SERVES **4**

- ½ **pound ground turkey**
- ½ **teaspoon dried oregano**
- 1 **tablespoon olive oil, plus more for the baking sheet**
  Kosher salt and black pepper
- 1 **pound pizza dough**
- 1 **cup roasted red peppers, sliced**
- 4 **ounces Feta, crumbled (1 cup)**
  Chopped fresh parsley, for serving

BROWN the turkey with the oregano in the oil in a large skillet over medium-high heat; season with ½ teaspoon salt and ¼ teaspoon black pepper.

SHAPE the dough into a large oval and place on an oiled baking sheet. Top with the turkey mixture, red peppers, and Feta. Bake at 400°F until golden, 30 to 35 minutes. Sprinkle with chopped parsley.

8

Turkey-Barley Vegetable Soup

HANDS-ON: **15 MINUTES** TOTAL: **45 MINUTES** SERVES **4**

- ½ **pound ground turkey**
- 1 **tablespoon olive oil**
- 1 **onion, chopped**
- 1 **carrot, sliced**
- 1 **stalk celery, chopped**
- 6 **cups chicken broth**
- ½ **cup pearl barley**
  Kosher salt and black pepper
- 3 **cups baby spinach, chopped**

BROWN the turkey in the oil in a saucepan over medium-high heat; remove. Add the onion, carrot, and celery to the saucepan and cook, stirring often, until softened, 3 to 5 minutes.

RETURN the turkey to the saucepan and add the broth and barley; season with ¾ teaspoon each salt and pepper. Simmer until the barley is tender, 25 to 30 minutes. Stir in the spinach.

9

Pasta with Turkey and Broccoli

HANDS-ON: **15 MINUTES** TOTAL: **20 MINUTES** SERVES **4**

- ¾ pound orecchiette
- 2 cups broccoli florets
- 1 pound ground turkey
- 2 cloves garlic, chopped
- 1 teaspoon fennel seed
- ½ teaspoon crushed red pepper
- 3 tablespoons olive oil
  Kosher salt
  Parmesan, grated, for serving

COOK the pasta according to the package directions, adding the broccoli during the last minute. Drain and return to the pot.

BROWN the turkey with the garlic, fennel seed, and red pepper in 1 tablespoon of the oil in a large skillet over medium-high heat; season with ½ teaspoon salt. Toss with the pasta and broccoli and the remaining 2 tablespoons of olive oil. Serve with grated Parmesan.

10

Thai Turkey Salad

HANDS-ON: **20 MINUTES** TOTAL: **20 MINUTES** SERVES **4**

- 1 pound ground turkey
- 1 tablespoon canola oil
- 2 tablespoons fish sauce
- 2 tablespoons brown sugar
- 4 cups shredded cabbage
- ¼ English cucumber, sliced
- ½ cup fresh mint leaves
- ½ cup chopped peanuts
- 2 tablespoons fresh lime juice
  Lime wedges, for serving

BROWN the turkey in the oil in a large skillet over medium-high heat. Add the fish sauce, brown sugar, and ¼ cup water and cook, stirring, until the liquid has almost evaporated, 2 to 4 minutes.

TOSS the cabbage, cucumber, mint, and peanuts with the lime juice. Top with the turkey and serve with lime wedges.

TIP
Link sausages burst open when cooked too quickly. Don't pierce them with a fork (which releases their juices); just turn down the heat, and turn throughout cooking for even browning.

GRILLED SAUSAGE AND FENNEL SALAD
PAGE 145

Italian Sausage

You can make these dishes with either sweet or hot Italian pork sausage. When the recipe indicates that the sausage casings should be removed, just cut down the length of the links with a paring knife or kitchen shears and remove the meat.

1
Sausage with White Beans and Tarragon

HANDS-ON: **30 MINUTES** TOTAL: **30 MINUTES** SERVES **4**

8 small Italian sausage links (about 1½ pounds)

2 tablespoons olive oil

2 medium carrots, thinly sliced on the bias

1 onion, chopped
  Kosher salt and black pepper

1 15-ounce can white beans, rinsed

¾ cup dry white wine

1 tablespoon fresh tarragon

COOK the sausages in the oil in a skillet over medium-high heat for 10 to 12 minutes; remove and slice. Add the carrots, onion, ½ teaspoon salt, and ¼ teaspoon pepper to the skillet and cook over medium heat until tender, 8 to 10 minutes.

ADD the beans and wine; simmer for 5 minutes. Fold in the sausage and tarragon.

2

Mediterranean
Stuffed Zucchini

HANDS-ON: **15 MINUTES** TOTAL: **35 MINUTES** SERVES **4**

½ **pound Italian sausage links, casings removed**

1 **tablespoon olive oil**

¼ **cup grated Asiago (1 ounce)**

2 **tablespoons pine nuts**

2 **tablespoons chopped sun-dried tomatoes**

2 **scallions, chopped**

4 **medium zucchini, halved lengthwise**

BROWN the sausage, breaking it up with a spoon, in the oil in a skillet over medium-high heat, 5 to 7 minutes. Mix in the Asiago, pine nuts, tomatoes, and scallions.

HOLLOW out the zucchini and fill with the sausage mixture. Roast at 400°F until tender, 12 to 15 minutes.

3

Shrimp with Sausage and Tomatoes

HANDS-ON: **25 MINUTES** TOTAL: **30 MINUTES** SERVES **4**

- 1 cup long-grain white rice
- 1 pound Italian sausage links, casings removed
- 2 medium onions, sliced
- 2 tablespoons olive oil
- 1 28-ounce can diced fire-roasted tomatoes
- 20 peeled and deveined medium shrimp
- 1 cup frozen peas
  Kosher salt and black pepper

COOK the rice according to the package directions.

BROWN the sausage and onions in the oil in a skillet over medium heat for 10 minutes. Add the tomatoes, shrimp, and peas; season with ½ teaspoon salt and ¼ teaspoon pepper. Simmer until the shrimp are opaque, 3 to 5 minutes. Serve over the rice.

4

Cauliflower and Sausage Flatbread

HANDS-ON: **10 MINUTES** TOTAL: **35 MINUTES** SERVES **4**

- ½ head cauliflower, sliced
- 1 red chili pepper, thinly sliced
- 1 cup fresh flat-leaf parsley leaves
- 1 tablespoon olive oil, plus more for the baking sheet
  Kosher salt and black pepper
- 1 pound pizza dough, thawed if frozen
- 2 cups grated Gruyère (8 ounces)
- ½ pound Italian sausage links, casings removed and broken into small pieces

TOSS the cauliflower, chili pepper, and parsley with the oil, ½ teaspoon salt, and ¼ teaspoon black pepper.

SHAPE the pizza dough into an oval; place on an oiled baking sheet. Top with the cauliflower mixture, Gruyère, and sausage. Bake at 425°F until golden, 25 to 30 minutes.

5

Sautéed Sausage and Swiss Chard over Polenta

HANDS-ON: 20 MINUTES TOTAL: 20 MINUTES SERVES 4

- 8 small Italian sausage links (about 1½ pounds total)
- 2 tablespoons olive oil
- 1 cup instant polenta
- 4 cloves garlic, sliced
- 1 bunch Swiss chard, stems discarded and leaves cut into 1-inch strips
   Kosher salt and black pepper

BROWN the sausages in 1 tablespoon of the oil in a skillet over medium-high heat, 10 to 12 minutes; remove and slice.

COOK the polenta according to the package directions.

COOK the garlic in the remaining tablespoon of oil in the skillet over medium heat for 1 minute. Add the chard, ½ teaspoon salt, and ¼ teaspoon pepper; cook, tossing, until wilted, 3 to 4 minutes. Fold in the sausage. Serve over the polenta.

6

Roasted Sausage and Grapes

HANDS-ON: 5 MINUTES TOTAL: 30 MINUTES SERVES 4

- 2 pounds seedless red grapes
- 8 sprigs fresh thyme
- 1 tablespoon olive oil
   Kosher salt and black pepper
- 8 small Italian sausage links (about 1½ pounds)

TOSS the grapes and thyme with the oil, ½ teaspoon salt, and ¼ teaspoon pepper on a rimmed baking sheet.

NESTLE the sausages among the grapes. Roast at 400°F, tossing occasionally, until the sausages are cooked, 20 to 25 minutes.

7

Fettuccine with Sausage and Cabbage

HANDS-ON: **20 MINUTES** TOTAL: **20 MINUTES** SERVES **4**

- 8 ounces fettuccine (½ box)
- ¾ pound Italian sausage links, casings removed
- 2 tablespoons olive oil
- ½ small Savoy cabbage, thinly sliced (about 6 cups)
- 3 shallots, sliced
  Kosher salt and black pepper
- ¾ cup low-sodium chicken broth
- ¼ cup chopped fresh chives

COOK the pasta according to the package directions; drain.

BROWN the sausage, breaking it up with a spoon, in 1 tablespoon of the oil in a skillet over medium-high heat, 5 to 6 minutes; remove.

WIPE out the skillet. Add the remaining tablespoon of oil, the cabbage, shallots, ½ teaspoon salt, and ¼ teaspoon pepper to the skillet; cook over medium heat for 6 minutes. Add the broth and simmer until tender, 3 to 4 minutes. Toss with the pasta, sausage, and chives.

8

Sausage, Pepper, and Cheddar Omelet

HANDS-ON: **10 MINUTES** TOTAL: **10 MINUTES** SERVES **1**

- 2 ounces Italian sausage links, casings removed
- ¼ red bell pepper, chopped
- 1 tablespoon olive oil
- 2 large eggs, beaten
- 1 teaspoon unsalted butter
- ¼ cup grated extra-sharp Cheddar (about 1 ounce)
  Kosher salt and black pepper

BROWN the sausage with the bell pepper in the oil in a skillet over medium-high heat.

COOK the eggs in the butter in a nonstick skillet over medium heat, stirring and tilting the pan, until just set, about 3 minutes. Sprinkle with the sausage mixture and Cheddar; fold the eggs over the filling and top with a pinch of salt and black pepper.

9
Sausage Heroes

HANDS-ON: **15 MINUTES** TOTAL: **15 MINUTES** SERVES **4**

- 4 Italian sausage links
- 4 rolls, split
- 1 medium beefsteak tomato, chopped
- ¼ cup marinated bocconcini (fresh mozzarella balls), quartered
- ¼ cup torn fresh basil
- 1 tablespoon olive oil
  Kosher salt and black pepper

GRILL the sausages over medium-high heat until cooked, 10 to 12 minutes. During the last 5 minutes of cooking, grill the rolls, 2 to 3 minutes.

TOSS the tomato and bocconcini with the basil, oil, and ¼ teaspoon each salt and pepper.

SERVE the sausages on grilled rolls and top with the tomato mixture.

10
Grilled Sausage and Fennel Salad

HANDS-ON: **20 MINUTES** TOTAL: **20 MINUTES** SERVES **4**

- 2 red onions, cut into rounds
- 1 fennel bulb, cut into wedges
- 2 tablespoons olive oil
  Kosher salt and black pepper
- 8 small Italian sausage links (about 1½ pounds)
- 6 cups spinach
- 1 tablespoon balsamic vinegar
- 4 ounces blue cheese, crumbled (1 cup)

COMBINE the red onions and fennel with 1 tablespoon of the oil, ½ teaspoon salt, and ¼ teaspoon pepper; grill, along with the sausages, over medium-high heat, turning, until cooked, 10 to 12 minutes.

TOSS the grilled vegetables with the spinach, vinegar, the remaining 1 tablespoon oil, and ¼ teaspoon each salt and pepper. Top with the sausages and blue cheese.

TIP
Kale stems can be
tough and woody.
Remove them with
a knife, or pull them
away from the leaves
before cooking.

**PAN-ROASTED
STEAK WITH
CREAMED KALE**
PAGE 153

Kale

It's the "it vegetable" for a reason: Bursting with vitamin C, kale makes a wicked Caesar salad, brightens up soups, and even supercharges a pesto.

1
Kale, Lemon, Artichoke, and Caper Fish Packets

HANDS-ON: **15 MINUTES** TOTAL: **30 MINUTES** SERVES **4**

4 **6-ounce pieces boneless, skinless cod, salmon, or bass**

4 **cups kale, stems discarded and leaves torn**

1 **lemon, sliced**

1 **cup halved artichoke hearts**

¼ **cup olive oil**
   Kosher salt and black pepper

2 **tablespoons capers**

DIVIDE the fish, kale, lemon, artichoke hearts, oil, 1 teaspoon salt, and ½ teaspoon pepper among 4 large pieces of parchment paper. Fold the parchment over the fish, then seal each packet by folding the edges over twice.

BAKE on a baking sheet at 425°F until the fish is opaque throughout, 12 to 14 minutes. Top with the capers.

2

Kale and Manchego Frittata with Potatoes

HANDS-ON: **20 MINUTES** TOTAL: **35 MINUTES** SERVES **4**

1½ **pounds fingerling or new potatoes, halved**

¼ **cup olive oil**
Kosher salt and black pepper

1 **small onion, chopped**

3 **cloves garlic, chopped**

1 **small bunch kale, stems discarded and leaves torn into ½-inch pieces (about 7 cups)**

8 **large eggs, beaten**

4 **ounces Manchego, grated (1 cup)**

TOSS the potatoes, 3 tablespoons of the oil, and ¼ teaspoon each salt and pepper on 2 rimmed baking sheets. Roast at 400°F, tossing once, for 15 to 18 minutes.

COOK the onion, garlic, and ¼ teaspoon each salt and pepper in the remaining tablespoon of oil in an ovenproof skillet over medium-high heat until golden. Add the kale; cook until tender. Remove from heat; stir in the eggs and ¾ cup of the cheese. Top with the remaining cheese. Transfer to oven.

BAKE until almost set, 6 to 8 minutes. Broil for 1 to 2 minutes. Serve with the potatoes.

3
Herb-Crusted Chicken with Kale and Croutons

HANDS-ON: **20 MINUTES** TOTAL: **1 HOUR** SERVES **4**

- 4 pounds bone-in, skin-on chicken pieces
- 2 cloves garlic, finely chopped
- 2 tablespoons chopped fresh rosemary leaves
- 2 tablespoons olive oil
- 1 teaspoon finely grated lemon zest plus 2 whole lemons, quartered
  Kosher salt and black pepper
- 4 thick slices country bread, torn into 1- to 2-inch pieces
- 4 cups baby kale leaves

TOSS the chicken, garlic, rosemary, oil, lemon zest and quarters, ¾ teaspoon salt, and ¼ teaspoon pepper on a rimmed baking sheet.

ROAST at 450°F, skin-side up, until the thickest part of the chicken registers 165°F, 35 to 40 minutes. Transfer to a serving dish. Reserve the baking sheet.

TOAST the bread in the drippings on the baking sheet until golden brown, 5 to 7 minutes. Toss with the kale. Serve with the chicken and lemons for squeezing.

4
Kale and Pepper Stir-Fry

HANDS-ON: **25 MINUTES** TOTAL: **25 MINUTES** SERVES **4**

- 1 red bell pepper, sliced
- 2 teaspoons grated fresh ginger
  Kosher salt
- 2 tablespoons canola oil
- 1 medium bunch kale, stems discarded and leaves torn into bite-size pieces (about 10 cups)
- 1 tablespoon soy sauce
- ½ teaspoon sesame oil
- 1 teaspoon toasted sesame seeds

COOK the bell pepper, ginger, and ½ teaspoon salt in the canola oil in a large skillet over medium-high heat until tender, 2 to 3 minutes. Add the kale and soy sauce; cook, tossing occasionally, until tender, 6 to 8 minutes. Mix in the sesame oil and sprinkle with the sesame seeds.

5

Kale and Mushroom
Skillet Pizza

HANDS-ON: **25 MINUTES** TOTAL: **40 MINUTES** SERVES **4**

2 sprigs fresh rosemary

4 tablespoons olive oil

1 bunch kale, stems discarded and leaves chopped

6 ounces shiitake mushrooms, thinly sliced (3 cups)

3 cloves garlic, thinly sliced
  Kosher salt and black pepper

1 pound whole-wheat pizza dough

1 teaspoon cornmeal

6 ounces fontina, grated (1½ cups)

HEAT the rosemary in 2 tablespoons of the oil in a large skillet over low heat until fragrant. Reserve the oil.

COOK the kale, mushrooms, garlic, and ½ teaspoon each salt and pepper in the remaining 2 tablespoons of oil over medium heat until softened, 5 minutes.

SHAPE the dough into a 12-inch round, then place in a cornmeal-dusted ovenproof skillet. Cook over medium heat until golden underneath. Top with the cheese and kale mixture. Bake at 450°F until the crust is cooked through, 10 to 15 minutes. Drizzle with the rosemary oil.

6

Mustardy Kale and
Butternut Squash

HANDS-ON: **30 MINUTES** TOTAL: **30 MINUTES** SERVES **4**

1 small butternut squash, cut into ¾-inch pieces

2 tablespoons olive oil

1 medium bunch kale, stems discarded and leaves torn into bite-size pieces (about 10 cups)

1 cup low-sodium chicken broth

1 tablespoon whole-grain mustard
  Kosher salt and black pepper

COOK the squash in the oil in a Dutch oven over medium heat, tossing occasionally, until beginning to soften, 10 to 12 minutes.

ADD the kale, broth, mustard, ¾ teaspoon salt, and ¼ teaspoon pepper. Cook, tossing occasionally, until tender, 8 to 10 minutes.

7

Sautéed Kale with Apples and Bacon

HANDS-ON: **20 MINUTES** TOTAL: **30 MINUTES** SERVES **4**

- 4 slices bacon
- 1 onion, sliced
- 1 apple, sliced
- 1 medium bunch kale, stems discarded and leaves torn into bite-size pieces (about 10 cups)
  Kosher salt and black pepper
- 1 tablespoon cider vinegar

COOK the bacon in a large skillet over medium heat until crisp, 6 to 8 minutes; remove and crumble.

ADD the onion and apple to the drippings in the skillet and cook until tender, 4 to 6 minutes. Add the kale; season with ¾ teaspoon salt and ¼ teaspoon pepper. Cook, tossing occasionally, until tender, 8 to 10 minutes. Mix in the bacon and vinegar.

8

Creamy Baked Pasta with Kale and Parmesan

HANDS-ON: **20 MINUTES** TOTAL: **45 MINUTES** SERVES **4**

- ¾ pound pasta shells or other short pasta
- ½ pound sweet Italian sausage, casings removed
- 2 tablespoons olive oil
- 1 bunch kale, stems discarded and leaves torn
- 1 14.5-ounce can diced tomatoes
- ⅔ cup heavy cream
- 4 ounces Asiago or fontina, grated (1 cup)
- 2 ounces Parmesan, grated (½ cup), plus more for serving
  Kosher salt and black pepper

COOK the pasta for 3 minutes less than the package directions specify; drain.

BROWN the sausage in the oil in a large skillet over medium heat, 4 to 5 minutes. Add the kale and toss until wilted. Combine with the pasta, tomatoes (and their juices), cream, cheeses, ⅓ cup water, ½ teaspoon salt, and ¼ teaspoon pepper. Transfer to an 8-inch baking dish. Bake at 450°F until the top is brown, 15 to 18 minutes. Let rest for 5 minutes. Top with more Parmesan.

9

Kale Caesar Salad

HANDS-ON: **20 MINUTES** TOTAL: **20 MINUTES** SERVES **4**

- ¼ cup mayonnaise
- ¼ cup finely grated Parmesan (1 ounce)
- 2 tablespoons lemon juice
- 2 tablespoons olive oil
- 1 teaspoon Dijon mustard
- 1 teaspoon Worcestershire sauce
     Kosher salt and black pepper
- ½ medium bunch kale, stems discarded and leaves thinly sliced (about 5 cups)
- 2 hard-cooked eggs, chopped
- ¼ small red onion, thinly sliced

WHISK together the mayonnaise, Parmesan, lemon juice, oil, mustard, Worcestershire sauce, ¾ teaspoon salt, and ¼ teaspoon pepper. Add the kale, eggs, and onion and toss to combine.

10

Pan-Roasted Steak with Creamed Kale

HANDS-ON: **25 MINUTES** TOTAL: **35 MINUTES** SERVES **4**

- 2 strip steaks (1 inch thick; about 2 pounds total)
     Kosher salt and black pepper
- ¼ cup olive oil
- 4 cloves garlic, sliced
- 2 bunches curly kale, stems discarded and leaves torn
- ½ cup heavy cream
- 1 15-ounce can cannellini beans, rinsed
     Chopped fresh chives, for serving

SEASON the steak with ½ teaspoon each salt and pepper. Brown in 2 tablespoons of the oil in an ovenproof skillet over high heat, 3 to 4 minutes per side. Transfer to a 425°F oven and cook until the center registers 130°F, 4 to 6 minutes more. Let rest for 5 minutes, then thinly slice.

COOK the garlic in the remaining oil in a saucepan over medium heat, 2 minutes. Add the kale, ½ teaspoon salt, and ¼ teaspoon pepper; cook until wilted. Add the cream and ¼ cup water; cook until tender. Add the beans; cook until warm. Serve with the steak. Top with the chives.

TIP
To cut mozzarella neatly, use a serrated knife, or put the round in the freezer 30 minutes before slicing.

MOZZARELLA, PROSCIUTTO, AND MELON SALAD WITH MINT
PAGE 161

Mozzarella

Mangia! This beloved Italian classic is a happy addition to so many dishes. Like most cheeses, mozzarella tastes best at room temperature, unless you're cooking it (in pizzas, panini, or lasagna). Take it out of the refrigerator 30 minutes before serving.

1
Sicilian Caprese with Raisins

HANDS-ON: **10 MINUTES** TOTAL: **20 MINUTES** SERVES **4**

¾ cup chopped fresh flat-leaf parsley

½ cup golden raisins

¼ cup olive oil

2 tablespoons capers

2 tablespoons pine nuts, toasted

1 tablespoon red wine vinegar
  Kosher salt and black pepper

1 pound heirloom tomatoes, sliced

8 ounces fresh mozzarella, sliced

COMBINE the parsley, raisins, oil, capers, pine nuts, vinegar, ½ teaspoon salt, and ¼ teaspoon pepper. Serve spooned over the tomatoes and mozzarella.

2
Classic Margherita Pizza

HANDS-ON: **20 MINUTES** TOTAL: **40 MINUTES** SERVES **4**

1 **pound pizza dough, at room temperature**

1 **tablespoon olive oil, plus more for the baking sheets and for drizzling**

1 **cup marinara sauce**

8 **ounces fresh mozzarella, sliced**

¼ **cup grated Parmesan (1 ounce)**

Kosher salt and black pepper

2 **tablespoons fresh basil leaves**

SHAPE the dough into 4 rounds and place on 2 oiled baking sheets. Brush with 1 tablespoon of the oil.

TOP with the marinara, mozzarella, and Parmesan, dividing evenly; season with ¼ teaspoon salt and ½ teaspoon pepper. Bake at 450°F until golden, 16 to 18 minutes. Drizzle with oil. Top with the basil.

3

Chicken and Olive Bread Panzanella

HANDS-ON: 25 MINUTES TOTAL: 25 MINUTES SERVES 4

8 ounces olive bread, cut into 1-inch cubes
2 tablespoons plus ⅓ cup olive oil
2 tablespoons cider vinegar
   Kosher salt and black pepper
5 ounces baby arugula (about 6 cups), torn
2 cups sliced rotisserie chicken
8 ounces fresh mozzarella, torn into bite-size pieces
1 cup sliced roasted red peppers

TOSS the bread with 2 tablespoons of the oil on a rimmed baking sheet. Toast at 350°F until crisp, 14 to 16 minutes.

WHISK together the remaining ⅓ cup of oil and the vinegar; season with ¼ teaspoon salt and ½ teaspoon black pepper. Toss with the toasted bread, arugula, chicken, mozzarella, and red peppers.

4

Deep-Dish Eggplant Parmesan

HANDS-ON: 30 MINUTES

TOTAL: 1 HOUR, 15 MINUTES SERVES 4

2 medium eggplants (cut into ¼-inch slices)
¼ cup olive oil
   Kosher salt and black pepper
3 cups marinara sauce
12 ounces fresh mozzarella, sliced
⅓ cup grated Parmesan (about 2 ounces)
¼ cup panko bread crumbs
5 ounces mixed greens (about 6 cups)
1 pint cherry tomatoes, halved
3 tablespoons of your favorite vinaigrette

BRUSH the eggplant slices with the oil on 2 rimmed baking sheets; season with ¼ teaspoon salt and ½ teaspoon pepper. Bake at 400°F until tender, 20 to 25 minutes.

LAYER the eggplant, marinara, mozzarella, and Parmesan in an 8-inch baking dish; top with the panko. Bake until the cheese is melted, 30 to 35 minutes. Serve with the greens and tomatoes drizzled with the vinaigrette.

5

Pasta with Sausage and Mozzarella

HANDS-ON: **25 MINUTES** TOTAL: **25 MINUTES** SERVES **4**

¾ pound fettuccine
¾ pound Italian sausage, casings removed
1 tablespoon olive oil
1 bunch broccolini, chopped
1 teaspoon chopped fresh rosemary leaves
¼ teaspoon crushed red pepper
8 ounces bocconcini (fresh mozzarella balls)

COOK the pasta according to the package directions.

BROWN the sausage in the oil in a large skillet over medium-high heat, breaking it up with a spoon, 7 to 8 minutes; remove.

ADD the broccolini to the skillet; cook, stirring, until tender, 5 to 7 minutes. Mix in the rosemary and red pepper. Toss the pasta with the sausage, broccolini, and bocconcini.

6

Mozzarella, Orzo, and Snap Pea Salad

HANDS-ON: **20 MINUTES** TOTAL: **20 MINUTES** SERVES **4**

1 cup orzo
1 pint cherry tomatoes, halved
1 cup halved snap peas
8 ounces bocconcini (fresh mozzarella balls), halved
½ cup chopped fresh herbs (such as dill, tarragon, and chives)
3 tablespoons olive oil
2 teaspoons grated lemon zest, plus 1 tablespoon lemon juice
Kosher salt and black pepper

COOK the pasta according to the package directions; drain and let cool.

TOSS the pasta with the tomatoes, snap peas, bocconcini, herbs, oil, lemon zest, and lemon juice; season with ½ teaspoon each salt and pepper.

7

Corn and Mozzarella
Chef's Salad

HANDS-ON: **25 MINUTES** TOTAL: **25 MINUTES** SERVES **4**

1½ pounds new potatoes, halved
⅓ cup olive oil
¼ cup fresh lemon juice
2 tablespoons chopped fresh dill
   Kosher salt and black pepper
1 avocado, sliced
8 radishes, halved
4 hard-cooked eggs, halved
1 cup fresh or frozen corn kernels
8 ounces bocconcini (fresh mozzarella balls)
1 head radicchio, torn

STEAM the potatoes until tender, 15 to 18 minutes.

WHISK together the oil, lemon juice, and dill; season with ¾ teaspoon salt and ½ teaspoon pepper. Drizzle the dressing over the potatoes, avocado, radishes, eggs, corn, bocconcini, and radicchio.

8

Steak and Swiss Chard
Panini

HANDS-ON: **25 MINUTES** TOTAL: **25 MINUTES** SERVES **4**

¾ pound strip steak (½ inch thick)
   Kosher salt and black pepper
2 tablespoons olive oil, plus more for the grill
1 bunch Swiss chard, stems discarded and leaves torn
2 cloves garlic, sliced
4 ounces fresh mozzarella, sliced
4 soft rolls
   Carrot sticks, for serving

SEASON the steak with ¼ teaspoon salt and ½ teaspoon pepper. Cook in the oil in a large skillet over medium-high heat, 6 to 10 minutes for medium-rare; let rest for 5 minutes and slice.

ADD the chard and garlic to the skillet and cook until tender, 4 to 6 minutes.

DIVIDE the chard, steak, and mozzarella among 4 soft rolls. Grill, pressing, until the cheese is melted, 8 to 12 minutes. Serve with carrot sticks.

9

Mozzarella, Salami, and Green Olive Salad

HANDS-ON: **15 MINUTES** TOTAL: **15 MINUTES** SERVES **4**

- 3 tablespoons olive oil
- 2 tablespoons red wine vinegar
   Kosher salt and black pepper
- 1 head red leaf lettuce, torn
- 8 ounces fresh mozzarella, torn into bite-size pieces
- 4 ounces salami, chopped
- ¼ small red onion, sliced
- ¼ cup pitted green olives, halved

WHISK together the oil, vinegar, and ¼ teaspoon each salt and pepper. Toss with the lettuce, mozzarella, salami, onion, and olives.

10

Mozzarella, Prosciutto, and Melon Salad with Mint

HANDS-ON: **15 MINUTES** TOTAL: **15 MINUTES** SERVES **4**

- ½ cantaloupe or honeydew melon, sliced
- 3 ounces prosciutto
- 8 ounces fresh mozzarella, torn into bite-size pieces
- 2 tablespoons olive oil
- 1 tablespoon Champagne vinegar
   Kosher salt and black pepper
   Fresh mint leaves, for serving

TOP the cantaloupe with the prosciutto and mozzarella. Drizzle with the oil and vinegar; season with ¼ teaspoon each salt and pepper. Top with mint leaves.

TIP
For extra creamy
and delicious
oatmeal, cook it in a
combination of half
water and half milk
(cow's milk, soy milk,
or almond milk). Serve
with additional milk
for drizzling.

**OATMEAL WITH
BLUEBERRIES,
SUNFLOWER SEEDS,
AND AGAVE**
PAGE 169

Oatmeal

Let's face facts—a bowl of oatmeal may be healthy, but it isn't always the most thrilling breakfast in the world. These easy, inventive hot-cereal upgrades will give you new reasons to rise and shine.

1
Oatmeal with Fried Egg and Avocado

HANDS-ON: **10 MINUTES** TOTAL: **10 MINUTES** SERVES **1**

1 serving quick-cooking or
old-fashioned rolled oats

1 large egg
Kosher salt and black pepper

2 teaspoons olive oil

¼ avocado, sliced

2 tablespoons fresh salsa

PREPARE the oats according to the package directions.

COOK the egg with ⅛ teaspoon each salt and pepper in the oil in a small nonstick skillet over medium heat, covered, 2 to 4 minutes for slightly runny sunny-side-up. Serve on the oatmeal with the avocado and salsa.

2

Oatmeal with
Pineapple and Mint

HANDS-ON: **10 MINUTES** TOTAL: **10 MINUTES** SERVES **1**

1 serving quick-cooking or
   old-fashioned rolled oats
½ cup chopped pineapple
1 tablespoon fresh mint leaves
1 teaspoon cinnamon sugar
2 tablespoons 1% milk

PREPARE the oats according to
the package directions. Top with
the pineapple, mint, and cinnamon
sugar. Drizzle with the milk.

3
—
Oatmeal with Banana and Molasses

HANDS-ON: 10 MINUTES TOTAL: **10 MINUTES** SERVES **1**

- 1 **serving quick-cooking or old-fashioned rolled oats**
- ½ **banana, sliced**
- 2 **tablespoons chopped toasted pecans**
- 2 **tablespoons 1% milk**
- 1 **tablespoon molasses**

PREPARE the oats according to the package directions. Top with the banana and pecans. Drizzle with the milk and molasses.

4
—
Oatmeal with Yogurt and Marmalade

HANDS-ON: 10 MINUTES TOTAL: **10 MINUTES** SERVES **1**

- 1 **serving quick-cooking or old-fashioned rolled oats**
- 2 **tablespoons plain low-fat Greek yogurt**
- 2 **tablespoons orange marmalade**

PREPARE the oats according to the package directions. Top with the yogurt and marmalade.

5

Oatmeal with Dried Fruit and Pistachios

HANDS-ON: 10 MINUTES TOTAL: **10 MINUTES** SERVES **1**

1 serving quick-cooking or old-fashioned rolled oats
1 pinch nutmeg
1 tablespoon dried cranberries
1 tablespoon dried cherries
1 tablespoon roasted pistachios
1 tablespoon honey

PREPARE the oats according to the package directions.
Stir in the nutmeg. Top with the cranberries, cherries,
and pistachios. Drizzle with the honey.

6

Oatmeal with Cheddar and Scallion

HANDS-ON: 10 MINUTES TOTAL: **10 MINUTES** SERVES **1**

1 serving quick-cooking or old-fashioned rolled oats
¼ cup grated extra-sharp Cheddar (1 ounce)
¼ teaspoon paprika
  Kosher salt and black pepper
1 scallion, chopped

PREPARE the oats according to the package directions.
Stir in the Cheddar and paprika; season with ⅛ teaspoon
each salt and pepper. Top with the scallion.

7

Oatmeal with
Peanut Butter and Grapes

HANDS-ON: **10 MINUTES** TOTAL: **10 MINUTES** SERVES **1**

1 **serving quick-cooking or old-fashioned rolled oats**
2 **tablespoons creamy natural peanut butter**
½ **cup red grapes**

PREPARE the oats according to the package directions.
Stir in the peanut butter. Top with the grapes.

8

Oatmeal with Bacon
and Maple Syrup

HANDS-ON: **15 MINUTES** TOTAL: **15 MINUTES** SERVES **1**

1 **slice bacon**
1 **serving quick-cooking or old-fashioned rolled oats**
1 **tablespoon maple syrup**

COOK the bacon in a large skillet over medium heat until
crisp, 6 to 8 minutes; break in half.

PREPARE the oats according to the package directions.
Drizzle with the maple syrup and top with the bacon.

9

Oatmeal with Mango and Coconut

HANDS-ON: **15 MINUTES** TOTAL: **15 MINUTES** SERVES **1**

- 2 **tablespoons unsweetened flaked coconut**
- 1 **serving quick-cooking or old-fashioned rolled oats**
- 1 **tablespoon brown sugar**
- ½ **cup mango, chopped**
- 2 **tablespoons cashews, chopped**

TOAST the coconut on a rimmed baking sheet at 350°F, tossing occasionally, until golden, 3 to 5 minutes.

PREPARE the oats according to the package directions. Stir in the brown sugar. Top with the mango, cashews, and toasted coconut.

10

Oatmeal with Blueberries, Sunflower Seeds, and Agave

HANDS-ON: **10 MINUTES** TOTAL: **10 MINUTES** SERVES **1**

- 1 **serving quick-cooking or old-fashioned rolled oats**
- ½ **cup blueberries**
- 1 **tablespoon sunflower seeds**
- 1 **tablespoon agave nectar**

PREPARE the oats according to the package directions. Top with the blueberries and sunflower seeds. Drizzle with the agave.

TIP
To make it easier
to stretch, let
the dough sit,
covered, at room
temperature for
1 hour before
following the recipe
instructions.

**PESTO, SAUSAGE,
AND TOMATO PIZZA**
PAGE 177

Pizza Dough

Craving something more nuanced than, say, a plain cheese pie? These creative recipes—starring the humble, ready-to-bake ball of pizza dough—will rise to any occasion.

1
Sausage and Broccoli Calzones

HANDS-ON: **15 MINUTES** TOTAL: **45 MINUTES** SERVES **4**

1 **pound Italian sausage links (about 8)**

1 **teaspoon olive oil, plus more for the baking sheet and for brushing**

1 **pound plain or whole-wheat pizza dough, thawed if frozen**

3 **cups grated mozzarella (12 ounces)**

2 **cups chopped broccoli**

1 **cup marinara sauce**

COOK the sausages in 1 teaspoon of the oil in a large skillet over medium-high heat for 10 to 12 minutes; slice.

SHAPE the dough into four 8-inch rounds. Top half of each round with the sausage, mozzarella, and broccoli, dividing evenly; fold over the dough and seal. Place the dough on an oiled baking sheet; brush with oil. Bake at 425°F until golden brown, 25 to 30 minutes. Serve with the marinara.

2
Garlic Butter Rolls

HANDS-ON: **10 MINUTES** TOTAL: **30 MINUTES** MAKES **12**

1 pound plain or whole-wheat
  pizza dough, thawed if frozen
4 cloves garlic, chopped
2 tablespoons olive oil
2 tablespoons unsalted butter,
  melted
  Chopped fresh flat-leaf
  parsley
  Kosher salt

TEAR the dough into 12 pieces and place in the cups of a 12-cup muffin tin. Divide the garlic among the pieces of dough, pressing into the centers. Drizzle with the oil and bake at 425°F until golden brown, 15 to 18 minutes. Toss in a bowl with the butter and parsley; season with 1 teaspoon salt.

3

Potato and Rosemary Flatbread

HANDS-ON: **15 MINUTES** TOTAL: **40 MINUTES** SERVES **4**

- 1 **pound plain or whole-wheat pizza dough, thawed if frozen**
   Cornmeal, for the baking sheet
- 4 **baby red potatoes, thinly sliced**
- 2 **cloves garlic, thinly sliced**
- 2 **tablespoons fresh rosemary leaves**
- 2 **tablespoons olive oil**
   Kosher salt and black pepper

SHAPE the dough into a large oval; place on a cornmeal-dusted baking sheet.

TOSS the potatoes, garlic, rosemary, and oil; season with ½ teaspoon salt and ¼ teaspoon pepper. Scatter evenly over the dough and bake at 425°F until golden brown, 25 to 30 minutes.

4

Salami and Spinach Stromboli

HANDS-ON: **10 MINUTES** TOTAL: **40 MINUTES** SERVES **4**

- 1 **pound plain or whole-wheat pizza dough, thawed if frozen**
- ¼ **pound thinly sliced salami**
- 4 **cups baby spinach**
- ½ **pound thinly sliced provolone**
- 1 **tablespoon olive oil, plus more for the baking sheet**

SHAPE the dough into a 12-by-15-inch rectangle. Top with the salami, spinach, and provolone.

ROLL up the dough, working from a short end. Place the rolled dough seam-side down on an oiled baking sheet and brush with the olive oil. Bake at 425°F until golden brown, 25 to 30 minutes.

5
Fried Dough with Chocolate Sauce

HANDS-ON: **15 MINUTES** TOTAL: **15 MINUTES** SERVES **4**

- 1 **pound plain or whole-wheat pizza dough, thawed if frozen**
  Canola oil
- 2 **tablespoons confectioners' sugar**
  Chocolate sauce

TEAR the dough into 16 pieces. Fry in ½ inch of oil in a skillet over medium heat until golden brown and cooked through, about 3 minutes per side. Dust with the sugar. Serve with chocolate sauce.

6
Cinnamon Twists

HANDS-ON: **10 MINUTES** TOTAL: **40 MINUTES** SERVES **8**

- 1 **pound plain or whole-wheat pizza dough, thawed if frozen**
- ½ **cup sugar**
- 2 **teaspoons cinnamon**
- ¼ **cup unsalted butter, melted**

SHAPE the dough into an 8-by-10-inch rectangle. Starting along the short edge and using a sharp knife, slice the dough into eight ¾-inch-wide lengths.

WHISK together the sugar and cinnamon. Brush all sides of the dough with the melted butter and roll in the cinnamon sugar. Twist the ends in opposite directions, then transfer to a greased or parchment-lined baking sheet. Let rest for 10 minutes. Bake at 375°F until golden brown, 18 to 20 minutes.

7

Bell Pepper and Feta Pizza

HANDS-ON: **15 MINUTES** TOTAL: **35 MINUTES** SERVES **4**

- 1 pound plain or whole-wheat pizza dough, thawed if frozen
  Cornmeal, for the baking sheets
- 1 cup marinara sauce
- 1 bell pepper, sliced
- 2 cups crumbled Feta (8 ounces)
- ½ cup halved pitted kalamata olives
  Kosher salt and black pepper
- ¼ cup fresh flat-leaf parsley leaves

SHAPE the dough into 4 rounds and place on 2 cornmeal-dusted baking sheets.

TOP with marinara, bell pepper, Feta, and olives, dividing evenly; season with ¼ teaspoon each salt and pepper. Bake at 475°F until the crust is golden brown, 18 to 20 minutes. Sprinkle with the parsley.

8

Spinach and Artichoke Pizza

HANDS-ON: **10 MINUTES** TOTAL: **30 MINUTES** SERVES **4**

- 1 pound plain or whole-wheat pizza dough, thawed if frozen
  Cornmeal, for the baking sheets
- 2 cups marinated artichoke hearts, drained and quartered
- 2 cups baby spinach (about 2 ounces)
- 4 ounces mozzarella, grated (1 cup)
- ½ 8-ounce bar cream cheese, cut up
- ½ cup grated Parmesan (2 ounces)
  Kosher salt and black pepper

SHAPE the dough into 4 rounds and place on 2 cornmeal-dusted baking sheets.

TOP with the artichokes, spinach, mozzarella, cream cheese, and Parmesan, dividing evenly; season with ¼ teaspoon each salt and pepper. Bake at 475°F until the crust is golden brown, 18 to 20 minutes.

9

Mushroom and Pea Pizza

HANDS-ON: **15 MINUTES** TOTAL: **35 MINUTES** SERVES **4**

  1 **pound plain or whole-wheat pizza dough,
     thawed if frozen**
     Cornmeal, for the baking sheets
1½ **cups ricotta**
  4 **ounces mushrooms, thinly sliced (about 2 cups)**
 ½ **cup frozen peas**
     Kosher salt and black pepper
 ¼ **cup chopped fresh basil**
  2 **teaspoons chopped fresh thyme**

SHAPE the dough into 4 rounds and place on 2 cornmeal-dusted baking sheets.

TOP with the ricotta, mushrooms, and frozen peas, dividing evenly; season with ¼ teaspoon each salt and pepper. Bake at 475°F until the crust is golden brown, 18 to 20 minutes. Top with the basil and thyme.

10

Pesto, Sausage, and Tomato Pizza

HANDS-ON: **20 MINUTES** TOTAL: **40 MINUTES** SERVES **4**

 ½ **pound Italian sausage, casings removed**
  2 **teaspoons olive oil**
  1 **pound plain or whole-wheat pizza dough,
     thawed if frozen**
     Cornmeal, for the baking sheets
 ½ **cup prepared pesto**
  1 **cup grape tomatoes, halved**
  8 **ounces bocconcini (fresh mozzarella balls), halved**
     Kosher salt and black pepper

BROWN the sausage in the oil in a large skillet over medium-high heat, 6 to 8 minutes.

SHAPE the dough into 4 rounds and place on 2 cornmeal-dusted baking sheets.

TOP with the pesto, tomatoes, bocconcini, and sausage, dividing evenly; season with ¼ teaspoon each salt and pepper. Bake at 475°F until the crust is golden brown, 18 to 20 minutes.

TIP
If you aren't planning
to cook the tenderloin
within a day or two of
buying it, look for one
packaged in Cryovac.
The meat will last in
the refrigerator for up
to 5 days and is much
less likely to develop
freezer burn if frozen.

**GLAZED PORK AND
PINEAPPLE KEBABS**
PAGE 185

Pork Tenderloin

Bacon gets all the love, but this versatile part of the pig is no less worthy. Make one (or more) of these delicious dishes and you'll never take pork tenderloin for granted again.

1
Barbecue Pork Sandwiches

HANDS-ON: **10 MINUTES** TOTAL: **30 MINUTES** SERVES **4**

1¼ **pounds pork tenderloin,
cut crosswise into 4 pieces**
½ **cup barbecue sauce**
1 **tablespoon cider vinegar**
4 **hamburger buns, split
Coleslaw, dill pickles, and
potato chips, for serving**

PLACE the pork, barbecue sauce,
vinegar, and ¼ cup water in a
medium saucepan. Simmer,
covered, until fork-tender, 18 to
20 minutes.

SHRED the meat. Serve it on the
buns, with coleslaw, pickles, and
potato chips on the side.

2
Crispy Fried Pork Cutlets

HANDS-ON: **35 MINUTES** TOTAL: **35 MINUTES** SERVES **4**

1½ cups panko bread crumbs

½ cup grated Parmesan (2 ounces)

Kosher salt

1¼ pounds pork tenderloin, sliced ¾ inch thick, pounded ¼ inch thick

2 eggs, beaten

½ cup plus 2 tablespoons olive oil

4 cups mixed greens

Lemon wedges, for serving

COMBINE the panko, Parmesan, and ½ teaspoon salt. Dip the pork slices in the eggs, then coat with the bread crumb mixture.

FRY, in batches, in ½ cup of the oil in a large skillet over medium-high heat until golden, 2 to 3 minutes per side.

TOSS the greens with the remaining 2 tablespoons of oil and serve with the cutlets and lemon wedges.

3
Spicy Pork and Soba Noodles

HANDS-ON: **20 MINUTES** TOTAL: **20 MINUTES** SERVES **4**

  6 **ounces soba noodles**
1¼ **pounds pork tenderloin, thinly sliced**
     Kosher salt and black pepper
  1 **tablespoon vegetable oil**
  ½ **English cucumber, sliced**
  2 **scallions, chopped**
  1 **red chili pepper, sliced**
  2 **tablespoons rice vinegar**
  2 **teaspoons sesame oil**

COOK the noodles according to the package directions.

SEASON the pork with ½ teaspoon salt and ¼ teaspoon black pepper. Brown, in batches, in the vegetable oil in a large skillet over medium-high heat, 1 to 2 minutes per side.

TOSS the pork with the noodles, cucumber, scallions, chili pepper, vinegar, and sesame oil; season with ½ teaspoon salt.

4
Rosemary-Crusted Pork

HANDS-ON: **10 MINUTES** TOTAL: **40 MINUTES** SERVES **4**

  ¼ **cup bread crumbs**
  2 **cloves garlic, chopped**
  1 **teaspoon smoked paprika**
  1 **tablespoon chopped rosemary**
     Kosher salt and black pepper
1¼ **pounds pork tenderloin**
  1 **teaspoon plus 1 tablespoon olive oil**
  1 **pound green beans**
  ¼ **cup pitted kalamata olives, halved**

COMBINE the bread crumbs, garlic, paprika, rosemary, and ½ teaspoon salt.

RUB the pork with 1 teaspoon of the oil, then coat with the bread crumb mixture. Roast at 425°F until cooked through, 20 to 30 minutes. Slice.

BOIL the green beans in a large pan of salted water; cook until just tender, 3 to 5 minutes. Drain and toss with the olives, ¼ teaspoon each salt and pepper, and the remaining tablespoon of oil. Serve with the pork.

5

Pork Fajitas

HANDS-ON: 10 MINUTES TOTAL: **30 MINUTES** SERVES **4**

1¼ pounds pork tenderloin, thinly sliced
1 teaspoon ground cumin
  Kosher salt and black pepper
2 tablespoons olive oil
1 onion, sliced
2 bell peppers, sliced
8 flour tortillas, warmed
1 avocado, cut up
1 cup fresh cilantro
½ cup sour cream

SEASON the pork with the cumin, ½ teaspoon salt, and ¼ teaspoon black pepper. Brown, in batches, in 1 tablespoon of the oil in a large skillet over medium-high heat, 1 to 2 minutes per side.

COOK the onion and bell peppers in the remaining tablespoon of oil in a second skillet over medium heat until tender, 6 to 8 minutes. Serve the pork with the vegetables, tortillas, avocado, cilantro, and sour cream.

6

Pork Scaloppine

HANDS-ON: 20 MINUTES TOTAL: **20 MINUTES** SERVES **4**

8 ounces egg noodles
1¼ pounds pork tenderloin, sliced ¾ inch thick, pounded ¼ inch thick
  Kosher salt and black pepper
¼ cup all-purpose flour
2 tablespoons olive oil
⅔ cup white wine
2 tablespoons unsalted butter
2 tablespoons chopped fresh flat-leaf parsley

COOK the noodles according to the package directions.

SEASON the pork with ½ teaspoon salt and ¼ teaspoon pepper, then coat in the flour. Brown, in batches, in the oil in a large skillet over medium-high heat, 1 to 2 minutes per side; remove.

ADD the wine and butter to the skillet; cook for 1 minute. Add the pork and toss. Serve over the noodles and sprinkle with the parsley.

7

Caribbean Pork with Mango Salsa

HANDS-ON: 10 MINUTES TOTAL: **25 MINUTES** SERVES **4**

- 1 mango, chopped
- 2 scallions, chopped
- 1 tablespoon fresh lime juice
- ¼ teaspoon crushed red pepper
- 1 tablespoon plus 1 teaspoon olive oil
  Kosher salt
- 1¼ pounds pork tenderloin
- 1 teaspoon ground coriander
  Lime wedges, for serving

COMBINE the mango, scallions, lime juice, red pepper, 1 tablespoon of the oil, and ¼ teaspoon salt.

RUB the pork with the remaining 1 teaspoon of oil; season with the coriander and ½ teaspoon salt.

BROIL, turning occasionally, until cooked through, 12 to 15 minutes. Slice; serve with the salsa and lime wedges.

8

Thai Pork Salad

HANDS-ON: 15 MINUTES TOTAL: **20 MINUTES** SERVES **4**

- 1¼ pounds pork tenderloin, thinly sliced
  Kosher salt
- 3 tablespoons vegetable oil
- 5 cups shredded Napa cabbage
- 2 carrots, grated
- ¼ cup torn mint leaves
- 2 scallions, chopped
- 2 tablespoons lime juice
- 2 teaspoons fish sauce

SEASON the pork with ½ teaspoon salt. Brown, in batches, in 1 tablespoon of the oil in a large skillet over medium-high heat, 1 to 2 minutes per side.

TOSS the pork with the cabbage, carrots, mint, scallions, lime juice, fish sauce, and the remaining 2 tablespoons of oil.

9
Pork with Buttered Apples

HANDS-ON: **25 MINUTES** TOTAL: **30 MINUTES** SERVES **4**

1¼ pounds pork tenderloin
     Kosher salt and black pepper
 1 tablespoon olive oil
 3 tablespoons unsalted butter
 3 apples, sliced ¼ inch thick
 1 tablespoon fresh thyme leaves

SEASON the pork with ½ teaspoon salt and ¼ teaspoon pepper. Brown in the oil in a large skillet over medium-high heat, 6 to 8 minutes. Cover and cook over low heat until cooked through, 15 to 20 minutes.

MELT the butter in a second skillet. Cook the apples, stirring, until tender, 5 to 7 minutes.

SPRINKLE with the thyme and serve with the pork.

10
Glazed Pork and Pineapple Kebabs

HANDS-ON: **10 MINUTES** TOTAL: **20 MINUTES** SERVES **4**

 1 cup long-grain white rice
1¼ pounds pork tenderloin, cut into 1-inch chunks
 ½ medium pineapple, cut into 1-inch chunks
 1 red onion, cut into 1-inch chunks
 1 cup grape tomatoes
     Kosher salt and black pepper
 ¼ cup honey
 2 tablespoons chopped fresh cilantro

COOK the rice according to the package directions.

THREAD the pork, pineapple, onion, and tomatoes onto skewers; season with ½ teaspoon salt and ¼ teaspoon pepper. Broil on a foil-lined baking sheet, turning once and brushing occasionally with the honey, until browned, 8 to 10 minutes. Serve with the rice and sprinkle with the cilantro.

TIP
If you're peeling
or slicing potatoes
in advance, place
them in a bowl of cold
water to prevent them
from turning gray.

**MUSHROOM
AND THYME
MASHED POTATOES**
PAGE 193

Potatoes

Just when you thought everyone's favorite spud couldn't get any more tantalizing, it has. Ten times over.

1
Scallion and Potato Soup

HANDS-ON: **10 MINUTES** TOTAL: **30 MINUTES** SERVES **4**

1 tablespoon unsalted butter

18 scallions (white and light green parts), sliced

1½ pounds new potatoes, cut into ½-inch chunks

½ cup dry white wine

1½ cups heavy cream

1½ cups low-sodium chicken or vegetable broth

Kosher salt and black pepper

MELT the butter in a large saucepan over medium-low heat. Add the scallions and cook for 1 minute.

ADD the potatoes, wine, cream, broth, 1¼ teaspoons salt, and ¼ teaspoon pepper and bring to a boil.

REDUCE heat and simmer until the potatoes are tender, about 15 minutes. Ladle the soup into individual bowls and sprinkle with pepper.

2

Salmon, Potato, and Arugula Salad with Dill Dressing

HANDS-ON: **20 MINUTES** TOTAL: **30 MINUTES** SERVES **4**

1 **pound new potatoes (about 12)**

4 **6-ounce pieces boneless, skinless salmon**

Kosher salt and black pepper

5 **tablespoons olive oil**

4 **anchovies**

1 **small clove garlic**

3 **tablespoons fresh lemon juice**

⅓ **cup chopped fresh dill**

1 **bunch arugula**

STEAM the potatoes until tender, 16 to 18 minutes; drain.

SEASON the salmon with ½ teaspoon salt and ¼ teaspoon pepper. Cook in 1 tablespoon of the oil in a large nonstick skillet over medium-high heat until opaque throughout, 3 to 4 minutes per side. Break into large chunks.

MASH the anchovies and garlic into a paste. Combine with the lemon juice and the remaining 4 tablespoons of oil; season with ¼ teaspoon each salt and pepper. Stir in the dill.

TOSS the arugula and potatoes with half the dressing. Divide the salad among 4 plates and top with the salmon. Drizzle with the remaining dressing.

3

Creamy Dill Potato Salad

HANDS-ON: **10 MINUTES** TOTAL: **40 MINUTES** SERVES **8**

3 pounds new potatoes, halved
½ cup sour cream
⅓ cup mayonnaise
¼ cup chopped fresh dill
2 tablespoons lemon juice
6 scallions, thinly sliced
  Kosher salt and black pepper

STEAM the potatoes until tender, 15 to 20 minutes; let cool.

TOSS the potatoes with the sour cream, mayonnaise, dill, lemon juice, and scallions; season with 1 teaspoon salt and ½ teaspoon pepper. Refrigerate for up to 8 hours before serving.

4

Grilled Potato and Onion Salad

HANDS-ON: **20 MINUTES** TOTAL: **20 MINUTES** SERVES **4**

1½ pounds red potatoes, cut into 2-inch pieces
1 red onion, cut into ½-inch-thick rings
4 tablespoons olive oil
½ cup fresh flat-leaf parsley leaves
1 tablespoon balsamic vinegar
  Kosher salt and black pepper

COMBINE the potatoes, onion, and 2 tablespoons of the oil. Arrange in a single layer on the grill over medium heat. Cook, turning frequently, until tender and slightly charred, about 15 minutes. Transfer to a bowl.

TOSS with the parsley, vinegar, the remaining 2 table-spoons of oil, 1¼ teaspoons salt, and ¼ teaspoon pepper. Serve warm or at room temperature.

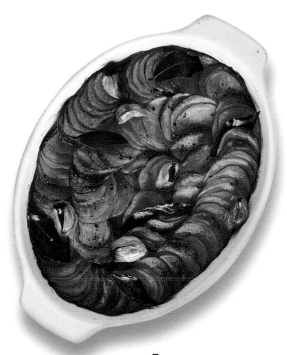

5

Crispy Accordion Potatoes

HANDS-ON: 20 MINUTES

TOTAL: 1 HOUR, 20 MINUTES SERVES **4**

- 3 pounds Yukon gold potatoes, thinly sliced
- 8 bay leaves
- 6 cloves garlic, unpeeled
- ⅓ cup olive oil
  Kosher salt and black pepper

ARRANGE the potatoes and bay leaves in an overlapping-shingle pattern in a 3-quart baking dish. Scatter the garlic on top and drizzle with the oil; season with 1½ teaspoons salt and ½ teaspoon pepper. Bake until the potatoes are tender and browned, 50 to 60 minutes.

6

Classic Latkes

HANDS-ON: 15 MINUTES TOTAL: **30 MINUTES** MAKES **24**

- 2 pounds (5 medium) peeled medium-starch potatoes (such as Yukon gold)
- 1 medium red onion, finely chopped (¾ cup)
- ¼ cup all-purpose flour
- 2 eggs, lightly beaten
- 2 tablespoons canola oil
  Kosher salt and black pepper
  Applesauce and sour cream, for serving

GRATE the potatoes with a box grater or food processor with the shredding blade. Toss with the onion, flour, eggs, 1 tablespoon of the oil, 1 teaspoon salt, and ¼ teaspoon pepper.

DROP by rounded tablespoonfuls onto 2 baking sheets brushed with the remaining 1 tablespoon of oil. Press lightly to make patties. Bake at 450°F until golden brown on the bottom, 10 minutes. Turn with a metal spatula and rotate the baking sheets. Bake another 5 minutes or until golden. Serve with applesauce and sour cream.

7

Brown Butter
Mashed Potatoes

HANDS-ON: **10 MINUTES** TOTAL: **30 MINUTES** SERVES **8**

2½ pounds russet potatoes, peeled and chopped
1½ cups whole milk
 ¾ cup (1½ sticks) unsalted butter, cubed
     Kosher salt and black pepper
     Chopped fresh chives, for serving

STEAM the potatoes until tender, 18 to 20 minutes; drain.
Mash with the milk. Fold in 4 tablespoons of the butter.
Season with 1½ teaspoons salt and ¾ teaspoon pepper.

COOK the remaining ½ cup of butter in a medium skillet
over medium heat, stirring occasionally, until the butter
foams and browns, 6 to 8 minutes. Top the potatoes with
the brown butter and chopped chives.

8

Bacon and Blue Cheese
Mashed Potatoes

HANDS-ON: **15 MINUTES** TOTAL: **40 MINUTES** SERVES **8**

3 pounds russet potatoes (about 6), peeled
   and cut into 2-inch chunks
   Kosher salt and black pepper
3 ounces bacon (6 slices)
¾ cup whole milk
½ cup (1 stick) unsalted butter, cut up
4 ounces blue cheese, crumbled (about 1 cup)

BOIL the potatoes with 2 teaspoons salt and enough
water to cover. Reduce heat and simmer until tender,
20 to 25 minutes; drain.

COOK the bacon in a large skillet over medium heat until
crisp, 5 to 8 minutes; remove and crumble.

MASH the potatoes with the milk and butter; season
with ½ teaspoon salt and ¼ teaspoon pepper. Fold in the
bacon and top with the blue cheese.

9

Chipotle and Cheddar
Mashed Potatoes

HANDS-ON: 15 MINUTES **TOTAL: 40 MINUTES** **SERVES 8**

- 3 pounds Yukon gold potatoes (about 6; peeled if desired), cut into 2-inch chunks
  Kosher salt and black pepper
- 8 ounces Cheddar, grated (2 cups)
- ¾ cup whole milk
- 1 to 2 tablespoons chopped chipotles in adobo sauce

BOIL the potatoes with 2 teaspoons salt and enough water to cover. Reduce heat and simmer until tender, 20 to 25 minutes; drain.

MASH with the Cheddar and milk; season with 1 teaspoon salt and ¼ teaspoon pepper. Fold in the chipotles just before serving.

10

Mushroom and Thyme
Mashed Potatoes

HANDS-ON: 15 MINUTES **TOTAL: 40 MINUTES** **SERVES 8**

- 3 pounds Yukon gold potatoes (about 6), peeled and cut into 2-inch chunks
  Kosher salt and black pepper
- 1 pound mushrooms, sliced
- 2 teaspoons fresh thyme leaves
- 1½ tablespoons olive oil
- ¾ cup whole milk
- ½ cup (1 stick) unsalted butter, cut up

BOIL the potatoes with 2 teaspoons salt and enough water to cover. Reduce heat and simmer until tender, 20 to 25 minutes; drain.

COOK the mushrooms with the thyme and ½ teaspoon salt in the oil in a large skillet over medium-high heat, tossing occasionally, until tender, 6 to 8 minutes.

MASH the potatoes with the milk and butter; season with ½ teaspoon salt and ¼ teaspoon pepper. Top with the mushroom mixture.

TIP
Quinoa takes about 15 minutes to cook. You can tell it's done when you see the white germ, which looks like a little white tail, sticking out. Fluff with a fork before serving.

QUINOA AND
VEGETABLE
SALAD WITH
TAHINI DRESSING
PAGE 201

Quinoa

Fast-cooking quinoa is a complete protein, containing all nine essential amino acids. Serve it in place of rice or pasta and make healthy eating second nature.

1

Steak with Cauliflower Puree and Crispy Quinoa

HANDS-ON: **35 MINUTES** TOTAL: **35 MINUTES** SERVES **4**

½ cup quinoa

3 tablespoons olive oil
Kosher salt and black pepper

1 tablespoon grated Parmesan

1 tablespoon chopped fresh flat-leaf parsley

1 small head cauliflower, cut into florets

½ cup heavy cream

2 tablespoons unsalted butter

2 strip steaks (1 inch thick)

COOK the quinoa, 2 tablespoons of the oil, ½ cup water, ½ teaspoon salt, and ¼ teaspoon pepper in a large skillet over medium heat until the water is absorbed, 12 to 14 minutes. Add the Parmesan and parsley.

STEAM the cauliflower in ½ inch of water until tender, 12 to 15 minutes. Puree the cauliflower, cream, butter, and ½ teaspoon each salt and pepper in a food processor, 30 seconds to 1 minute.

SEASON the steaks with ½ teaspoon salt and ¼ teaspoon pepper. Cook in the remaining tablespoon of oil in a large skillet over medium-high heat, 2 to 4 minutes per side for medium-rare. Let rest for 5 minutes; thinly slice against the grain. Serve with the quinoa over the puree.

2
Quinoa Breakfast Bowl

HANDS-ON: **20 MINUTES** TOTAL: **30 MINUTES** SERVES **4**

1 **cup quinoa**
4 **large eggs**
2 **tablespoons olive oil**
 Kosher salt and black pepper
1 **avocado, chopped**
6 **ounces smoked salmon**
 Fresh lemon juice, for serving
 Sliced scallions, for serving

COOK the quinoa according to the package directions.

COOK the eggs, covered, in the oil in a large nonstick skillet over medium heat for 2 to 4 minutes for slightly runny yolks. Season with ¼ teaspoon each salt and pepper. Serve the quinoa topped with the eggs, avocado, and salmon. Drizzle with lemon juice and top with sliced scallions.

3

Quinoa and Oat Porridge

HANDS-ON: **15 MINUTES** TOTAL: **45 MINUTES** SERVES **4**

½ cup quinoa

½ cup old-fashioned rolled oats

2 tablespoons brown sugar, plus more for serving

1 teaspoon ground cinnamon

1 cup milk, plus more for serving

½ cup raisins

   Toasted nuts and sliced banana, for serving

COMBINE the quinoa, oats, brown sugar, cinnamon, milk, and 1⅔ cups water in a small saucepan. Cook, stirring often, until very tender, 25 to 30 minutes. Stir in the raisins and cook until softened, 1 to 2 minutes.

SERVE with the nuts, banana, and more brown sugar and milk (if desired).

4

Chickpea and Quinoa Soup

HANDS-ON: **15 MINUTES** TOTAL: **25 MINUTES** SERVES **6**

1 red onion, chopped

3 cloves garlic, chopped

3 tablespoons olive oil

   Kosher salt and black pepper

8 cups low-sodium vegetable broth

1 cup red quinoa

2 15.5-ounce cans chickpeas, rinsed

1 cup fresh or frozen corn kernels

3 tomatoes, chopped

⅓ cup chopped fresh cilantro

1 avocado, sliced

   Grated Cheddar, lime wedges, and tortilla chips, for serving

COOK the onion and garlic in the oil in a large saucepan over medium-high heat until soft. Season with ½ teaspoon each salt and pepper. Add the broth and quinoa; bring to a boil, then simmer until the quinoa is tender. Add the chickpeas, corn, and tomatoes; cook until warm. Serve with the cilantro, avocado, cheese, lime, and tortilla chips.

5

Clementine, Fennel, and Quinoa Salad

HANDS-ON: 5 MINUTES TOTAL: **20 MINUTES** SERVES **4**

- ½ cup red quinoa
- 4 clementines, peeled and sliced
- 1 small head fennel, sliced
- ¼ cup olive oil
- 2 tablespoons golden raisins
- 2 tablespoons sherry vinegar
  Kosher salt and black pepper
- ½ cup chopped fresh herbs (such as cilantro and parsley)

COOK the quinoa according to the package directions.

COMBINE the clementines, fennel, oil, raisins, vinegar, ½ teaspoon salt, and ¼ teaspoon pepper. Toss with the herbs and quinoa just before serving.

6

Salmon with Creamed Spinach and Quinoa

HANDS-ON: 25 MINUTES TOTAL: **25 MINUTES** SERVES **4**

- ½ cup red quinoa
- 1 small onion, chopped
  Kosher salt and black pepper
- 2 tablespoons unsalted butter
- ½ cup heavy cream
- 5 ounces baby spinach
- 4 6-ounce pieces boneless, skinless salmon
- 1 tablespoon olive oil

COOK the quinoa according to the package directions.

COOK the onion and ½ teaspoon each salt and pepper in butter in a small saucepan over medium-high heat, stirring occasionally, until tender, 6 to 8 minutes. Add the cream and cook until thickened, 2 to 4 minutes. Stir in the spinach and cooked quinoa.

SEASON the salmon with ¼ teaspoon each salt and pepper. Cook in the oil in a large nonstick skillet over medium-high heat until opaque throughout, 3 to 4 minutes per side. Serve the salmon with the spinach and quinoa.

7

Zucchini with Quinoa Stuffing

HANDS-ON: **20 MINUTES** TOTAL: **55 MINUTES** SERVES **4**

½ cup quinoa

4 medium zucchini

1 15-ounce can cannellini beans, rinsed

1 cup grape or cherry tomatoes, quartered

½ cup almonds, chopped (about 2 ounces)

2 cloves garlic, chopped

¾ cup grated Parmesan (3 ounces)

4 tablespoons olive oil

COOK the quinoa according to the package directions.

CUT the zucchini in half lengthwise, scoop out the seeds, and place in a baking dish, cut-side up.

FLUFF the quinoa and add the beans, tomatoes, almonds, garlic, ½ cup of the Parmesan, and 3 tablespoons of the oil. Spoon the mixture into the zucchini. Top with the remaining tablespoon of oil and ¼ cup of Parmesan. Cover with foil and bake at 400°F until the zucchini is tender, 25 to 30 minutes. Remove foil and bake until golden, 8 to 10 minutes.

8

Quinoa with Mushrooms, Kale, and Sweet Potatoes

HANDS-ON: **15 MINUTES** TOTAL: **30 MINUTES** SERVES **4**

1 cup quinoa

2 small sweet potatoes (about 1 pound), peeled and cut into ¾-inch pieces

10 ounces button mushrooms, quartered

2 tablespoons olive oil

2 cloves garlic, thinly sliced

1 bunch kale, stems discarded and leaves torn into 2-inch pieces

¾ cup dry white wine
Kosher salt and black pepper

¼ cup grated Parmesan (1 ounce)

COOK the quinoa according to the package directions.

COOK the sweet potatoes and mushrooms in the oil in a large saucepan over medium heat, tossing occasionally, until beginning to soften, 5 to 6 minutes. Stir in the garlic and cook for 1 minute. Add the kale, wine, ¾ teaspoon salt, and ¼ teaspoon pepper. Cook, tossing often, until the vegetables are tender, 10 to 12 minutes. Serve over the quinoa and sprinkle with the Parmesan.

9

Tomato, Cucumber, and Quinoa Salad

HANDS-ON: 10 MINUTES **TOTAL: 20 MINUTES** **SERVES 4**

- ½ cup quinoa
- 3 tablespoons olive oil
- 2 tablespoons sherry vinegar or red wine vinegar
  Kosher salt and black pepper
- ½ pound tomatoes, chopped
- ½ English cucumber, sliced
- 4 cups baby arugula (about 3 ounces)

COOK the quinoa according to the package directions. Let cool.

WHISK together the oil, vinegar, ½ teaspoon salt, and ¼ teaspoon pepper. Add the quinoa, tomatoes, cucumber, and arugula and toss to combine; season with ¼ teaspoon each salt and pepper.

10

Quinoa and Vegetable Salad with Tahini Dressing

HANDS-ON: 30 MINUTES **TOTAL: 30 MINUTES** **SERVES 4**

- 1 cup quinoa
- 1 cup frozen shelled edamame
- ⅓ cup tahini
- 2 tablespoons fresh lemon juice
- 2 teaspoons grated fresh ginger
- 1 teaspoon honey
  Kosher salt and black pepper
- 1 bunch watercress, trimmed (about 4 cups)
- 1 pound raw beets (about 2 medium), peeled and coarsely grated
- 8 radishes, thinly sliced

COOK the quinoa according to the package directions. Transfer to a plate and refrigerate until cool. Cook the edamame according to the package directions.

WHISK together the tahini, lemon juice, ginger, honey, ½ cup water, ½ teaspoon salt, and ¼ teaspoon pepper.

DIVIDE the watercress, beets, radishes, edamame, and quinoa among plates and drizzle with the dressing.

TIP
Most grocery-store tubs of ricotta contain 8 ounces, just shy of 2 cups. Use it quickly for the creamiest, milkiest texture.

SPAGHETTI WITH RICOTTA AND TOMATOES
PAGE 209

Ricotta

Mild-tasting ricotta occasionally fades into the background—or between lasagna layers. But versatility is part of its appeal. Ricotta works in sweet and savory dishes.

1

Radishes with Creamy Ricotta

HANDS-ON: **5 MINUTES** TOTAL: **5 MINUTES** SERVES **4**

1 cup ricotta
1 tablespoon olive oil
  Kosher salt and black pepper
2 bunches radishes, trimmed
  (about 16)

PLACE the ricotta in a small bowl, drizzle with the oil, and sprinkle with ⅛ teaspoon each salt and pepper. Serve with the radishes for dipping.

2
Chard and Ricotta Frittata

HANDS-ON: **10 MINUTES** TOTAL: **45 MINUTES** SERVES **4**

1 **bunch Swiss chard, thick stems removed and sliced, leaves chopped (8 cups)**

1 **small onion, chopped**

2 **cloves garlic, chopped**
  Kosher salt and black pepper

2 **tablespoons olive oil**

8 **large eggs, whisked**

1 **cup ricotta**
  Hot sauce (optional), for serving

COOK the chard stems, onion, garlic, 1 teaspoon salt, and ¼ teaspoon pepper in the oil in a medium nonstick ovenproof skillet over medium-high heat until soft, 10 minutes.

ADD the chard leaves gradually and cook until wilted, 2 to 3 minutes. Add the eggs. Dollop with the ricotta. Bake at 400°F until just set in the middle, 14 to 16 minutes. Serve with hot sauce (if desired).

3

Ricotta, Olive Oil, and Honey Toasts

HANDS-ON: **10 MINUTES** TOTAL: **10 MINUTES** SERVES **4**

- 4 pieces halved baguette, toasted
- 1 tablespoon olive oil, plus more for serving
- ½ cup ricotta
- 2 teaspoons honey
  Flaky sea salt and black pepper

DRIZZLE the baguette with the oil. Divide the ricotta and honey among the toasts. Top with sea salt and pepper before serving.

4

Whipped Ricotta with Pomegranate and Mint

HANDS-ON: **15 MINUTES** TOTAL: **15 MINUTES** SERVES **8**

- 1 cup whole-milk ricotta
  Kosher salt and black pepper
- 2 tablespoons pomegranate seeds
- 1 tablespoon chopped fresh mint leaves
  Olive oil and flatbread, for serving

WHIP the ricotta in a food processor until very smooth, 1 to 2 minutes. Season with ½ teaspoon salt and ¼ teaspoon pepper. Top with the pomegranate seeds, mint, oil, and additional pepper. Serve with flatbread.

5

Orecchiette with Red Onions, Almonds, and Green Olives

HANDS-ON: **25 MINUTES** TOTAL: **25 MINUTES** SERVES **4**

- 12 ounces orecchiette
- 2 medium red onions, chopped
- 2 tablespoons olive oil, plus more for serving
  Kosher salt and black pepper
- ⅔ cup pitted green olives, chopped
- ⅔ cup roasted almonds, roughly chopped
- 2 tablespoons fresh lemon juice
- ½ cup finely grated Parmesan (about 2 ounces), plus more for serving
- 1 cup ricotta

COOK the pasta according to the package directions. Drain, reserving 1 cup of the cooking water.

COOK the onions in the oil in a large skillet over medium-high heat until tender. Season with ½ teaspoon each salt and pepper. Add the pasta, olives, almonds, lemon juice, Parmesan, ½ teaspoon salt, ¼ teaspoon pepper, and the cooking water; toss. Top with the ricotta, drizzle with olive oil, and sprinkle with Parmesan and pepper.

6

Baked Ricotta with Parmesan and Herbs

HANDS-ON: **20 MINUTES** TOTAL: **50 MINUTES** SERVES **4**

- 1 large egg, lightly beaten
- 1 cup ricotta
- ⅓ cup grated Parmesan
- 2 tablespoons olive oil
- 1 teaspoon chopped fresh thyme
  Kosher salt and black pepper
  Crudités, for serving

COMBINE the egg, ricotta, Parmesan, oil, thyme, and ¼ teaspoon each salt and pepper. Pour into a buttered 2-cup ovenproof dish. Bake at 350°F until golden and puffy, 25 to 30 minutes. Serve with crudités.

7
Watermelon-Ricotta Bites

HANDS-ON: **30 MINUTES** TOTAL: **30 MINUTES** SERVES **20**

1 **4-pound seedless watermelon,
   cut into ½-inch cubes (about 6 cups)**
4 **ounces ricotta**
2 **tablespoons olive oil**
   Kosher salt and black pepper
   Fresh mint leaves, for serving

SCOOP out the center of each watermelon cube and fill
with the ricotta. Top with the oil, 1 teaspoon salt, ½ teaspoon pepper, and mint leaves, dividing evenly.

8
Ricotta Cheesecake

HANDS-ON: **20 MINUTES**
TOTAL: **1 HOUR, 20 MINUTES** SERVES **8**

   Butter, for greasing pan
⅓ **cup finely crushed gingersnaps**
2 **15-ounce containers ricotta**
1 **8-ounce bar cream cheese**
2 **large eggs**
½ **cup sugar**
1 **tablespoon all-purpose flour**
1 **teaspoon lemon zest**
1 **teaspoon orange zest**
1 **teaspoon vanilla extract**
   Kosher salt

BUTTER a 9-inch springform cake pan generously. Line
the bottom and sides with the gingersnap crumbs.
Pulse the ricotta and cream cheese in a food processor
until smooth, 30 to 45 seconds. Add the eggs, sugar,
flour, zests, vanilla, and a pinch of salt. Pulse until well
combined. Pour into the prepared pan. Bake at 350°F
until just set in the middle, 50 to 60 minutes.

9

Wine-Poached Pears with Whipped Ricotta

HANDS-ON: **15 MINUTES** TOTAL: **55 MINUTES** SERVES **4**

1½ cups dry red wine
⅓ cup sugar
1 cinnamon stick
   Kosher salt
2 pears, peeled and halved
1 cup ricotta
¼ cup confectioners' sugar

COMBINE the wine, sugar, cinnamon stick, and a pinch of salt in a large saucepan over high heat. Simmer and stir to dissolve the sugar. Add the pears. Cook, turning occasionally, until the pears are tender and the liquid is syrupy, 30 to 40 minutes.

WHISK the ricotta, confectioners' sugar, and a pinch of salt until smooth. Serve the pears and syrup over the ricotta.

10

Spaghetti with Ricotta and Tomatoes

HANDS-ON: **20 MINUTES** TOTAL: **20 MINUTES** SERVES **4**

2 pints grape tomatoes
4 cloves garlic, smashed
2 teaspoons olive oil
¾ pound spaghetti
1 cup ricotta
¼ cup chopped fresh flat-leaf parsley
   Kosher salt and black pepper

TOSS the tomatoes and garlic with the oil on a rimmed baking sheet. Roast at 450°F until the tomatoes burst, 8 to 10 minutes.

COOK the pasta according to the package directions; drain, reserving ¾ cup of the cooking water. Toss the pasta with the ricotta, parsley, and the reserved cooking water; season with ¾ teaspoon salt and ¼ teaspoon pepper. Top with the tomatoes.

TIP
To shred a rotisserie chicken, pull off the breasts and legs. Remove the bones and, using 2 forks, pull the meat apart. A 2½-pound rotisserie bird will yield 3½ to 4 cups of meat.

**CHICKEN
NIÇOISE SALAD**
PAGE 217

Rotisserie Chicken

Who says dinner prep has to be a feather-ruffling experience? These quick, satisfying recipes, starring the supermarket savior, will get a meal on the table in a matter of minutes.

1
Gingery Peanut Noodles with Chicken

HANDS-ON: **20 MINUTES** TOTAL: **20 MINUTES** SERVES **4**

½ pound spaghetti

½ cup peanut butter

3 tablespoons rice vinegar

3 tablespoons low-sodium soy sauce

1 tablespoon brown sugar

1 teaspoon grated fresh ginger

1½ cups shredded rotisserie chicken

1 red bell pepper, sliced

½ English cucumber, cut into strips

2 scallions, sliced

2 tablespoons chopped unsalted roasted peanuts

COOK the pasta according to the package directions; drain.

BLEND 1 cup water, the peanut butter, rice vinegar, soy sauce, brown sugar, and ginger in a blender. Toss with the pasta, chicken, bell pepper, cucumber, and scallions. Sprinkle with the chopped peanuts.

2
Chicken and Gruyère Turnovers

HANDS-ON: **15 MINUTES** TOTAL: **40 MINUTES** SERVES **4**

1½ cups shredded rotisserie
chicken

1½ cups grated Gruyère

1 cup frozen peas

2 sheets (one 17.25-ounce
package) frozen puff pastry,
thawed

1 large egg, beaten

¼ cup Dijon mustard, for serving

COMBINE the chicken, Gruyère,
and peas.

CUT the 2 sheets of puff pastry in
half to form 4 rectangles; place on
a baking sheet. Top half of each
rectangle with the chicken mixture,
dividing evenly. Seal the pastries and
brush the tops with the beaten egg.
Bake at 400°F until golden, 20 to
25 minutes. Serve with the mustard.

3
Chicken, Pesto, and Fried Egg Pizza

HANDS-ON: **25 MINUTES** TOTAL: **25 MINUTES** SERVES **4**

- 1 pound store-bought pizza dough, at room temperature
- 2 tablespoons olive oil
- 1½ cups grated Asiago or Parmesan (6 ounces)
- 4 large eggs
- 1½ cups shredded rotisserie chicken, warmed
- 1 cup arugula
- ¼ cup prepared pesto
  Kosher salt and black pepper

SHAPE the pizza dough into 4 rounds; brush both sides with 1 tablespoon of the oil and place on 2 baking sheets. Sprinkle with the Asiago, dividing evenly, and bake at 425°F until golden, 12 to 15 minutes.

FRY the eggs in the remaining tablespoon of oil in a large skillet. Top the pizzas with the chicken, arugula, pesto, eggs, and ¼ teaspoon each salt and pepper.

4
Cajun Chicken and Rice

HANDS-ON: **25 MINUTES** TOTAL: **50 MINUTES** SERVES **4**

- 1 cup brown rice
- 1 small onion, sliced
- 2 cloves garlic, sliced
- 1 bay leaf
- 2 tablespoons olive oil
- 1 14.5-ounce can diced tomatoes
- 2 cups frozen cut okra
- 1 cup fresh or frozen corn kernels
- ¼ teaspoon cayenne pepper
  Kosher salt and black pepper
- 1½ cups shredded rotisserie chicken

COOK the rice according to the package directions.

COOK the onion, garlic, and bay leaf in the oil in a skillet over medium heat until softened, 8 to 10 minutes. Add the tomatoes, okra, corn, cayenne, ½ teaspoon salt, and ¼ teaspoon black pepper. Cook until tender, 6 to 7 minutes. Add the chicken and cook until heated through, 1 to 2 minutes. Serve over the rice.

5

Greek Lemon Soup
with Chicken

HANDS-ON: **15 MINUTES** TOTAL: **30 MINUTES** SERVES **4**

- 6 **cups low-sodium chicken broth**
- ⅓ **cup orzo**
- 6 **large egg yolks**
- 1½ **cups shredded rotisserie chicken**
- ¼ **cup fresh lemon juice**
  Kosher salt and black pepper

BRING the broth to a boil in a large saucepan. Add the orzo and cook until tender, 8 to 9 minutes.

BEAT the egg yolks; slowly whisk in 1 cup of the hot broth. Add the egg mixture to the saucepan and cook over medium heat, stirring, until thickened, 5 to 7 minutes. Add the chicken and lemon juice; season with ½ teaspoon salt and ¼ teaspoon pepper.

6

Chicken and Tortellini Soup

HANDS-ON: **20 MINUTES** TOTAL: **20 MINUTES** SERVES **4**

- 4 **carrots, cut into bite-size pieces**
- 5 **cups low-sodium chicken broth**
- 8 **ounces cheese tortellini (fresh or frozen)**
- 1½ **cups shredded rotisserie chicken**
  Kosher salt
- 2 **tablespoons chopped fresh flat-leaf parsley**

SIMMER the carrots in the broth in a large saucepan until tender, 10 to 12 minutes. Add the tortellini and simmer until tender, 2 to 4 minutes.

STIR in the chicken and cook until warmed through, 1 to 2 minutes more. Season with ¼ teaspoon salt and sprinkle with the parsley.

7

Buffalo Chicken Sandwiches

HANDS-ON: **10 MINUTES** TOTAL: **10 MINUTES** SERVES **4**

- 2 tablespoons unsalted butter
- ½ cup Buffalo wing sauce
- 3 cups shredded rotisserie chicken
- 4 hearty white rolls, split and toasted
- 4 ounces blue cheese, crumbled (1 cup)
  Celery stalks and leaves, for serving

MELT the butter in a medium skillet; stir in the wing sauce and chicken and cook until warmed through, 2 to 4 minutes.

FORM sandwiches with the rolls, chicken mixture, and blue cheese, dividing evenly. Serve with celery stalks; add the leaves to the sandwiches (if desired).

8

Chicken and Quinoa Burritos

HANDS-ON: **25 MINUTES** TOTAL: **25 MINUTES** SERVES **4**

- 4 burrito-size whole-wheat tortillas, warmed
- 1 cup shredded rotisserie chicken, warmed
- 1 cup black beans, rinsed and warmed
- 1 cup cooked quinoa or brown rice
- 1 cup grated Monterey Jack (4 ounces)
- 1 cup fresh cilantro sprigs
- ½ cup low-fat Greek yogurt
- 1 avocado, sliced
- 1 cup corn salsa

TOP the tortillas with the chicken, beans, quinoa, Monterey Jack, cilantro, yogurt, and avocado, dividing evenly. Roll into burritos and serve with the corn salsa.

9

Buttermilk Chicken and Tomato Salad

HANDS-ON: **10 MINUTES** TOTAL: **10 MINUTES** SERVES **4**

¼ cup buttermilk
¼ cup mayonnaise
1 tablespoon fresh lemon juice
4 plum tomatoes, roughly chopped
   Kosher salt and black pepper
2 romaine hearts, torn into bite-size pieces
1 2- to 2½-pound rotisserie chicken, cut up
½ tablespoon chopped fresh chives

WHISK together the buttermilk, mayonnaise, and lemon juice. Add the tomatoes, ¼ teaspoon salt, and ⅛ teaspoon pepper. Divide the lettuce among the plates and top with the chicken. Spoon the dressing and tomatoes over the salad and sprinkle with the chives.

10

Chicken Niçoise Salad

HANDS·ON: **25 MINUTES** TOTAL: **30 MINUTES** SERVES **4**

½ pound green beans, trimmed
½ pound new potatoes, halved
4 large eggs
6 cups salad greens
1½ cups shredded rotisserie chicken
½ small red onion, sliced
½ cup cured pitted black olives
3 tablespoons red wine vinaigrette

STEAM the green beans until tender, 4 to 5 minutes; rinse under cold water. Repeat with the potatoes, steaming until tender, 10 to 12 minutes.

HARD-COOK the eggs; peel and halve. Divide the greens among plates and top with the chicken, onion, olives, green beans, potatoes, and eggs. Dress with the vinaigrette.

SPINACH WITH
BACON AND CROUTONS
PAGE 225

TIP
To revive wilted
leaves, give greens
a cold bath in a
bowl of ice water
for 15 minutes.

Salad Greens

Which of these fast, fresh, leafy dishes will you want to make? It's a toss-up. For the healthiest greens, look for red and dark green leaves. And don't be afraid to branch out: Exotic-sounding varieties, like mâche and tatsoi, deliver a diversity of nutrients, textures, and tastes.

1

Herb Salad Mix with Tomatoes, Pepper, and Feta

HANDS-ON: **15 MINUTES** TOTAL: **15 MINUTES** SERVES **4**

3 tablespoons olive oil

1½ tablespoons fresh lemon juice

½ small clove garlic, crushed
Kosher salt and black pepper

5 ounces store-bought herb
salad mix (6 cups)

1 cup grape tomatoes, halved

1 yellow bell pepper, sliced

1 cup broken pita chips

2 ounces Feta, crumbled
(½ cup)

WHISK together the oil, lemon
juice, garlic, ¼ teaspoon salt, and
⅛ teaspoon black pepper.

TOSS the salad mix, tomatoes,
bell pepper, pita chips, and Feta
with the dressing.

2
Endive and Radicchio with Grapes

HANDS-ON: **10 MINUTES** TOTAL: **10 MINUTES** SERVES **4**

3 tablespoons olive oil

1½ tablespoons red wine vinegar

½ teaspoon Dijon mustard

½ teaspoon honey

Kosher salt and black pepper

1 small head radicchio, leaves torn (3 cups)

1 head endive, leaves sliced (1 cup)

½ cup halved green grapes

¼ cup fresh flat-leaf parsley leaves

¼ cup pitted kalamata olives, sliced

WHISK together the oil, vinegar, mustard, honey, ½ teaspoon salt, and ¼ teaspoon pepper.

TOSS the radicchio, endive, grapes, parsley, and olives with the dressing.

3

Watercress with Beets and Fennel

HANDS-ON: **20 MINUTES** TOTAL: **30 MINUTES** SERVES **4**

- 1 pound beets (about 2½ large), peeled and cut into ½-inch wedges
- 3 tablespoons olive oil
   Kosher salt and black pepper
- ¼ cup buttermilk
- 2 tablespoons mayonnaise
- 1 tablespoon chopped fresh herbs (such as chives, parsley, and dill)
- 1 bunch watercress (6 cups)
- 1 small bulb fennel, thinly sliced, plus ¼ cup chopped fennel fronds

TOSS the beets with the oil on a rimmed baking sheet; season with ¾ teaspoon salt and ¼ teaspoon pepper. Roast at 400°F until tender, 18 to 20 minutes. Let cool.

WHISK together the buttermilk, mayonnaise, herbs, ½ teaspoon salt, and ¼ teaspoon pepper. Toss with the watercress, fennel, and beets. Sprinkle with the fennel fronds.

4

Green Leaf with Chorizo and Apples

HANDS-ON: **10 MINUTES** TOTAL: **15 MINUTES** SERVES **4**

- 4 ounces Spanish chorizo, cut up
- 3 tablespoons plus 1 teaspoon olive oil
- 1½ tablespoons fresh lemon juice
- ½ small clove garlic, crushed
   Kosher salt and black pepper
- 1 small head green leaf lettuce, leaves torn (6 cups)
- ½ small apple, sliced
- 2 ounces Manchego, sliced

COOK the chorizo in 1 teaspoon of the oil in a medium skillet over medium heat until crisp, 3 to 4 minutes.

WHISK together the lemon juice, garlic, the remaining 3 tablespoons of oil, ¼ teaspoon salt, and ⅛ teaspoon pepper.

TOSS the lettuce, apple, Manchego, and chorizo with the dressing.

5

Arugula with Peaches and Cheddar

HANDS-ON: 15 MINUTES TOTAL: 15 MINUTES SERVES 4

- ¼ cup pecans
- 3 tablespoons olive oil
- 1½ tablespoons red wine vinegar
- ½ teaspoon Dijon mustard
- ½ teaspoon honey
  Kosher salt and black pepper
- 2 bunches arugula (6 cups)
- 1 peach, sliced
- 2 ounces sharp white Cheddar, cut into chunks

TOAST the pecans on a rimmed baking sheet at 350°F, tossing once, until fragrant, 4 to 5 minutes. Let cool, then chop.

WHISK together the oil, vinegar, mustard, honey, ½ teaspoon salt, and ¼ teaspoon pepper. Toss with the arugula, peach, Cheddar, and pecans.

6

Romaine with Pickled Vegetables

HANDS-ON: 10 MINUTES TOTAL: 10 MINUTES SERVES 4

- 3 tablespoons olive oil
- 1½ tablespoons fresh lemon juice
- ½ small clove garlic, crushed
  Kosher salt and black pepper
- 1 head romaine lettuce, leaves torn (6 cups)
- 1 15.5-ounce can cannellini beans, rinsed
- ¾ cup giardiniera (mixed pickled vegetables), drained
- ¼ small red onion, sliced

WHISK together the oil, lemon juice, garlic, ¼ teaspoon salt, and ⅛ teaspoon pepper.

TOSS the lettuce, beans, giardiniera, and red onion with the dressing.

7

Bibb with Radishes and Pine Nuts

HANDS-ON: **10 MINUTES** TOTAL: **15 MINUTES** SERVES **4**

¼ cup pine nuts

¼ cup buttermilk

2 tablespoons mayonnaise

1 tablespoon chopped fresh herbs (such as chives, parsley, and dill)

Kosher salt and black pepper

1 head Bibb lettuce, leaves torn (6 cups)

6 radishes, thinly sliced

TOAST the pine nuts on a rimmed baking sheet at 350°F, tossing once, until golden, 6 to 7 minutes. Let cool.

WHISK together the buttermilk, mayonnaise, herbs, ½ teaspoon salt, and ¼ teaspoon pepper. Toss the lettuce, radishes, and pine nuts with the dressing.

8

Red Leaf with Roasted Red Peppers and Pecorino

HANDS-ON: **10 MINUTES** TOTAL: **10 MINUTES** SERVES **4**

3 tablespoons olive oil

1½ tablespoons red wine vinegar

½ teaspoon Dijon mustard

½ teaspoon honey

Kosher salt and black pepper

1 small head red leaf lettuce, leaves torn (6 cups)

½ cup store-bought roasted red peppers, sliced

2 tablespoons capers

2 ounces pecorino, shaved

WHISK together the oil, vinegar, mustard, honey, ½ teaspoon salt, and ¼ teaspoon black pepper. Toss with the lettuce, red peppers, and capers. Top with the pecorino.

9

Frisée with Avocado and Blue Cheese

HANDS-ON: **10 MINUTES** TOTAL: **15 MINUTES** SERVES **4**

- ¼ cup sliced almonds
- 3 tablespoons olive oil
- 1½ tablespoons red wine vinegar
- ½ teaspoon Dijon mustard
- ½ teaspoon honey
  Kosher salt and black pepper
- 1 large head frisée, leaves torn (6 cups)
- 1 avocado, sliced
- 2 ounces blue cheese, crumbled (½ cup)

TOAST the almonds on a rimmed baking sheet at 350°F, tossing once, until golden, 3 to 5 minutes. Let cool.

WHISK together the oil, vinegar, mustard, honey, ½ teaspoon salt, and ¼ teaspoon pepper. Toss the frisée, avocado, blue cheese, and almonds with the dressing.

10

Spinach with Bacon and Croutons

HANDS-ON: **10 MINUTES** TOTAL: **20 MINUTES** SERVES **4**

- 4 slices bacon, cut up
- 2 slices sandwich bread, torn into 1-inch pieces
  Kosher salt and black pepper
- ¼ cup buttermilk
- 2 tablespoons mayonnaise
- 1 tablespoon fresh herbs (such as chives, parsley, and dill)
- 5 ounces baby spinach (6 cups)
- ½ cucumber, sliced

TOSS the bacon and bread on a rimmed baking sheet; season with ¼ teaspoon salt and ⅛ teaspoon pepper. Bake at 400°F until the bacon is crisp, 10 to 12 minutes. Let cool.

WHISK together the buttermilk, mayonnaise, herbs, ¼ teaspoon salt, and ⅛ teaspoon pepper. Toss the spinach, cucumber, and crouton mixture with the dressing.

TIP
Websites like montereybayaquarium.org can help you choose a sustainable salmon variety on the fly. Good for you, your family, and the environment.

SALMON WITH WARM TOMATOES AND DILL
PAGE 233

Salmon Fillets

Putting together a simple, delicious dinner shouldn't feel like swimming upstream. You'll love these quick, delectable meals featuring one of the healthiest types of fish around.

1

Roasted Salmon with Fennel and Carrots

HANDS-ON: **10 MINUTES** TOTAL: **45 MINUTES** SERVES **4**

1 bulb fennel, sliced, plus
   chopped fronds, for serving
2 carrots, sliced
1 shallot, sliced
¼ cup dry white wine
4 6-ounce salmon fillets
   Kosher salt and black pepper
1 lemon, sliced

TOSS the fennel with the carrots, shallot, and wine in a 9-by-13-inch baking dish. Top with the salmon; season with ¾ teaspoon salt and ¼ teaspoon pepper. Top with the lemon.

COVER with foil and roast at 400°F until the salmon is opaque throughout, 30 to 35 minutes. Sprinkle with fennel fronds.

2

Spiced Salmon Tacos with Cabbage Slaw

HANDS-ON: **20 MINUTES** TOTAL: **20 MINUTES** SERVES **4**

1 **pound skinless salmon fillet**
1 **teaspoon ground cumin**
  Kosher salt and black pepper
3 **tablespoons olive oil**
2 **cups thinly sliced red cabbage**
1 **avocado, chopped**
3 **tablespoons lime juice**
8 **corn tortillas, warmed**
  Fresh cilantro, for serving

SEASON the salmon with the cumin and ¼ teaspoon each salt and pepper. Cook in 1 tablespoon of the oil in a large nonstick skillet over medium-high heat until opaque throughout, 4 to 6 minutes per side; flake.

TOSS the cabbage and avocado with the lime juice, the remaining 2 tablespoons of oil, and ½ teaspoon salt. Serve the salmon in the warm tortillas with the slaw and cilantro.

3

Horseradish
Salmon Burgers

HANDS-ON: **15 MINUTES** TOTAL: **25 MINUTES** SERVES **4**

1 pound skinless salmon fillet
2 scallions, sliced
2 large eggs
⅓ cup bread crumbs
3 tablespoons prepared horseradish
  Kosher salt and black pepper
2 tablespoons olive oil
4 soft buns
½ cup mayonnaise
  Lettuce
  Beet chips, for serving (optional)

PLACE the salmon, scallions, eggs, bread crumbs, horseradish, ¾ teaspoon salt, and ¼ teaspoon pepper in a food processor; coarsely chop. Form the mixture into 4 patties. Cook in the oil in a large nonstick skillet over medium heat until opaque throughout, 6 to 7 minutes per side. Assemble sandwiches with the buns, mayonnaise, and lettuce. Serve with beet chips.

4

Mustard-Glazed Salmon
with Peas

HANDS-ON: **20 MINUTES** TOTAL: **25 MINUTES** SERVES **4**

4 6-ounce skinless salmon fillets
2 tablespoons Dijon mustard
1 teaspoon olive oil
1 teaspoon chopped fresh thyme
2 slices bacon, cut up
1 10-ounce bag frozen peas
  Kosher salt and black pepper

PLACE the salmon on a rimmed baking sheet. Combine the mustard, oil, and thyme. Spread on the salmon and roast at 450°F until opaque throughout, 8 to 10 minutes.

BROWN the bacon in a medium skillet over medium heat, 12 to 14 minutes. Add the peas and ¼ teaspoon each salt and pepper; cook until heated through, 2 to 3 minutes. Serve with the salmon.

5

Salmon, Radicchio, and Farro Salad

HANDS-ON: 15 MINUTES **TOTAL: 25 MINUTES** **SERVES 4**

- 1 **cup farro**
- ¾ **pound skinless salmon fillet**
  Kosher salt and black pepper
- 1 **tablespoon olive oil, plus ⅓ cup for the dressing**
- 1 **small head radicchio, chopped**
- ⅓ **cup raisins**
- ¼ **cup chopped fresh flat-leaf parsley**
- 3 **tablespoons lemon juice**

COOK the farro according to the package directions.

SEASON the salmon with ¼ teaspoon each salt and pepper. Cook in 1 tablespoon of the oil in a large nonstick skillet over medium-high heat until opaque throughout, 4 to 6 minutes per side; flake. Toss with the farro, radicchio, raisins, the remaining ⅓ cup of oil, the parsley, lemon juice, and ½ teaspoon each salt and pepper.

6

Roasted Salmon with Pesto Vegetables

HANDS-ON: 10 MINUTES **TOTAL: 25 MINUTES** **SERVES 4**

- 2 **bell peppers, thinly sliced**
- 1 **small red onion, thinly sliced**
- 4 **slices bread, torn**
- 2 **tablespoons olive oil**
- 4 **6-ounce skinless salmon fillets**
  Kosher salt and black pepper
- ¼ **cup prepared pesto**

TOSS the peppers, onion, and bread with the oil on a rimmed baking sheet. Nestle the salmon in the mixture; season with ¾ teaspoon salt and ¼ teaspoon pepper.

ROAST at 450°F until the salmon is opaque throughout and the vegetables are tender, 8 to 10 minutes. Serve topped with the pesto.

7
Salmon and Arugula Salad

HANDS-ON: **15 MINUTES** TOTAL: **25 MINUTES** SERVES **4**

¾ **pound skinless salmon fillet**
   Kosher salt and black pepper
1 **tablespoon olive oil**
2 **bunches arugula**
1 **15.5-ounce can chickpeas, rinsed**
¼ **small red onion, sliced**
½ **cucumber, sliced**
¼ **cup pitted kalamata olives, sliced**
¼ **cup vinaigrette**

SEASON the salmon with ¼ teaspoon each salt and pepper. Cook in the oil in a large nonstick skillet over medium-high heat until opaque throughout, 4 to 6 minutes per side; cool and flake.

TOSS with the arugula, chickpeas, red onion, cucumber, olives, and vinaigrette.

8
Buttery Pasta with Salmon and Leeks

HANDS-ON: **15 MINUTES** TOTAL: **20 MINUTES** SERVES **4**

¾ **pound spaghetti**
1 **pound skinless salmon fillet**
   Kosher salt and black pepper
4 **tablespoons unsalted butter**
2 **leeks, sliced**
   Chives, chopped

COOK the pasta according to the package directions.

SEASON the salmon with ¾ teaspoon salt and ¼ teaspoon pepper. Cook in 2 tablespoons of the butter in a large nonstick skillet over medium-high heat until opaque throughout, 4 to 6 minutes per side; remove and flake. Add the leeks to the skillet and cook until tender, 4 to 6 minutes. Toss the pasta with the salmon, leeks, and the remaining 2 tablespoons of butter. Top with chives.

9

Spicy Salmon with Bok Choy and Rice

HANDS-ON: 10 MINUTES **TOTAL: 20 MINUTES** SERVES **4**

- 1 cup long-grain white rice
- 2 tablespoons honey
- 1 tablespoon low-sodium soy sauce
- ¼ teaspoon crushed red pepper
- 4 6-ounce skinless salmon fillets
- 1 pound baby bok choy, quartered

COOK the rice according to the package directions.

COMBINE the honey, soy sauce, and red pepper.

BROIL the salmon on a foil-lined rimmed baking sheet until opaque throughout, 8 to 10 minutes, basting with the honey mixture during the last 3 minutes.

STEAM the bok choy until tender, 8 to 10 minutes. Serve with the salmon and rice.

10

Salmon with Warm Tomatoes and Dill

HANDS-ON: 25 MINUTES **TOTAL: 25 MINUTES** SERVES **4**

- 1 cup couscous
- 2 pints grape tomatoes
  Kosher salt and black pepper
- 2 tablespoons olive oil
- ¼ cup fresh dill, chopped
- 4 6-ounce skinless salmon fillets

COOK the couscous according to the package directions.

COOK the tomatoes with ¼ teaspoon salt in 1 tablespoon of the oil in a large nonstick skillet over medium-high heat until soft, 4 to 6 minutes. Fold in the dill; transfer to a plate.

SEASON the salmon with ½ teaspoon each salt and pepper. Cook in the remaining tablespoon of oil in the skillet until opaque throughout, 4 to 6 minutes per side. Serve with the tomatoes and couscous.

TIP
Shrimp sizes vary.
For these recipes, look
for a 31 to 40 count
per pound for medium
shrimp and a 26 to
30 count per pound
for large.

**SHRIMP AND
VEGETABLE SOUP**
PAGE 241

Shrimp

Casting your net for new weeknight options? Reel in the family with these tasty, easy-to-fix shrimp dishes.

1
Spiced Shrimp with Beans

HANDS-ON: **20 MINUTES** TOTAL: **25 MINUTES** SERVES **4**

1 cup couscous

1 pound peeled and deveined
medium shrimp

1 shallot, chopped

½ teaspoon ground coriander

½ teaspoon ground paprika
Kosher salt

1 tablespoon olive oil

1 15.5-ounce can white
beans, rinsed

¼ cup white wine vinegar

2 tablespoons chopped fresh
flat-leaf parsley

COOK the couscous according to
the package directions.

COOK the shrimp, shallot, coriander,
paprika, and ½ teaspoon salt in
the oil in a large skillet over
medium-high heat until the shrimp
are opaque; transfer to a plate.

ADD the beans, vinegar, and
½ cup water to the skillet; cook
until warm. Serve with the
shrimp, couscous, and parsley.

2

Shrimp and Hummus Sandwiches

HANDS-ON: **10 MINUTES** TOTAL: **20 MINUTES** SERVES **4**

¾ **pound peeled and deveined medium shrimp**

Kosher salt

½ **English cucumber, sliced**

1 **tablespoon lemon juice**

1 **tablespoon olive oil**

8 **slices pumpernickel bread, toasted**

1 **cup hummus**

Vegetable chips, for serving (optional)

BOIL the shrimp in salted water in a large saucepan until opaque; halve lengthwise. Toss with the cucumber, lemon juice, and oil.

TOP the bread with the hummus and shrimp mixture, dividing evenly. Serve with vegetable chips (if desired).

3

Shrimp and Broccoli Tempura

HANDS-ON: 30 MINUTES TOTAL: **30 MINUTES** SERVES **4**

- 1 8-ounce package soba noodles
- ¼ cup low-sodium soy sauce
- 3 tablespoons lime juice
- 2 tablespoons light brown sugar
- 2 cups all-purpose flour
- 2 cups seltzer
- ¼ teaspoon baking soda
- ¾ pound peeled and deveined large shrimp
- 3 cups broccoli florets
- 8 cups canola oil
- 2 scallions, sliced

COOK the noodles according to the package directions.

WHISK the soy sauce, lime juice, sugar, and ¼ cup water; set aside. Whisk the flour, seltzer, and baking soda. Dip the shrimp and broccoli in the batter. Heat the oil over medium heat until a deep-fry thermometer reads 360°F. Fry the shrimp and broccoli in batches until golden. Serve with the noodles and soy-lime dip. Top with the scallions.

4

Crispy Shrimp Cakes

HANDS-ON: 10 MINUTES TOTAL: **40 MINUTES** SERVES **4**

- 1 pound peeled and deveined medium shrimp, finely chopped
- ⅓ cup mayonnaise
- ¼ cup bread crumbs
- 1 large egg
- 1 tablespoon chopped fresh chives
- 1 tablespoon prepared horseradish
  Kosher salt and black pepper
- 3 tablespoons olive oil
- 6 cups mixed greens
- 1 cup cherry tomatoes, quartered
- 4 radishes, thinly sliced
- 3 tablespoons of your favorite vinaigrette

MIX together the shrimp, mayonnaise, bread crumbs, egg, chives, horseradish, 1 teaspoon salt, and ¼ teaspoon pepper. Form the mixture into 8 patties; chill until firm.

COOK the patties in the oil in a large nonstick skillet until cooked through. Toss the greens, tomatoes, and radishes with the vinaigrette. Serve with the shrimp cakes.

5

Shrimp and Sausage
with Polenta

HANDS-ON: 20 MINUTES TOTAL: **20 MINUTES** SERVES **4**

- ½ pound andouille sausage, sliced
- 3 tablespoons olive oil
- 1 pound peeled and deveined medium shrimp
- 1 green bell pepper, sliced
  Kosher salt and black pepper
- 4 tablespoons unsalted butter
- 1 cup instant polenta
- ½ teaspoon chopped fresh oregano

COOK the sausage in the oil in a large skillet over medium-high heat until browned, 3 to 4 minutes. Add the shrimp, bell pepper, ½ teaspoon salt, and ¼ teaspoon black pepper and cook until the shrimp are opaque, 3 to 4 minutes more. Add the butter and cook until melted.

COOK the polenta according to the package directions. Serve with the shrimp mixture, sprinkled with the oregano.

6

Tandoori Shrimp with
Rice and Peas

HANDS-ON: 20 MINUTES TOTAL: **40 MINUTES** SERVES **4**

- 1 pound peeled and deveined large shrimp
- 1 cup plain yogurt
- 2 teaspoons garam masala
- ½ teaspoon cayenne pepper
- 1 cup long-grain white rice
- ½ cup frozen peas
- 1 carrot, grated
  Kosher salt and black pepper

MARINATE the shrimp in the yogurt, garam masala, and cayenne for 30 minutes.

COOK the rice according to the package directions, adding the peas and carrot in the last 5 minutes.

THREAD the shrimp onto skewers; season with ½ teaspoon salt and ¼ teaspoon black pepper. Broil until opaque, 4 to 5 minutes. Serve with the rice.

7

Shrimp and Mango Lettuce Wraps

HANDS-ON: **15 MINUTES** TOTAL: **25 MINUTES** SERVES **4**

- 1 pound peeled and deveined medium shrimp, chopped
- 2 cloves garlic, sliced
- 2 tablespoons canola oil
- 2 teaspoons Asian fish sauce
- 8 large Bibb lettuce leaves
- 1 mango, sliced
- ¼ cup peanuts, chopped
- ¼ cup fresh mint leaves
  Lime wedges and Sriracha or Asian chili-garlic sauce, for serving (optional)

COOK the shrimp and garlic in the oil in a large skillet over medium-high heat until the shrimp are opaque. Add the fish sauce and toss to combine.

TOP the lettuce leaves with the shrimp mixture, mango, peanuts, and mint. Serve with lime wedges and Sriracha (if desired).

8

Pasta with Shrimp and Spinach

HANDS-ON: **10 MINUTES** TOTAL: **25 MINUTES** SERVES **4**

- ¾ pound penne
- ¾ pound peeled and deveined medium shrimp
- 2 cloves garlic, sliced
- ¼ teaspoon crushed red pepper
  Kosher salt
- 2 tablespoons olive oil
- 2 cups baby spinach
- 2 ounces Feta, crumbled (½ cup)
- ¼ cup halved pitted kalamata olives

COOK the pasta according to the package directions.

COOK the shrimp, garlic, red pepper, and ¼ teaspoon salt in the oil in a large skillet over medium-high heat until the shrimp are opaque. Toss with the pasta, spinach, Feta, and olives.

9

Baked Risotto with Shrimp and Watercress

HANDS-ON: **40 MINUTES** TOTAL: **40 MINUTES** SERVES **4**

- 1 onion, chopped
  Kosher salt and black pepper
- 2 tablespoons unsalted butter
- ½ cup dry white wine
- 3 cups chicken broth
- 1 cup Arborio rice
- 1 pound peeled and deveined medium shrimp, chopped
- 1 bunch watercress, torn

COOK the onion, ½ teaspoon salt, and ¼ teaspoon pepper in the butter in a Dutch oven over medium heat until tender, 3 to 5 minutes. Add the wine; cook until syrupy, 6 to 7 minutes.

ADD the broth and rice. Bake, covered, at 425°F until the rice is almost tender, 15 to 20 minutes. Add the shrimp and cook until opaque, 6 to 7 minutes more. Fold in the watercress before serving.

10

Shrimp and Vegetable Soup

HANDS-ON: **15 MINUTES** TOTAL: **30 MINUTES** SERVES **4**

- 1 onion, chopped
- 1 carrot, chopped
- 1 fennel bulb, chopped, plus fronds for serving
- 2 tablespoons olive oil
- 2 tablespoons tomato paste
- 1 pound peeled and deveined medium shrimp
- 2 8-ounce bottles clam juice
- 1 14.5-ounce can diced tomatoes
  Kosher salt and black pepper

COOK the onion, carrot, and chopped fennel in the oil in a large saucepan over medium heat until softened, 6 to 8 minutes; stir in the tomato paste. Add the shrimp, clam juice, tomatoes (with their juices), and 1½ cups water; season with ½ teaspoon salt and ¼ teaspoon pepper. Simmer until the shrimp are opaque, about 2 minutes. Sprinkle with fennel fronds.

TIP
For the most tender steak, slice thinly against the grain: Look for the long fibers running along the meat. (They resemble the grain in a piece of wood.) With a sharp knife, cut straight across the fibers to break them up.

SPICED BEEF KEBABS
WITH YOGURT
PAGE 249

Sirloin

Sirloin delivers taste and tenderness at a low price. Fully preheat the grill, skillet, or broiler before cooking to achieve a better sear.

1

Steak with Mozzarella and Tomatoes

HANDS-ON: **20 MINUTES** TOTAL: **20 MINUTES** SERVES **4**

1½ **pounds sirloin steak (1 inch thick)**
    Kosher salt and black pepper
1   **tablespoon olive oil**
1   **pint cherry tomatoes, halved**
½   **cup bocconcini (fresh mozzarella balls), halved**
½   **cup fresh basil leaves**
    Country bread, for serving

SEASON the steak with ½ teaspoon salt and ¼ teaspoon pepper. Cook in the oil in a large skillet over medium-high heat for 3 to 5 minutes per side for medium-rare; remove. Let rest for 5 minutes; slice.

COOK the tomatoes in the skillet, tossing, until softened, 2 to 4 minutes. Stir in the bocconcini and basil. Serve with the steak and country bread.

<u>2</u>

Beef and Broccoli Stir-Fry

HANDS-ON: **30 MINUTES** TOTAL: **30 MINUTES** SERVES **4**

1 cup white rice
1 pound sirloin steak, sliced
2 tablespoons canola oil
1 tablespoon chopped fresh
    ginger
2 cups broccoli florets
3 tablespoons oyster sauce
3 tablespoons rice vinegar
¼ cup roasted peanuts

COOK the rice according to the package directions.

BROWN the steak, in 2 batches, in the oil in a large skillet over medium-high heat, 2 to 3 minutes; remove.

ADD the ginger, broccoli, and 1 cup water to the skillet. Cook, tossing, until tender, 6 to 8 minutes. Add the steak, oyster sauce, and vinegar; cook, tossing, until thickened, 1 to 2 minutes. Serve over the rice with the peanuts.

3

Steak Salad with Avocado and Onion

HANDS-ON: **20 MINUTES** TOTAL: **45 MINUTES** SERVES **4**

- 1 pound sirloin steak (1 inch thick)
- ⅓ cup low-sodium soy sauce
- 3 tablespoons plus 2 teaspoons olive oil
- 1 small head romaine, chopped
- ½ cup fresh cilantro leaves
  Crumbled queso fresco or Feta
- ¼ small red onion, sliced
- 1 avocado, sliced
- 3 tablespoons lime juice
  Kosher salt

MARINATE the steak in the soy sauce for 30 minutes. Cook in 2 teaspoons of the oil in a large skillet over medium-high heat for 3 to 5 minutes per side for medium-rare. Let rest for 5 minutes; slice.

TOSS the steak with the romaine, cilantro, queso fresco, red onion, avocado, the remaining 3 tablespoons of oil, and the lime juice; season with ½ teaspoon salt.

4

Thai Red Curry and Beef Soup

HANDS-ON: **20 MINUTES** TOTAL: **30 MINUTES** SERVES **4**

- 8 ounces rice noodles
- 1 pound sirloin steak, cut into 1-inch pieces
- 1 sweet potato, peeled and cut into 1-inch pieces
- 1 onion, sliced
- 2 tablespoons canola oil
- 4 cups low-sodium chicken broth
- 1 15-ounce can coconut milk
- 2 tablespoons red curry paste
- 2 tablespoons Asian fish sauce
- 1 tablespoon lime juice
  Fresh basil leaves
- 1 red chili pepper, sliced

COOK the noodles according to the package directions.

BROWN the steak, sweet potato, and onion in the oil in a large saucepan over medium-high heat. Add the broth, coconut milk, curry paste, and fish sauce; simmer until the potato is tender, 8 to 10 minutes. Stir in the noodles and lime juice. Top with the basil and chili pepper.

5
Steak with Mustard-Shallot Sauce

HANDS-ON: 15 MINUTES **TOTAL: 25 MINUTES** **SERVES 4**

- 1½ **pounds sirloin steak (1 inch thick)**
  Kosher salt and black pepper
- 2 **teaspoons olive oil**
- 2 **tablespoons Dijon mustard**
- 2 **tablespoons red wine vinegar**
- 1 **shallot, chopped**
- 1 **pound green beans**

SEASON the steak with ¾ teaspoon salt and ¼ teaspoon pepper. Cook in the oil in a large skillet over medium-high heat for 3 to 5 minutes per side for medium-rare. Let rest for 5 minutes; slice.

WHISK together the mustard, vinegar, and shallot.

STEAM the green beans until tender, 4 to 6 minutes. Top the steak with the mustard sauce and serve with the green beans.

6
Herb-Crusted Steak with Fries

HANDS-ON: 20 MINUTES **TOTAL: 30 MINUTES** **SERVES 4**

- ¾ **pound frozen French fries**
- ½ **cup sour cream**
- 2 **tablespoons prepared horseradish**
  Kosher salt and black pepper
- 1½ **pounds sirloin steak (1 inch thick)**
- 2 **tablespoons herbes de Provence**
- 2 **teaspoons olive oil**

COOK the French fries according to the package directions.

MIX together the sour cream, horseradish, and ¼ teaspoon pepper.

RUB the steak with the herbes de Provence; season with ½ teaspoon each salt and pepper. Cook in the oil in a large skillet over medium-high heat for 3 to 5 minutes per side for medium-rare. Let rest for 5 minutes; slice. Serve with the French fries and horseradish cream.

7
Beef Paprikash with Egg Noodles

HANDS-ON: **25 MINUTES** TOTAL: **40 MINUTES** SERVES **4**

¾ **pound egg noodles**
1 **pound sirloin steak, cut into 1-inch pieces**
  Kosher salt and black pepper
2 **tablespoons olive oil**
2 **onions, sliced**
2 **tablespoons paprika**
2 **cups low-sodium chicken broth**
⅔ **cup sour cream**
  Chopped fresh flat-leaf parsley

COOK the noodles according to the package directions.

SEASON the steak with ½ teaspoon each salt and pepper. Brown in the oil in a large skillet over medium-high heat, 5 to 7 minutes. Add the onions and paprika and cook, tossing, until softened, 4 to 6 minutes. Add the broth and simmer until thickened, 10 to 12 minutes. Stir in the sour cream. Serve over the noodles with parsley.

8
Open-Faced Steak Reubens

HANDS-ON: **20 MINUTES** TOTAL: **25 MINUTES** SERVES **4**

1 **pound sirloin steak (1 inch thick)**
  Kosher salt and black pepper
2 **teaspoons olive oil**
4 **slices rye bread**
½ **cup Russian dressing**
1 **cup sauerkraut**
8 **slices Swiss cheese**
  Vegetable chips, for serving

SEASON the steak with ½ teaspoon each salt and pepper. Cook in the oil in a large skillet over medium-high for 3 to 5 minutes per side for medium-rare. Let rest for 5 minutes; slice.

TOAST the bread. Top the bread with the dressing, steak, sauerkraut, and Swiss cheese, dividing evenly. Broil until the cheese melts, 3 to 5 minutes. Serve with vegetable chips.

9
Chicken-Fried Steak with Carrot Slaw

HANDS-ON: **30 MINUTES** TOTAL: **30 MINUTES** SERVES **4**

1½ pounds sirloin steak (1 inch thick),
   cut into 4 pieces
   Kosher salt and black pepper
1 cup buttermilk
1 cup all-purpose flour
¼ cup canola oil
4 carrots, grated
¼ cup mayonnaise
1 tablespoon lemon juice
1 tablespoon chopped fresh dill
   Lemon wedges, for serving

POUND each piece of steak to a ½-inch thickness. Season with ½ teaspoon each salt and pepper. Dip in the buttermilk, then the flour. Fry the steak, in 2 batches, in the oil in a large nonstick skillet over medium heat until golden, 2 to 3 minutes per side.

COMBINE the carrots, mayonnaise, lemon juice, and dill. Serve with the steak and lemon wedges.

10
Spiced Beef Kebabs with Yogurt

HANDS-ON: **20 MINUTES** TOTAL: **30 MINUTES** SERVES **4**

1½ pounds sirloin steak, cut into 1½-inch pieces
2 bell peppers, cut into 1½-inch pieces
1 red onion, cut into 1½-inch pieces
1 tablespoon olive oil
2 teaspoons ground coriander
   Kosher salt and black pepper
½ cup plain yogurt
2 tablespoons lemon juice
4 pitas, warmed, for serving
¼ cup fresh mint leaves
   Hot sauce, for serving

TOSS the steak, bell peppers, and onion with the oil and coriander; season with ¾ teaspoon salt and ¼ teaspoon black pepper. Thread onto 8 skewers and broil, turning occasionally, until cooked through, 6 to 8 minutes.

MIX together the yogurt and lemon juice. Serve the kebabs with the warm pitas and top with the yogurt sauce, mint, and hot sauce.

TIP
Separating slices
of smoked salmon
can be tricky. Use
the tine of a fork to
gently lift away thin
slices.

SMOKED SALMON
WITH CREAMY
CUCUMBER SALAD
PAGE 257

Smoked Salmon

This delicacy often appears on brunch menus, but it's easy to serve smoked salmon at home any time of the day. These recipe variations on the king of fish are as inventive as they are numerous.

1

Smoked Salmon on Crispy Crushed Potatoes with Dill

HANDS-ON: **15 MINUTES** TOTAL: **20 MINUTES** SERVES **4**

1 pound fingerling potatoes
   Kosher salt and black pepper
3 tablespoons olive oil
½ cup sour cream
4 ounces sliced smoked salmon
1 tablespoon chopped fresh dill

BOIL the potatoes in a large saucepan of salted water until just tender, 12 to 15 minutes. Press each potato to flatten slightly.

COOK the potatoes in the oil in a large skillet over medium-high heat until browned and crisp, 4 to 5 minutes per side. Season with 1 teaspoon salt and ½ teaspoon pepper. Top with the sour cream, smoked salmon, and dill.

2

Deviled Eggs with Smoked Salmon and Fried Capers

HANDS-ON: **10 MINUTES** TOTAL: **15 MINUTES** SERVES **4**

- 2 **tablespoons drained capers**
- 1 **tablespoon canola oil**
- 6 **hard-cooked eggs**
- ¼ **cup mayonnaise**
- 1½ **ounces chopped smoked salmon, plus more for serving**
- 2 **tablespoons plain Greek yogurt**
- 1 **tablespoon Dijon mustard Kosher salt and black pepper**

COOK the capers in the oil in a small skillet over medium heat, stirring, until crisp, 4 to 5 minutes.

HALVE the eggs. Scoop out the yolks; combine with the mayonnaise, smoked salmon, yogurt, mustard, ½ teaspoon salt, and ¼ teaspoon pepper. Spoon back into the egg whites. Top with more chopped smoked salmon and the capers.

3
Smoked Salmon and Horseradish Cream

HANDS-ON: **5 MINUTES** TOTAL: **5 MINUTES** SERVES **8**

- 1 8-ounce bar cream cheese, at room temperature
- 2 tablespoons prepared horseradish
- 2 tablespoons heavy cream
  Chopped fresh dill (optional)
- 1 pound thinly sliced smoked salmon
- 1 15-ounce package potato chips

COMBINE the cream cheese, horseradish, and heavy cream, stirring until smooth. Sprinkle with dill (if desired). Serve with the smoked salmon and potato chips.

4
Smoked Salmon Pizzettes

HANDS-ON: **15 MINUTES** TOTAL: **35 MINUTES** SERVES **4**

- 1 pound plain or whole-wheat pizza dough, at room temperature
  Cornmeal, for the baking sheet
- 2 shallots, sliced
- ½ cup crème fraîche or sour cream
- 4 ounces sliced smoked salmon
- 2 tablespoons capers
- 2 tablespoons chopped fresh chives

SHAPE the dough into 4 small rounds; place on a cornmeal-dusted baking sheet. Sprinkle on the shallots and press them in gently. Spread with the crème fraîche. Bake at 425°F until golden brown, 20 to 25 minutes. Top with the salmon and sprinkle with the capers and chives.

5

Salmon "Tartare" and Avocado with Sesame Dressing

HANDS-ON: **20 MINUTES** TOTAL: **20 MINUTES** SERVES **4**

- 1 tablespoon finely chopped scallion, plus sliced scallion greens for serving
- 1 tablespoon low-sodium soy sauce
- 2 teaspoons lemon juice
- 1 teaspoon Dijon mustard
- 1 teaspoon toasted sesame seeds, plus more for serving
- 1 avocado, chopped
- 4 ounces smoked salmon, roughly chopped

COMBINE the scallion, soy sauce, lemon juice, mustard, and sesame seeds. Drizzle the dressing over the avocado and smoked salmon. Serve topped with additional sesame seeds and scallion greens.

6

Smoked Salmon, Yogurt, and Radish Tartine with Chives

HANDS-ON: **10 MINUTES** TOTAL: **10 MINUTES** SERVES **4**

- ¼ cup plain Greek yogurt
- 4 slices toasted dark rye bread
- 4 ounces sliced smoked salmon
- 2 radishes, sliced
- ¼ small red onion, sliced
  Chopped fresh chives, flaky sea salt, and lemon wedges, for serving

SPREAD the yogurt on the bread and top with the smoked salmon, radishes, and onion. Serve topped with chives and sea salt, with lemon wedges on the side.

7

Creamy Smoked
Salmon Dip

HANDS-ON: **10 MINUTES** TOTAL: **10 MINUTES** SERVES **4**

4 ounces cream cheese

2 ounces chopped smoked salmon

1 tablespoon prepared horseradish

½ teaspoon finely grated lemon zest

1 tablespoon lemon juice

Kosher salt and black pepper

Crudités (like endive, carrot, and broccolini), toast, or crackers, for serving

COMBINE the cream cheese, smoked salmon, horseradish, lemon zest, lemon juice, and ¼ teaspoon each salt and pepper. Serve with crudités, toast, or crackers.

8

Smoked Salmon and
Pickled Vegetable Salad

HANDS-ON: **15 MINUTES** TOTAL: **30 MINUTES** SERVES **4**

¼ cup white wine vinegar

1 tablespoon sugar

½ teaspoon crushed caraway seeds

Kosher salt

½ English cucumber, sliced

½ small fennel bulb, sliced

4 ounces sliced smoked salmon

2 cups torn frisée

Olive oil and flaky sea salt, for serving

COMBINE the vinegar, sugar, caraway seeds, 1 teaspoon salt, and ¼ cup water in a saucepan and bring to a boil; remove from heat. Add the cucumber and fennel. Let cool, tossing occasionally; drain.

TOP the smoked salmon with the frisée and pickled vegetables. Serve with a drizzle of olive oil and sea salt.

9

Smoked Salmon
Potato Bites

HANDS-ON: 15 MINUTES TOTAL: 30 MINUTES SERVES 8

- 2 Yukon gold potatoes (about 8 ounces), thinly sliced
- 3 tablespoons olive oil
  Kosher salt and black pepper
- ⅓ cup plain Greek yogurt
- 4 ounces smoked salmon, sliced
  Chopped fresh chives, for serving

TOSS the potatoes with the oil on a baking sheet; season with ½ teaspoon each salt and pepper. Roast at 400°F, turning once, until golden brown, 18 to 22 minutes. Transfer to a wire rack to cool. Divide the yogurt and smoked salmon among the potatoes. Sprinkle with chives.

10

Smoked Salmon with
Creamy Cucumber Salad

HANDS-ON: 15 MINUTES TOTAL: 15 MINUTES SERVES 6

- 2 teaspoons prepared horseradish
- 2 teaspoons coarse-grain mustard
- ½ cup sour cream
- ¼ cup fresh lemon juice
  Kosher salt and black pepper
- ½ English cucumber or 1 regular cucumber, quartered lengthwise and sliced
- 2 bunches watercress, stems removed
- 1 pound thinly sliced smoked salmon
- 2 tablespoons finely chopped fresh dill
- 1 lemon, cut into wedges (optional)
  Bagel chips or 1 thinly sliced baguette

COMBINE the horseradish, mustard, sour cream, lemon juice, ½ teaspoon salt, and ¼ teaspoon pepper. Reserve half the dressing and set aside.

TOSS the cucumber with the dressing. Divide the watercress and salmon among 6 plates; top with the cucumber and dill. Serve with the reserved dressing, lemon wedges (if desired), and bagel chips.

TIP
For a ready-on-cue pasta dinner every time, heed the old adage: The sauce can wait for the pasta, not vice versa. Bring pasta water to a boil while you make the sauce. Cook the pasta as the sauce is finishing up; drain, toss, and enjoy.

**ARTICHOKE AND
SARDINE SPAGHETTI**
PAGE 265

Spaghetti

Yes, marinara is nice. But may we recommend bacon and escarole? These dishes put something new (and noteworthy) on top of spaghetti.

1

Cauliflower and Ricotta Spaghetti

HANDS-ON: **20 MINUTES** TOTAL: **45 MINUTES** SERVES **4**

¾ **pound spaghetti**
1 **head cauliflower, cut into florets (8 cups)**
¼ **cup olive oil**
1 **28-ounce can diced tomatoes**
2 **cloves garlic, chopped**
6 **anchovies**
  Kosher salt and black pepper
1 **cup ricotta**
¼ **cup toasted pine nuts**

COOK the pasta according to the package directions; drain.

TOSS the cauliflower with 2 tablespoons of the oil. Roast on a baking sheet at 425°F until tender, 25 to 35 minutes.

COOK the tomatoes, garlic, and anchovies in the remaining 2 tablespoons of oil in a large skillet over medium heat, stirring occasionally, until thick, 20 to 25 minutes. Season with ¾ teaspoon salt and ½ teaspoon pepper. Toss with the pasta and cauliflower. Serve topped with the ricotta and pine nuts.

2
Kimchi Chicken Noodle Soup

HANDS-ON: **20 MINUTES** TOTAL: **45 MINUTES** SERVES **4**

½ **pound spaghetti**

4 **cloves garlic, sliced**

3 **tablespoons chopped fresh ginger**

2 **tablespoons canola oil**

6 **cups low-sodium chicken broth**

1 **pound boneless, skinless chicken thighs**

1 **cup sliced kimchi Kosher salt**

1 **cup snow peas, sliced lengthwise, for serving**

4 **fried eggs, for serving**

COOK the pasta according to the package directions; drain.

COOK the garlic and ginger in the oil in a large saucepan over medium heat until fragrant, 1 to 2 minutes. Add the broth and chicken and bring to a boil. Reduce heat and simmer until chicken is cooked through, 20 to 25 minutes. Shred the chicken and return to the pan. Add the pasta, kimchi, and ½ teaspoon salt. Serve with the snow peas and eggs.

3
—
Creamy Brussels Sprouts Spaghetti

HANDS-ON: **20 MINUTES** TOTAL: **20 MINUTES** SERVES **4**

- ¾ **pound spaghetti**
- ¾ **pound Brussels sprouts, trimmed and sliced**
- 4 **tablespoons (½ stick) unsalted butter**
- 2 **cloves garlic, sliced**
- ¼ **cup heavy cream**
  Kosher salt and black pepper
- 3 **ounces ricotta salata, thinly sliced**

COOK the pasta according to the package directions; drain, reserving ½ cup of the cooking water.

COOK the Brussels sprouts in 2 tablespoons of the butter in a large skillet over medium heat, tossing occasionally, until crisp-tender, 4 to 6 minutes. Add the garlic; cook until fragrant, 1 minute. Toss with the pasta, heavy cream, the remaining 2 tablespoons of butter, and the reserved cooking water. Season with ½ teaspoon salt and ¼ teaspoon pepper. Serve topped with the ricotta salata.

4
—
Cold Sesame Noodles

HANDS-ON: **20 MINUTES** TOTAL: **20 MINUTES** SERVES **4**

- ¾ **pound spaghetti**
- 1 **teaspoon crushed red pepper**
- ¼ **cup canola oil**
- 4 **scallions, chopped, plus more sliced, for serving**
- ¼ **cup tahini**
- 3 **tablespoons rice vinegar**
- 3 **tablespoons low-sodium soy sauce**
  Kosher salt
  Toasted sesame seeds, for serving

COOK the pasta according to the package directions; drain and rinse under cold water.

COOK the red pepper in the oil in a large saucepan over medium heat until sizzling, 2 to 3 minutes. Remove from heat and stir in the scallions, tahini, vinegar, soy sauce, and 3 tablespoons water. Season with ½ teaspoon salt. Toss with the pasta. Serve topped with sesame seeds and sliced scallions.

5

Mushroom and Radicchio Spaghetti

HANDS-ON: **20 MINUTES** TOTAL: **20 MINUTES** SERVES **4**

¾ **pound spaghetti**
8 **ounces button mushrooms, halved**
1 **tablespoon olive oil**
  Kosher salt and black pepper
1 **head radicchio, torn**
4 **ounces fontina, grated (about 1 cup)**
2 **tablespoons Dijon mustard**
  Chopped fresh chives, for serving

COOK the pasta according to the package directions; drain.

COOK the mushrooms in the oil in a large skillet over high heat, tossing often, until browned, 5 to 7 minutes. Season with ½ teaspoon salt and ¼ teaspoon pepper. Toss with the pasta, radicchio, fontina, and mustard. Season with ¼ teaspoon each salt and pepper. Serve topped with the chives.

6

Shrimp and Tarragon Spaghetti

HANDS-ON: **15 MINUTES** TOTAL: **15 MINUTES** SERVES **4**

¾ **pound spaghetti**
1 **pound peeled and deveined large shrimp**
8 **radishes, quartered**
1 **tablespoon olive oil**
  Kosher salt and black pepper
¼ **cup (½ stick) unsalted butter**
1 **tablespoon chopped fresh tarragon leaves**
1 **teaspoon finely grated lemon zest**

COOK the pasta according to the package directions; drain, reserving ½ cup of the cooking water.

COOK the shrimp and radishes in the oil in a large skillet over medium-high heat, tossing occasionally, until the shrimp are opaque, 4 to 6 minutes. Season with ½ teaspoon salt and ¼ teaspoon pepper. Toss with the pasta, butter, tarragon, zest, and reserved cooking water.

7

Mexican Taco-Bowl Spaghetti

HANDS-ON: 20 MINUTES **TOTAL: 30 MINUTES** SERVES **4**

½ pound spaghetti
½ pound ground beef chuck
1 onion, chopped
2 teaspoons chili powder
2 tablespoons olive oil
   Kosher salt
1¼ cups fresh or frozen corn kernels
1 14.5-ounce can diced tomatoes
   Chopped avocado, chopped fresh cilantro leaves, crumbled Cotija or Feta, and lime wedges, for serving

COOK the pasta according to the package directions; drain.

COOK the beef, onion, and chili powder in the oil in a large skillet over high heat, stirring often, until browned, 6 to 8 minutes. Season with ¾ teaspoon salt.

ADD the corn and tomatoes. Cook, stirring, until heated through, 2 to 4 minutes. Toss with the pasta. Serve with avocado, cilantro, Cotija, and lime wedges.

8

Bacon and Escarole Spaghetti

HANDS-ON: 30 MINUTES **TOTAL: 30 MINUTES** SERVES **4**

¾ pound spaghetti
4 slices thick-cut bacon, chopped
1 tablespoon olive oil
1 onion, chopped
1 tablespoon fresh thyme leaves
   Kosher salt and black pepper
1 28-ounce can diced tomatoes
1 head escarole, torn
   Grated Parmesan, for serving

COOK the pasta according to the package directions; drain.

COOK the bacon in the oil in a large saucepan over medium-high heat, tossing often, until crisp, 6 to 8 minutes. Add the onion and thyme. Cook, stirring often, until soft, 8 to 10 minutes. Season with ¼ teaspoon salt and ½ teaspoon pepper. Add the tomatoes and escarole. Cook until the escarole is tender, 2 to 4 minutes. Serve over the pasta, topped with Parmesan.

9

Crispy Chickpea and Caper Spaghetti

HANDS-ON: 15 MINUTES TOTAL: 35 MINUTES SERVES 4

¾ **pound spaghetti**
1 **15-ounce can chickpeas, rinsed**
½ **cup panko bread crumbs**
¼ **cup capers, drained**
¼ **cup olive oil, plus more for drizzling**
2 **cloves garlic, chopped**
½ **teaspoon ground coriander**
   Kosher salt and black pepper
¼ **cup finely chopped fresh cilantro leaves**
2 **tablespoons fresh lemon juice**

COOK the pasta according to the package directions; drain.

COMBINE the chickpeas, bread crumbs, capers, oil, garlic, coriander, and ½ teaspoon each salt and pepper. Roast on a rimmed baking sheet at 400°F, tossing once, until crispy, 18 to 22 minutes. Toss with the pasta, cilantro, and lemon juice. Drizzle with additional oil.

10

Artichoke and Sardine Spaghetti

HANDS-ON: 15 MINUTES TOTAL: 30 MINUTES SERVES 4

¾ **pound spaghetti**
1 **cup roughly chopped marinated artichokes**
4 **ounces sardines, chopped (about ½ cup)**
3 **ounces pecorino, finely grated (about ¾ cup), plus more for serving**
¾ **cup finely chopped fresh flat-leaf parsley leaves**
½ **cup roasted almonds, chopped**
¼ **cup olive oil**
3 **tablespoons lemon juice**
   Kosher salt and black pepper

COOK the pasta according to the package directions; drain.

COMBINE the artichokes, sardines, pecorino, parsley, almonds, oil, and lemon juice. Season with ¼ teaspoon salt and ½ teaspoon pepper. Toss with the pasta. Serve topped with additional pecorino.

**TILAPIA WITH
CAPER-PARSLEY SAUCE**
PAGE 273

TIP
Tilapia is one of
the mildest-tasting
varieties of white
fish. (No trace of fishy
flavor!) It's a great
option for people who
normally don't like fish.

Tilapia

Farm-raised tilapia is generally a low-mercury, healthy, and earth-friendly choice. Dive into recipes featuring this family-friendly fish.

1
Blackened Tilapia with Buttered Carrots

HANDS-ON: **25 MINUTES** TOTAL: **25 MINUTES** SERVES **4**

1½ pounds carrots, cut into
    sticks if large

1 tablespoon unsalted butter

1 tablespoon chopped fresh
    oregano

    Kosher salt

4 6-ounce tilapia fillets, split
    lengthwise

2 tablespoons blackening
    seasoning

3 tablespoons canola oil, plus
    more if needed

    Corn bread, for serving

STEAM the carrots until tender, 6 to 8 minutes. Toss with the butter, oregano, and ½ teaspoon salt.

RUB the tilapia with the blackening seasoning. Cook, in batches, in the oil in a nonstick skillet over medium-high heat until cooked through, 2 to 3 minutes per side. Serve with the carrots and corn bread.

<u>2</u>
Fish Tacos with Cucumber Relish

HANDS-ON: **20 MINUTES** TOTAL: **20 MINUTES** SERVES **4**

4 **6-ounce tilapia fillets**
1 **teaspoon ground coriander**
   Kosher salt and black pepper
1 **tablespoon olive oil, plus**
   more for the grill
6 **radishes, sliced**
1 **cucumber, halved and sliced**
2 **tablespoons fresh lime juice,**
   plus lime wedges for serving
8 **corn tortillas, warmed**
1 **cup fresh cilantro leaves**
¼ **cup sour cream**

SEASON the tilapia with the coriander, ½ teaspoon salt, and ¼ teaspoon pepper. Grill on an oiled grill rack over high heat until cooked through, 1 to 2 minutes per side; break into pieces.

TOSS together the radishes, cucumber, lime juice, and 1 tablespoon oil. Serve in the tortillas with the tilapia, cilantro leaves, lime wedges, and sour cream.

3

Teriyaki Tilapia with Herb Salad

HANDS-ON: **15 MINUTES** TOTAL: **1 HOUR, 5 MINUTES** SERVES **4**

- 1 cup brown rice
- 4 6-ounce tilapia fillets
- ¼ cup teriyaki sauce
- ¼ cup fresh cilantro leaves
- ¼ cup fresh mint leaves
- 2 scallions, thinly sliced
- 1 tablespoon fresh lime juice
- 1 teaspoon crushed red pepper

COOK the rice according to the package directions.

BROIL the tilapia on a foil-lined rimmed baking sheet, basting occasionally with the teriyaki sauce, until cooked through, 7 to 9 minutes; break into pieces.

COMBINE the cilantro, mint, scallions, and lime juice. Serve the tilapia over the rice and top with the herb salad and red pepper.

4

Garlicky Grilled Tilapia with Couscous

HANDS-ON: **15 MINUTES** TOTAL: **20 MINUTES** SERVES **4**

- 4 6-ounce tilapia fillets, split lengthwise
- 2 tablespoons fresh lemon juice
- 1 tablespoon olive oil, plus more for the grill
- 2 cloves garlic, chopped
  Kosher salt and black pepper
- 1 cup couscous
- 1 tablespoon chopped fresh flat-leaf parsley
- 2 tablespoons chopped sun-dried tomatoes

MARINATE the tilapia in the lemon juice, oil, and garlic for 10 minutes. Season with ½ teaspoon salt and ¼ teaspoon pepper. Grill on an oiled grill rack over high heat until cooked through, 1 to 2 minutes per side.

COOK the couscous according to the package directions. Remove from heat and stir in the parsley and tomatoes. Serve with the tilapia.

5
Dijon Fish Cakes with Greens

HANDS-ON: 15 MINUTES **TOTAL: 1 HOUR, 15 MINUTES** SERVES **4**

- 4 6-ounce tilapia fillets
  Kosher salt and black pepper
- ½ cup mayonnaise
- 2 large eggs
- 2 tablespoons chopped fresh dill
- 1 tablespoon Dijon mustard
- ¾ cup panko bread crumbs
- 2 tablespoons canola oil
  Salad greens and tomatoes, for serving

SEASON the tilapia with ¾ teaspoon salt and ¼ teaspoon pepper. Bake at 400°F until cooked through, 10 to 12 minutes. Let cool; flake.

COMBINE the mayonnaise, eggs, dill, and mustard. Fold in the tilapia and bread crumbs. Form into 8 cakes; chill 30 minutes.

COOK in the oil in a nonstick skillet over medium heat for 3 to 5 minutes per side. Serve with the greens and tomatoes.

6
Crispy Fish Sticks with Coleslaw

HANDS-ON: 30 MINUTES **TOTAL: 30 MINUTES** SERVES **4**

- ⅓ cup sour cream
- 1 tablespoon red wine vinegar
  Kosher salt and black pepper
- ½ small head green cabbage, thinly sliced
- 2 carrots, grated
- 4 6-ounce tilapia fillets, split lengthwise
- ½ cup all-purpose flour
- 2 large eggs, beaten
- 1½ cups panko bread crumbs
- 1¾ cups canola oil, plus more if needed
- ½ cup ketchup

WHISK together the sour cream, vinegar, ½ teaspoon salt, and ¼ teaspoon pepper. Toss with the cabbage and carrots.

SEASON the tilapia with ½ teaspoon salt and ¼ teaspoon pepper. Dredge in the flour, dip in the eggs, then coat with the bread crumbs. Fry in the oil in a nonstick skillet over medium-high heat for 2 to 3 minutes per side. Serve with the coleslaw and ketchup.

7

Tilapia Salad with Apples and Almonds

HANDS-ON: **10 MINUTES** TOTAL: **25 MINUTES** SERVES **4**

 4 6-ounce tilapia fillets
   Kosher salt and black pepper
 4 tablespoons olive oil
 2 tablespoons fresh lime juice
 1 tablespoon Dijon mustard
 2 teaspoons honey
 6 cups arugula, thick stems removed
   (about 8 ounces)
 2 heads endive, sliced
 1 apple, cored and thinly sliced
 ¼ cup sliced almonds, toasted

SEASON the tilapia with ½ teaspoon salt and ¼ teaspoon pepper. Cook in 2 tablespoons of the oil in a nonstick skillet over medium-high heat until cooked through, 2 to 3 minutes per side. Let cool; break into pieces.

WHISK the lime juice, mustard, honey, the remaining oil, and ¼ teaspoon each salt and pepper. Add the arugula, endive, apple, and almonds and toss. Top with the tilapia.

8

Tilapia Po'boys

HANDS-ON: **20 MINUTES** TOTAL: **30 MINUTES** SERVES **4**

 3 6-ounce tilapia fillets, cut into strips
 ½ cup all-purpose flour
 1 tablespoon seafood seasoning
 2 tablespoons canola oil
 ¼ cup mayonnaise
 1 baguette, split and quartered
 1 cup shredded lettuce
16 pickle chips
   Hot sauce and potato chips, for serving

DREDGE the tilapia in a mixture of the flour and seafood seasoning. In batches, cook in the oil in a nonstick skillet over medium heat until cooked through, 3 to 4 minutes per side.

SPREAD the mayonnaise on the baguette pieces. Form sandwiches with the lettuce, pickles, and tilapia. Serve with hot sauce and potato chips.

9

Prosciutto-Wrapped Tilapia

HANDS-ON: **20 MINUTES** TOTAL: **20 MINUTES** SERVES **4**

- 3 bell peppers, sliced
- 2 cloves garlic, sliced
- 3 tablespoons olive oil
- ½ cup fresh basil leaves
- 4 6-ounce tilapia fillets
  Kosher salt and black pepper
- 4 large slices prosciutto

COOK the bell peppers and garlic in 1½ tablespoons of the oil in a skillet over medium-high heat, tossing frequently, until tender, 8 to 10 minutes. Fold in the basil.

SEASON the tilapia with ¼ teaspoon each salt and black pepper. Wrap each fillet in a slice of prosciutto. Cook in the remaining 1½ tablespoons of oil in a nonstick skillet over medium-high heat until cooked through, 2 to 3 minutes per side. Serve with the bell peppers.

10

Tilapia with Caper-Parsley Sauce

HANDS-ON: **10 MINUTES** TOTAL: **45 MINUTES** SERVES **4**

- 1½ pounds fingerling or new potatoes, halved
- 1 tablespoon olive oil
  Kosher salt and black pepper
- 4 6-ounce tilapia fillets, split lengthwise
- 4½ tablespoons unsalted butter
- 1 cup dry white wine
- 2 tablespoons capers
- ¼ cup chopped fresh flat-leaf parsley

TOSS the potatoes with the oil, ½ teaspoon salt, and ¼ teaspoon pepper on a rimmed baking sheet. Roast at 450°F, tossing once, until tender, 30 to 35 minutes.

SEASON the tilapia with ½ teaspoon salt and ¼ teaspoon pepper. In batches, cook in 1½ tablespoons butter in a nonstick skillet over medium-high heat until cooked through, 2 to 3 minutes per side; remove.

ADD the wine to skillet and reduce by half, 2 to 3 minutes. Whisk in the remaining 3 tablespoons of butter, the capers, and parsley. Serve with the tilapia and potatoes.

TIP
Tomatoes can be tricky to cut neatly. A serrated knife gets the job done without tearing the skin or crushing the flesh.

SAUTÉED TOMATOES,
SAUSAGE, AND OKRA
PAGE 281

Tomatoes

"A world without tomatoes is like a string quartet without violins," novelist Laurie Colwin once wrote. Hear, hear! These easy dishes offer a delicious symphony of flavors. Any tomato variety will work in these recipes unless otherwise specified.

1

Tomato Soup with Parmesan and Croutons

HANDS-ON: **10 MINUTES** TOTAL: **30 MINUTES** SERVES **4**

2 onions, chopped

2 tablespoons olive oil
  Kosher salt

1 28-ounce can whole peeled
  tomatoes, with juices

4 cups low-sodium chicken broth

1 teaspoon dried oregano

1 cup croutons

2 ounces Parmesan, shaved

COOK the onions in the oil with ½ teaspoon salt in a large saucepan over medium heat, stirring occasionally, until softened, 4 to 6 minutes.

ADD the tomatoes (with their juices), broth, and oregano. Simmer until beginning to thicken, 10 to 15 minutes. Puree in a blender. Top with the croutons and Parmesan.

2

Tomato, Cantaloupe, and Mint Salad

HANDS-ON: 10 MINUTES TOTAL: **30 MINUTES** SERVES **4**

1 cup balsamic vinegar

2 tablespoons light brown sugar

1 pound tomatoes, cut up

¼ cantaloupe, cut up

2 tablespoons olive oil

½ cup fresh mint leaves

   Kosher salt and black pepper

SIMMER the vinegar and brown sugar in a small saucepan until reduced to ¼ cup; transfer to a small bowl and let cool.

DIVIDE the tomatoes and cantaloupe among 4 plates. Drizzle with the oil and balsamic syrup, sprinkle with the mint, and season with ¼ teaspoon each salt and pepper.

3
Baked Tomatoes Provençal

HANDS-ON: **10 MINUTES** TOTAL: **30 MINUTES** SERVES **4**

- ½ cup panko bread crumbs
- ½ cup grated Parmesan (2 ounces)
- 2 tablespoons olive oil
- 1 tablespoon dried oregano
  Kosher salt and black pepper
- 1½ pounds beefsteak tomatoes, sliced ½ inch thick

TOSS together the bread crumbs, Parmesan, oil, and oregano; season with ¾ teaspoon salt and ¼ teaspoon pepper.

PLACE the tomatoes in a baking dish, overlapping slightly. Sprinkle with the bread crumb mixture and bake at 350°F until golden brown, 20 to 25 minutes.

4
Tomato, Corn, and Red Cabbage Salad

HANDS-ON: **15 MINUTES** TOTAL: **20 MINUTES** SERVES **4**

- 3 tablespoons fresh lime juice
- 2 tablespoons olive oil
  Kosher salt and black pepper
- ½ pound cherry tomatoes, halved
- 2 cups corn kernels (from 2 ears)
- 1 avocado, cut up
- ¼ head red cabbage (about ½ pound), thinly sliced
- 4 scallions, sliced

WHISK together the lime juice and oil; season with ½ teaspoon salt and ¼ teaspoon pepper. Add the tomatoes, corn, avocado, cabbage, and scallions and toss to combine.

5

Mediterranean Pasta Salad

HANDS-ON: **10 MINUTES** TOTAL: **30 MINUTES** SERVES **4**

6 ounces gemelli pasta (or other short pasta)
3 tablespoons olive oil
2 tablespoons lemon juice
2 tablespoons chopped fresh flat-leaf parsley
2 anchovy fillets, chopped
1 tablespoon chopped capers
1 teaspoon grated lemon zest
    Kosher salt and black pepper
½ pound tomatoes, cut up

COOK the pasta according to the package directions; drain and let cool.

WHISK together the oil, lemon juice, parsley, anchovies, capers, and lemon zest; season with ½ teaspoon salt and ¼ teaspoon pepper. Add the pasta and tomatoes and toss to combine.

6

Roasted Tomatoes and Fennel

HANDS-ON: **5 MINUTES** TOTAL: **1 HOUR** SERVES **4**

1 pound tomatoes, cut into wedges
2 medium bulbs fennel, cut into thin wedges, plus fennel fronds for sprinkling (optional)
3 tablespoons olive oil
    Kosher salt and black pepper

TOSS the tomatoes and fennel with the oil on 2 rimmed baking sheets; season with ¼ teaspoon each salt and pepper. Roast at 375°F until the fennel is tender, 40 to 50 minutes. Sprinkle with fennel fronds (if desired).

7

Tomatoes with Ranch Dressing

HANDS-ON: **10 MINUTES** TOTAL: **15 MINUTES** SERVES **4**

- 2 slices bacon
- ¼ cup mayonnaise
- ¼ cup sour cream
- 2 tablespoons milk
  Kosher salt and black pepper
- 1½ pounds tomatoes, sliced
- ¼ small red onion, finely chopped
  Fresh dill, chopped, for serving

COOK the bacon in a large skillet over medium heat until crisp. Let cool, then crumble.

WHISK together the mayonnaise, sour cream, and milk; season with ½ teaspoon salt and ¼ teaspoon pepper. Drizzle the dressing over the tomatoes. Sprinkle with the bacon, onion, and dill.

8

Tomato and Rye Panzanella

HANDS-ON: **15 MINUTES** TOTAL: **20 MINUTES** SERVES **4**

- ¼ pound rye bread, cut into ½-inch cubes
- ¼ cup plus 2 tablespoons olive oil
- 1 tablespoon red wine vinegar
  Kosher salt and black pepper
- ½ pound tomatoes, cut up
- ½ cup torn fresh basil leaves
- ½ cup cubed Havarti

TOSS the bread with 2 tablespoons of the oil on a rimmed baking sheet. Toast at 350°F, tossing once, until crisp, 10 to 12 minutes.

WHISK together the vinegar and the remaining ¼ cup of oil; season with ¾ teaspoon salt and ¼ teaspoon pepper. Add the tomatoes, bread, basil, and Havarti and toss to combine.

9

Curried Tomatoes and Chickpeas

HANDS-ON: **10 MINUTES** TOTAL: **15 MINUTES** SERVES **4**

  4 scallions, sliced, white and light green parts separated
  1 tablespoon grated fresh ginger
  1 teaspoon curry powder
  2 tablespoons olive oil
  2 pints grape tomatoes
  1 15.5-ounce can chickpeas, rinsed
  1 tablespoon fresh lime juice
     Kosher salt and black pepper

COOK the white parts of the scallions, the ginger, and curry powder in the oil in a large skillet over medium heat for 2 minutes. Add the tomatoes and cook until beginning to burst, 5 to 7 minutes.

ADD the chickpeas and lime juice, sprinkle with the scallion greens, and season with ½ teaspoon salt and ¼ teaspoon pepper.

10

Sautéed Tomatoes, Sausage, and Okra

HANDS-ON: **25 MINUTES** TOTAL: **25 MINUTES** SERVES **4**

  6 ounces andouille sausage, thinly sliced
  ½ pound fresh okra, halved lengthwise
  2 cloves garlic, thinly sliced
  2 tablespoons olive oil
  1 pound cherry tomatoes
     Fresh cilantro, chopped, for serving
     Kosher salt and black pepper

COOK the sausage, okra, and garlic in the oil in a large skillet over medium heat, until the sausage is browned and the okra is almost tender, 9 minutes. Add the tomatoes and cook until beginning to burst, 4 to 6 minutes. Sprinkle with cilantro and season with ¾ teaspoon salt and ¼ teaspoon pepper.

TIP
Warm tortillas are more pliable and easier to work with. Warm in a lightly oiled cast-iron skillet, or wrap tortillas in a damp paper towel and microwave for 30 to 60 seconds.

CHILAQUILES
PAGE 289

Tortillas

Ready to think beyond the burrito?
Just wrap your head around these
recipes—they're easy, fast to fix, and
flat-out delicious.

1
Beef and Pineapple Tacos

HANDS-ON: 30 MINUTES TOTAL: **30 MINUTES** SERVES **4**

1 pound skirt steak, cut into
  3 pieces
  Kosher salt and black pepper
1 tablespoon olive oil
2 cups chopped pineapple
½ red chili pepper, sliced
8 6-inch corn tortillas, warmed
  Fresh cilantro and lime
  wedges, for serving

SEASON the steak with 1 teaspoon salt and ¼ teaspoon pepper. Cook in the oil in a skillet over medium-high heat until medium-rare, 2 to 3 minutes per side. Let rest; slice.

ADD the pineapple and chili to the skillet; cook until tender, 6 to 8 minutes. Serve the steak and pineapple in the tortillas with cilantro and lime wedges.

2
Spiced Tortilla Crisps with Hummus

HANDS-ON: **5 MINUTES** TOTAL: **15 MINUTES** SERVES **4**

4 8-inch flour tortillas, cut into 2-inch strips

2 tablespoons olive oil, plus more for drizzling

1 teaspoon dried thyme

1 teaspoon dried oregano

1 teaspoon sesame seeds
   Kosher salt and black pepper
   Hummus and paprika, for serving

TOSS the tortilla strips with the oil, thyme, oregano, and sesame seeds on 2 baking sheets; season with ½ teaspoon each salt and pepper. Bake at 425°F, switching the sheets halfway through, until crisp, 5 to 7 minutes. Serve with hummus drizzled with oil and sprinkled with paprika.

3

Shrimp and
Avocado Tostadas

HANDS-ON: 20 MINUTES TOTAL: **20 MINUTES** SERVES **4**

1½ pounds cooked small shrimp
 2 avocados, chopped
 ½ medium red onion, chopped
 2 tablespoons lime juice
 ½ cup plus 2 tablespoons olive oil
    Kosher salt
 8 6-inch corn tortillas

TOSS together the shrimp, avocados, onion, lime juice, and 2 tablespoons of the oil; season with ½ teaspoon salt.

FRY the tortillas one at a time in ½ inch of oil in a medium skillet over medium-high heat until crisp, 1 to 2 minutes per side; drain and season with ¼ teaspoon salt. Top with the shrimp mixture.

4

Margherita Tortilla Pizzas

HANDS-ON: 10 MINUTES TOTAL: **30 MINUTES** SERVES **4**

 4 8-inch whole-wheat tortillas
 2 tablespoons olive oil
 1 cup marinara sauce
1½ cups grated mozzarella (6 ounces)
 ¼ cup fresh basil leaves

BRUSH the tortillas on both sides with the oil; prick all over with a fork. Bake on 2 rimmed baking sheets at 425°F, switching the sheets halfway through, until golden, 5 to 7 minutes per side.

TOP the tortillas with the marinara sauce and mozzarella, dividing evenly. Bake until the cheese melts, 7 to 9 minutes. Sprinkle with the basil.

5

Salami and Roasted Red Pepper Wraps

HANDS-ON: 15 MINUTES TOTAL: 15 MINUTES SERVES 4

- 4 cups shredded romaine lettuce
- 1 cup sliced roasted red peppers
- 2 tablespoons olive oil
- 2 tablespoons red wine vinegar
  Kosher salt and black pepper
- 4 10-inch whole-wheat tortillas
- 4 ounces cream cheese
- 8 ounces sliced salami
  Potato chips, for serving

TOSS the lettuce and red peppers with the oil and vinegar; season with ¼ teaspoon each salt and pepper. Dividing evenly, spread the tortillas with the cream cheese. Top with the salami and romaine mixture; roll up. Serve with potato chips.

6

Quesadillas Rancheros

HANDS-ON: 15 MINUTES TOTAL: 15 MINUTES SERVES 4

- 8 8-inch whole-wheat tortillas
- 2 tablespoons olive oil
- 3 cups grated Cheddar (12 ounces)
- 4 large eggs, fried
  Salsa verde, sliced scallions, and hot sauce, for serving

BRUSH the tortillas on one side with the oil. Dividing evenly, form sandwiches with the tortillas (oiled-sides out) and the Cheddar.

BROIL the sandwiches, in batches, on 2 foil-lined rimmed baking sheets until the tortillas are crisp and the cheese melts, 1 to 2 minutes per side. Top with the eggs, salsa verde, scallions, and hot sauce.

7

Chicken Salad with Crispy Tortillas

HANDS-ON: **20 MINUTES** TOTAL: **20 MINUTES** SERVES **4**

- 6 6-inch corn tortillas, cut into ½-inch strips
- ¾ cup olive oil
  Kosher salt
- 1 small head romaine lettuce, torn
- 3 cups shredded rotisserie chicken
- 1 carrot, shredded
- 4 radishes, sliced
- ¼ cup of your favorite vinaigrette

FRY the tortilla strips in ½ inch of oil in a large skillet over medium-high heat until crisp, 3 to 4 minutes; drain and season with ½ teaspoon salt.

TOSS together the lettuce, chicken, carrot, radishes, and vinaigrette. Top with the tortilla strips.

8

Bean and Cheese Taquitos

HANDS-ON: **25 MINUTES** TOTAL: **25 MINUTES** SERVES **4**

- 1 cup black beans, drained and rinsed
- ½ cup grated Cheddar (2 ounces)
- 8 6-inch corn tortillas, warmed
- ¾ cup olive oil
- ½ cup fresh salsa
- ¼ cup sour cream

MASH the beans with the Cheddar. Dividing evenly, roll up the mixture in the tortillas.

FRY the rolls, in batches, seam-side down, in ½ inch of oil in a large skillet over medium-high heat until crisp, 2 to 3 minutes per side. Serve with the salsa and sour cream.

9

Cinnamon Tortilla Sundaes

HANDS-ON: **5 MINUTES** TOTAL: **25 MINUTES** SERVES **4**

4 8-inch flour tortillas
2 tablespoons butter, melted
1 tablespoon sugar
1 teaspoon cinnamon
   Vanilla ice cream, maraschino cherries, chopped
   peanuts, and hot fudge sauce, for serving

BRUSH the tortillas on both sides with the butter; sprinkle
with the sugar and cinnamon. Bake on 2 baking sheets
at 425°F, switching the sheets halfway through, until
golden, 5 to 7 minutes per side. Cool; break into pieces.
Top with vanilla ice cream, maraschino cherries, peanuts,
and hot fudge sauce.

10

Chilaquiles

HANDS-ON: **15 MINUTES** TOTAL: **15 MINUTES** SERVES **4**

6 6-inch corn tortillas, cut into wedges
¾ cup olive oil
¾ cup red enchilada sauce
¼ cup crumbled Feta (1 ounce)
¼ small white onion, chopped
¼ cup fresh cilantro leaves

FRY the tortillas in ½ inch of oil in a large skillet over
medium-high heat until crisp, 3 to 4 minutes; drain.

WIPE the skillet clean and warm the enchilada sauce
and ¼ cup water over medium heat. Add the crisped
tortillas to the skillet and cook until most of the sauce is
absorbed, 5 to 6 minutes. Top with the Feta, onion,
and cilantro.

ROASTED ZUCCHINI,
POTATO, AND
BURRATA SALAD
PAGE 297

TIP
If your cooked zucchini is soggy instead of crispy, try lightly salting the slices 15 minutes before cooking. Place the slices in a colander to drain—the salt will draw out water.

Zucchini

Pizza, gazpacho, a grilled zucchini sandwich: These transformative recipes add a little zing to summer's most versatile squash.

1
Pan-Fried Chicken Cutlets with Zucchini Salad

HANDS-ON: **30 MINUTES** TOTAL: **30 MINUTES** SERVES **4**

1 zucchini, shaved with a vegetable peeler

1 cup halved grape tomatoes

¼ small red onion, sliced

1 tablespoon cider vinegar

6 tablespoons olive oil
Kosher salt and black pepper

8 chicken cutlets (about 1½ pounds total)

2 large eggs, beaten

2 cups panko bread crumbs

TOSS together the zucchini, tomatoes, onion, vinegar, 1 tablespoon of the oil, and ¼ teaspoon each salt and pepper.

SEASON the chicken with ½ teaspoon each salt and pepper; dip in the eggs, then coat in the bread crumbs. Fry, in batches, in the remaining 5 tablespoons of oil in a large skillet over medium heat until golden brown, 2 to 4 minutes per side. Serve over the zucchini salad.

2

Zucchini and Corn Pizzas

HANDS-ON: 15 MINUTES TOTAL: **35 MINUTES** SERVES **4**

- 1 **pound pizza dough, at room temperature**
- 2 **tablespoons olive oil, plus more for the baking sheets**
- 1 **cup ricotta**
- 1 **zucchini, thinly sliced**
  Kosher salt and black pepper
- 1 **cup fresh or frozen corn kernels**
- ¼ **cup torn fresh cilantro**
- 1 **tablespoon fresh lemon juice**

SHAPE the dough into 4 rounds and place on 2 oiled baking sheets. Brush with 1 tablespoon of the oil. Divide the ricotta, zucchini, and ½ teaspoon each salt and pepper among the rounds. Bake at 450°F until golden brown, 15 to 18 minutes.

TOP with the corn and cilantro. Drizzle with the lemon juice and the remaining tablespoon of oil; season with ¼ teaspoon each salt and pepper.

3

Zucchini Gazpacho with Basil and Yogurt

HANDS-ON: **15 MINUTES** TOTAL: **15 MINUTES** SERVES **4**

4 scallions, chopped
3 cucumbers, sliced
2 zucchini, sliced
¾ cup olive oil, plus more for drizzling
½ cup fresh basil, plus more for serving
⅓ cup fresh lemon juice
½ cup plain yogurt, plus more for serving
    Kosher salt and black pepper

PUREE the scallions, cucumbers, zucchini, oil, basil, and lemon juice in a blender until smooth. Add the yogurt and 1 teaspoon each salt and pepper and pulse to combine. Serve topped with additional plain yogurt, torn basil, pepper, and a drizzle of oil.

4

Gnocchi with Zucchini, Red Chilies, and Parmesan

HANDS-ON: **20 MINUTES** TOTAL: **25 MINUTES** SERVES **4**

1 pound gnocchi
2 zucchini, chopped
1 large onion, chopped
1 Fresno chili pepper, thinly sliced
    Kosher salt and black pepper
2 tablespoons olive oil
2 ounces Parmesan, grated (about ½ cup),
    plus more for serving
2 tablespoons fresh lemon juice

COOK the gnocchi according to the package directions; drain.

COOK the zucchini, onion, chili, and ¼ teaspoon each salt and pepper in the oil in a large skillet over medium-high heat, stirring often, until tender, 8 to 10 minutes. Toss with the gnocchi, Parmesan, and lemon juice. Season with ¼ teaspoon each salt and pepper. Serve topped with additional Parmesan.

5
Zucchini and
Sausage Frittata

HANDS-ON: **25 MINUTES** TOTAL: **40 MINUTES** SERVES **4**

- ½ **pound Italian sausage, casings removed**
- 2 **tablespoons olive oil**
- 2 **zucchini, sliced**
- 1 **small onion, chopped**
  Kosher salt and black pepper
- 8 **large eggs, beaten**
- 2 **ounces Cheddar, grated (about ½ cup)**
  Green salad, for serving

COOK the sausage, breaking it up with a spoon, in the oil in a medium nonstick ovenproof skillet over medium-high heat until golden, 3 to 5 minutes. Add the zucchini, onion, and ¾ teaspoon each salt and pepper. Cook, stirring often, until tender, 6 to 8 minutes. Remove from heat and stir in the eggs and Cheddar.

TRANSFER to oven and bake at 400°F until just set, 10 to 13 minutes. Serve with a green salad.

6
Turkey, Cheddar, and
Grilled Zucchini Sandwich

HANDS-ON: **25 MINUTES** TOTAL: **25 MINUTES** SERVES **4**

- 2 **zucchini, cut into ½-inch planks**
- 3 **tablespoons olive oil**
  Kosher salt and black pepper
  Canola oil, for the grill
- 8 **slices country bread**
- 2 **tablespoons mayonnaise**
- 2 **tablespoons Dijon mustard**
- 6 **ounces sliced roasted turkey**
- 4 **ounces sliced Cheddar**
  Lettuce, for serving

TOSS the zucchini with 1 tablespoon of the olive oil and ½ teaspoon each salt and pepper. Grill on an oiled grate over medium heat until tender, 2 to 3 minutes per side.

BRUSH the bread with the remaining 2 tablespoons of olive oil and grill until golden brown, 30 seconds per side. Divide the mayonnaise, mustard, turkey, Cheddar, lettuce, and zucchini among the grilled bread slices.

7

Fried Zucchini with Chive Mayo

HANDS-ON: **25 MINUTES** TOTAL: **25 MINUTES** SERVES **4**

- 1¼ cups buttermilk
- 1 large egg, beaten
- 1½ cups all-purpose flour
  Kosher salt and black pepper
- 4 cups canola oil
- 2 zucchini, halved and cut into spears
- ½ cup mayonnaise
- ¼ cup chopped fresh chives
- ¾ teaspoon seafood seasoning
  Lemon wedges, for serving

WHISK the buttermilk, egg, 1 cup of the flour, 1 teaspoon salt, and ½ teaspoon pepper in a large bowl. Heat the oil in a large saucepan over medium heat until a deep-fry thermometer reads 350°F. Toss the zucchini in ½ cup of the flour, then coat the zucchini in the batter. Fry, in batches, until golden, 4 to 6 minutes.

COMBINE the mayonnaise, chives, and seafood seasoning. Serve with the zucchini and lemon wedges.

8

Seared Snapper with Sautéed Zucchini and Tomatoes

HANDS-ON: **25 MINUTES** TOTAL: **25 MINUTES** SERVES **4**

- 3 zucchini, chopped
- 3 beefsteak tomatoes, chopped
- 4 cloves garlic, crushed
- 1 tablespoon fresh thyme, plus more for serving
  Kosher salt and black pepper
- ¼ cup olive oil
- 4 6-ounce pieces boneless, skin-on snapper or bass

COOK the zucchini, tomatoes, garlic, thyme, and ½ teaspoon each salt and pepper in 2 tablespoons of the oil in a large skillet over medium heat, tossing often, until tender, 12 to 15 minutes.

SEASON the snapper with ¼ teaspoon each salt and pepper. Cook, skin-side down, in the remaining 2 tablespoons of oil in a large nonstick skillet over medium-high heat until opaque, 3 to 4 minutes per side. Serve over the vegetables.

9
Steak and Zucchini with Greek Beans

HANDS-ON: **20 MINUTES** TOTAL: **20 MINUTES** SERVES **4**

1½   pounds skirt steak, cut into 4 pieces
1   teaspoon smoked paprika
    Kosher salt
4   zucchini, cut lengthwise into quarters
2   tablespoons olive oil
    Canola oil, for the grill
1   15.5-ounce can butter beans, drained and rinsed
2   ounces Feta, crumbled (about ½ cup)
1   tablespoon white wine vinegar
1   tablespoon chopped fresh flat-leaf parsley leaves

SEASON the steak with the paprika and ½ teaspoon salt. Toss the zucchini with 1 tablespoon of the olive oil and ¼ teaspoon salt. Grill on an oiled rack over medium-high heat until the steak is medium-rare and the zucchini is tender, 3 to 4 minutes per side for each. Let the steak rest; slice.

TOSS together the beans, Feta, vinegar, parsley, the remaining tablespoon of oil, and ¼ teaspoon salt. Serve with the steak and zucchini.

10
Roasted Zucchini, Potato, and Burrata Salad

HANDS-ON: **20 MINUTES** TOTAL: **50 MINUTES** SERVES **4**

4   zucchini, cut into 1½-inch pieces
1½   pounds small Yukon gold potatoes, quartered
4   tablespoons olive oil
    Kosher salt and black pepper
6   cups trimmed watercress
¼   cup pine nuts, toasted
¼   cup torn fresh basil leaves
8   ounces burrata (or fresh mozzarella), torn
2   tablespoons red wine vinegar

TOSS the zucchini and potatoes with 3 tablespoons of the oil and ½ teaspoon each salt and pepper. Bake on a rimmed baking sheet at 375°F until tender, 25 to 30 minutes. Let cool.

TOP the watercress with the pine nuts, basil, burrata, and roasted vegetables. Drizzle with the vinegar and the remaining tablespoon of oil. Season with ¼ teaspoon each salt and pepper.

Sweet
Endings

TIP
For best results every time you bake, be sure to spoon and level flour into your measuring cup, rather than dipping the cup directly into the flour.

CACAO NIB AND PUMPKIN SEED TOFFEE
PAGE 307

Cookies, Bars, and Beyond

These 10 recipes cover all the tasty bases, from classic crowd-pleasers to delectable new additions. Whatever direction you choose to go (lemon bars or pumpkin seed toffee?), assume the results will disappear quickly.

1

Tangy Lemon Bars

HANDS-ON: **30 MINUTES** TOTAL: **2 HOURS, 30 MINUTES** MAKES **24**

CRUST

Nonstick cooking spray

1½ cups all-purpose flour,
spooned and leveled

½ cup (1 stick) cold unsalted
butter, cut into pieces

⅓ cup granulated sugar

¼ teaspoon salt

FILLING

3 large eggs

1 large egg yolk

⅔ cup granulated sugar

⅓ cup fresh lemon juice

2 teaspoons finely grated
lemon zest

2 tablespoons all-purpose flour

2 tablespoons heavy cream

⅛ teaspoon salt

Confectioners' sugar,
for dusting

SPRAY an 8-inch square pan
with cooking spray and line with
parchment, leaving an overhang;
spray the parchment.

PULSE the flour, butter, granulated
sugar, and salt in a food processor
until fine crumbs form to make the
crust. Press into the bottom of the
prepared pan and bake at 350°F
until pale golden, 25 to 30 minutes.

WHISK together the eggs, egg yolk,
granulated sugar, lemon juice,
lemon zest, flour, cream, and salt to
make the filling. Pour onto the hot
crust. Bake at 350°F until just set,
15 to 18 minutes. Cool completely,
then refrigerate for 2 hours. Cut
into 24 rectangles. Dust with the
confectioners' sugar.

2

Jam and Pistachio Icebox Cookies

HANDS-ON: **45 MINUTES** TOTAL: **4 HOURS** MAKES **40**

1½ **cups all-purpose flour, spooned and leveled, plus more for rolling**

½ **teaspoon ground cardamom**

¼ **teaspoon salt**

12 **tablespoons (1½ sticks) unsalted butter, softened**

⅓ **cup granulated sugar**

½ **cup shelled unsalted pistachios, finely chopped**

½ **cup thick lingonberry jam or other thick red berry jam**

COMBINE the flour, cardamom, and salt.

BEAT the butter and sugar with an electric mixer until fluffy, 2 to 3 minutes. Gradually add the flour mixture. Mix until the dough forms clumps. Stir in the pistachios.

PRESS the dough into a rectangle on a sheet of lightly floured parchment paper. Roll it into a ¼-inch-thick 12-by-8-inch rectangle with a lightly floured rolling pin. With a long side facing you, spread the jam over the bottom half of the dough in an even layer. Fold the top half of the dough over to sandwich the jam. Wrap the

dough in parchment and plastic wrap and refrigerate until very firm, at least 2 hours.

TRIM off the uneven ends of dough, then cut crosswise into ¼-inch slices. Place the slices 1½ inches apart on 2 parchment-lined baking sheets. Bake at 350°F until golden brown, 15 minutes. Cool slightly on the baking sheets, then transfer to a wire rack to cool completely.

3

Double Chocolate Chip Cookies

HANDS-ON: **15 MINUTES** TOTAL: **35 MINUTES**

MAKES **36**

½ cup (1 stick) unsalted butter, at room temperature

½ cup granulated sugar

½ cup brown sugar

1 large egg

1 teaspoon pure vanilla extract

1½ cups all-purpose flour, spooned and leveled

¼ cup unsweetened cocoa powder

½ teaspoon baking soda

½ teaspoon baking powder

½ teaspoon salt

½ cup milk chocolate chips

½ cup semisweet chocolate chips

BEAT the butter and sugars with an electric mixer until fluffy, 2 to 3 minutes. Add the egg and vanilla. Sift together the flour, cocoa, baking soda, baking powder, and salt. Gradually add the flour mixture to the butter mixture. Mix to combine. Stir in the chocolate chips.

FORM the dough into 1½-inch balls and place 2 inches apart on parchment-lined baking sheets. Bake at 350°F until the centers are set, about 12 minutes. Cool slightly on the baking sheets, then transfer to a wire rack to cool completely.

4

Black and White Cookies

HANDS-ON: **45 MINUTES** TOTAL: **1 HOUR, 30 MINUTES**

MAKES **24**

5 cups cake flour, spooned and leveled

1 teaspoon baking powder

1 teaspoon salt

1 cup (2 sticks) unsalted butter

1¾ cups granulated sugar

4 large eggs

1 cup milk

1 teaspoon pure vanilla extract

4 cups confectioners' sugar

2 tablespoons fresh lemon juice

3 ounces bittersweet chocolate

1 tablespoon light corn syrup

WHISK together the flour, baking powder, and salt.

BEAT the butter and sugar with an electric mixer until fluffy, 2 to 3 minutes. Add the eggs, milk, and vanilla. Gradually add the flour mixture. Stir to combine.

SCOOP the dough using a ¼-cup measuring cup and place 2 inches apart on 2 parchment-lined baking sheets. Bake at 375°F, rotating once, until the edges begin to brown, 15 to 17 minutes. Cool slightly on the baking sheets, then transfer to a wire rack to cool completely.

WHISK together the confectioners' sugar, ⅓ cup boiling water, and the lemon juice until smooth. Divide the mixture between 2 heatproof bowls. Set one bowl over a saucepan of gently simmering water; add the chocolate and corn syrup and stir until melted. On each cookie, spread half the flat side with white frosting and half with chocolate frosting. Let the cookies set, about 10 minutes.

5
Buckeyes

HANDS-ON: **30 MINUTES** TOTAL: **1 HOUR, 15 MINUTES**

MAKES **30**

¾ **cup creamy peanut butter**

½ **cup (1 stick) unsalted butter, softened**

2 **cups confectioners' sugar**

½ **teaspoon pure vanilla extract**

¼ **teaspoon salt**

½ **pound bittersweet chocolate, chopped**

BEAT the peanut butter and butter with an electric mixer until creamy. Gradually add the confectioners' sugar, vanilla, and salt. Mix to combine. (The mixture will be crumbly.)

FORM tablespoonfuls of the dough into balls and place on a wax paper–lined baking sheet. Freeze until firm, about 15 minutes.

MELT the chocolate in a glass bowl in the microwave, stopping and stirring every 30 seconds, until smooth. Let cool slightly. Resting each ball on the tines of a fork, lower it into the chocolate until it is two-thirds covered. Refrigerate on the baking sheet until the chocolate is firm, about 30 minutes.

6
Salted Oatmeal Cookies with Dark Chocolate

HANDS-ON: **20 MINUTES** TOTAL: **55 MINUTES** MAKES **24**

2 **cups old-fashioned rolled oats (not quick-cooking)**

1 **cup all-purpose flour, spooned and leveled**

¾ **teaspoon baking soda**

¼ **teaspoon ground cinnamon**

2 **teaspoons flaky sea salt (such as Maldon)**

¾ **cup (1½ sticks) unsalted butter, at room temperature**

½ **cup granulated sugar**

½ **cup packed light brown sugar**

1 **large egg**

1 **teaspoon pure vanilla extract**

6 **ounces bittersweet chocolate, coarsely chopped**

COMBINE the oats, flour, baking soda, cinnamon, and 1 teaspoon of the salt in a medium bowl; set aside.

BEAT the butter, granulated sugar, and brown sugar with an electric mixer until fluffy, 2 to 3 minutes. Beat in the egg and vanilla. Gradually add the flour mixture. Mix to combine. Stir in the chocolate.

DROP tablespoonfuls of the dough 2 inches apart onto 2 parchment-lined baking sheets. Sprinkle with the remaining 1 teaspoon of salt.

BAKE at 375°F, rotating once, until lightly brown around the edges, about 10 to 12 minutes. Cool slightly on the baking sheets, then transfer to a wire rack to cool completely.

7

Chocolate-Dipped Marshmallows

HANDS ON: 10 MINUTES TOTAL: **30 MINUTES** MAKES **12**

- 12 marshmallows
- 2 ounces semisweet chocolate, melted
- 3 tablespoons toppings (such as chopped pistachios, shredded coconut, and crumbled graham crackers)

DIP half of each marshmallow in the melted chocolate, letting the excess drip off, then sprinkle with the desired toppings. Chill until firm, about 20 minutes.

8

Pecan Bars

HANDS-ON TIME: 20 MINUTES

TOTAL TIME: **2 HOURS, 10 MINUTES** MAKES **24**

CRUST
- ½ cup (1 stick) cold unsalted butter, cut into pieces, plus more for the baking pan
- 1½ cups all-purpose flour, spooned and leveled, plus more for pressing in the dough
- ⅓ cup granulated sugar
- ¼ teaspoon salt

FILLING
- ½ cup packed light brown sugar
- ¼ cup granulated sugar
- 4 tablespoons (½ stick) unsalted butter, cut into pieces
- ¼ cup honey
- 2 tablespoons heavy cream
- 2 cups pecans, toasted and chopped
- 1 teaspoon pure vanilla extract

LINE a buttered 8-inch square baking pan with parchment, leaving an overhang; butter the parchment. Process the flour, butter, sugar, and salt in a food processor until fine crumbs form. With floured fingers, press the dough into the prepared pan. Bake at 350°F until just beginning to brown, 25 to 30 minutes.

BRING the sugars, butter, honey, and cream to a boil in a medium saucepan; reduce heat and simmer until slightly thickened, 4 to 5 minutes. Stir in the pecans and vanilla. Spread over the crust and let cool for 1 hour. Cut into 24 rectangles.

9

Sugared Pecan Balls

HANDS-ON: **25 MINUTES**

TOTAL: **1 HOUR, 20 MINUTES** MAKES **36**

- 2 cups pecans, toasted
- 2 cups all-purpose flour, spooned and leveled
- 1 teaspoon salt
- 1 cup (2 sticks) unsalted butter, at room temperature
- ⅔ cup confectioners' sugar
- 1 teaspoon pure vanilla extract

GRIND the pecans in a food processor. Whisk together the finely ground pecans, flour, and salt; set aside.

BEAT the butter and ⅓ cup of the sugar with an electric mixer until fluffy, 2 to 3 minutes. Beat in the vanilla. Gradually add the flour mixture. Mix to combine.

SHAPE the dough into balls (about 1 tablespoon each) and space 2 inches apart on parchment-lined baking sheets. Bake at 350°F, rotating once, until just beginning to brown, 12 to 14 minutes. Cool slightly on the baking sheets, then transfer to a wire rack to cool completely.

PLACE the remaining ⅓ cup of sugar on a plate. A few at a time, roll the balls in the sugar to coat.

10

Cacao Nib and Pumpkin Seed Toffee

HANDS-ON: **20 MINUTES**

TOTAL: **1 HOUR, 30 MINUTES** SERVES **16**

- 55 Club crackers
  Nonstick cooking spray
- 1½ cups granulated sugar
- 1½ cups (3 sticks) unsalted butter
- 2 tablespoons cane sugar syrup
- 8 ounces bittersweet chocolate, chopped
- 1 cup roasted salted pumpkin seeds (pepitas)
- ½ cup cacao nibs

ARRANGE the crackers in a single layer on a baking sheet coated with cooking spray. Break them to fit if necessary.

STIR the sugar, butter, and syrup in a large saucepan over medium-low heat until the sugar is melted. Cook without stirring until it starts to brown around the edge. Simmer until a candy thermometer registers 300°F. Spread carefully over the crackers in an even layer; let cool for 2 minutes.

SPRINKLE the chocolate over the toffee and spread evenly with a spatula. Sprinkle the pumpkin seeds and cacao nibs evenly over the chocolate.

FREEZE the toffee until set, about 15 minutes. Invert onto a work surface and break into large shards.

TIP
When baking cup-
cakes, fill each cup no
more than ⅔ full to
ensure modestly sized,
gently curved tops—
and to avoid messy
spillovers that will
stick to the pan.

CARROT CAKE
CUPCAKES
PAGE 315

Cupcakes

Batter up! When it's your turn to bring dessert, hit a home run with one of these easy, adorable treats.

<u>1</u>

Gingerbread Cupcakes with Lemon Cream Cheese Frosting

HANDS-ON: **45 MINUTES** TOTAL: **1 HOUR, 25 MINUTES** MAKES **24**

CUPCAKES

2½ cups all-purpose flour, spooned and leveled

1½ teaspoons baking powder

¼ teaspoon baking soda

1½ teaspoons ground ginger

1½ teaspoons ground cinnamon

½ teaspoon salt

1 cup (2 sticks) unsalted butter, at room temperature

¾ cup packed dark brown sugar

¾ cup light molasses

1 tablespoon grated ginger

3 large eggs, at room temperature

1 cup whole milk

FROSTING

1 8-ounce bar cream cheese, at room temperature

½ cup (1 stick) unsalted butter, at room temperature

1 pound confectioners' sugar (about 3¾ cups)

2 tablespoons fresh lemon juice, plus 2 teaspoons lemon zest

¼ teaspoon salt

WHISK together the flour, baking powder, baking soda, ground ginger, cinnamon, and salt; set aside.

BEAT the butter and sugar with an electric mixer until fluffy, 2 to 3 minutes. Beat in the molasses and grated ginger, then the eggs one at a time. Alternate adding in the flour mixture and the milk; mix to combine.

BAKE in 2 lined 12-cup muffin tins at 350°F for 15 to 20 minutes. Let cool.

BEAT the cream cheese and butter with an electric mixer until smooth, 2 minutes. Add the sugar, lemon juice, and salt; beat until fluffy, 5 minutes. Chill for 10 minutes. Frost the cupcakes and sprinkle with the lemon zest.

2

Hot Chocolate Cupcakes with Marshmallow Frosting

HANDS-ON: **55 MINUTES** TOTAL: **1 HOUR, 45 MINUTES** MAKES **24**

CUPCAKES

- ¾ cup unsweetened cocoa powder (not Dutch)
- ⅔ cup boiling water
- 2 large eggs
- 1½ cups granulated sugar
- ⅓ cup vegetable oil
- 1 teaspoon pure vanilla extract
- ¼ teaspoon salt
- 1⅓ cups all-purpose flour, spooned and leveled
- ⅔ cup whole milk
- ¾ teaspoon baking powder
- ½ teaspoon baking soda

FROSTING

- 2½ cups granulated sugar
- 6 large egg whites
- ¼ teaspoon pure vanilla extract
- ½ teaspoon cream of tartar
  Chocolate shavings and miniature marshmallows, for garnish

WHISK the cocoa into the hot water until dissolved. Let cool.

BEAT the eggs and sugar with an electric mixer until light, 3 minutes. Whisk in the oil, vanilla, and salt. Whisk in the cocoa mixture.

WHISK together the flour, milk, baking powder, and baking soda.

Add to the egg mixture; mix to combine.

BAKE in 2 lined 12-cup muffin tins at 350°F for 15 to 20 minutes. Let cool.

WHISK the sugar, egg whites, vanilla, and cream of tartar in a heatproof bowl over a saucepan with 1 inch of gently simmering water until the whites feel warm and the sugar dissolves, 2 minutes. Whip with an electric mixer with the whisk attachment until soft peaks form, 4 to 5 minutes.

DOLLOP or pipe the frosting onto the cupcakes. Top with chocolate shavings and marshmallows.

3

Snickerdoodle Cupcakes

HANDS-ON: **45 MINUTES** TOTAL: **1 HOUR, 25 MINUTES**
MAKES **24**

CUPCAKES

2½ cups all-purpose flour, spooned and leveled

1½ teaspoons ground cinnamon

1½ teaspoons baking powder

¼ teaspoon baking soda

½ teaspoon salt

1 cup (2 sticks) unsalted butter, at room temperature

1½ cups granulated sugar

1 teaspoon pure vanilla extract

3 large eggs, at room temperature

1 cup whole milk

FROSTING

2 cups (4 sticks) unsalted butter, at room temperature

1½ cups confectioners' sugar

1 teaspoon pure vanilla extract

1 teaspoon ground cinnamon, plus more for dusting

¼ teaspoon salt

WHISK together the flour, cinnamon, baking powder, baking soda, and salt; set aside.

BEAT the butter and sugar with an electric mixer until fluffy, 3 minutes. Add the vanilla, then the eggs, one at a time. Add in the flour mixture, alternating with the milk; mix to combine. Bake in 2 lined 12-cup muffin tins at 350°F for 15 to 20 minutes. Let cool.

BEAT the butter until fluffy, 3 to 5 minutes. Add the sugar, vanilla, cinnamon, and salt. Frost the cupcakes, then dust with cinnamon.

4

Salted Caramel Cupcakes

HANDS-ON: **55 MINUTES** TOTAL: **1 HOUR, 40 MINUTES**
MAKES **24**

CUPCAKES

2¾ cups all-purpose flour, spooned and leveled

1 teaspoon baking powder

½ teaspoon baking soda

¾ teaspoon salt

1 cup (2 sticks) unsalted butter, at room temperature

1½ cups light brown sugar

2 teaspoons pure vanilla extract

2 large eggs, at room temperature

1 cup whole milk

FROSTING

½ cup (1 stick) unsalted butter

1 cup light brown sugar

3 tablespoons whole milk

1½ cups confectioners' sugar

Caramel corn and flaky sea salt, for garnish

WHISK together the flour, baking powder, baking soda, and salt; set aside.

BEAT the butter and brown sugar with an electric mixer until fluffy, 3 minutes. Add the vanilla, then the eggs, one at a time. Add in the flour mixture, alternating with the milk; mix to combine. Bake in 2 lined 12-cup muffin tins at 350°F for 15 to 20 minutes. Let cool.

COOK the butter, brown sugar, and milk in a medium saucepan until the sugar is dissolved. Beat, in a bowl, with the sugar until smooth. Frost the cupcakes and garnish with caramel corn and sea salt.

5
Lemon Cupcakes

HANDS-ON: **20 MINUTES** TOTAL: **1 HOUR** MAKES **24**

CUPCAKES

- 3 cups all-purpose flour, spooned and leveled
- 2 tablespoons finely grated lemon zest
- 2½ teaspoons baking powder
- ½ teaspoon salt
- 1 cup (2 sticks) unsalted butter, at room temperature
- 1½ cups granulated sugar
- 1 teaspoon pure vanilla extract
- 4 large eggs, at room temperature
- 1 cup whole milk

FROSTING

- 1 cup (2 sticks) unsalted butter, at room temperature
- 1½ cups confectioners' sugar
- 1 tablespoon fresh lemon juice, 1 tablespoon finely grated lemon zest, plus thinly sliced lemon zest, for garnish
- ¼ teaspoon salt

WHISK together the flour, lemon zest, baking powder, and salt; set aside.

BEAT the butter and sugar with an electric mixer until fluffy, 2 to 3 minutes. Add the vanilla, then the eggs, one at a time. Add in the flour mixture, alternating with the milk; mix to combine. Bake in 2 lined 12-cup muffin tins at 350°F, 15 to 20 minutes. Let cool.

BEAT the butter and sugar until fluffy, 3 to 5 minutes. Beat in the lemon juice, lemon zest, and salt. Frost the cupcakes and sprinkle with additional lemon zest.

6
Maple-Pumpkin Cupcakes

HANDS-ON: **30 MINUTES** TOTAL: **50 MINUTES** MAKES **24**

CUPCAKES

- 2½ cups all-purpose flour, spooned and leveled
- 2 teaspoons baking soda
- ½ teaspoon salt
- 1 teaspoon ground cinnamon
- ½ teaspoon ground ginger
- ¼ teaspoon ground allspice
- 1 15-ounce can pure pumpkin puree
- 2 large eggs, at room temperature
- 1½ cups granulated sugar
- ⅔ cup vegetable oil

FROSTING

- 1 8-ounce bar cream cheese, at room temperature
- ¼ cup (½ stick) unsalted butter, at room temperature
- 2 cups confectioners' sugar
- ¼ cup pure maple syrup
- ¼ teaspoon salt

WHISK together the flour, baking soda, salt, cinnamon, ginger, and allspice; set aside.

MIX together the pumpkin puree, eggs, granulated sugar, and oil until uniform in color. Add the flour mixture. Mix to combine. Bake in 2 lined 12-cup muffin tins at 350°F until a toothpick inserted in the center comes out clean, 20 to 24 minutes. Let cool.

BEAT the cream cheese, butter, sugar, maple syrup, and salt with an electric mixer until fluffy, 3 to 5 minutes. Frost the cupcakes.

7

Double Chocolate Cupcakes (Vegan)

HANDS ON: **20 MINUTES** TOTAL: **55 MINUTES** MAKES **12**

CUPCAKES

 1 **cup white whole-wheat flour, spooned and leveled**
 ¾ **cup granulated sugar**
 ⅓ **cup unsweetened cocoa powder**
 ¾ **teaspoon baking soda**
 ½ **teaspoon baking powder**
 ½ **teaspoon salt**
 1 **cup soy milk**
 2 **teaspoons cider vinegar**
 ¼ **cup canola oil**
 2 **teaspoons pure vanilla extract**

FROSTING

 ¼ **cup soy milk**
 1 **3.5-ounce bar semisweet chocolate, chopped**
 Raspberries, for garnish

WHISK together the flour, sugar, cocoa, baking soda, baking powder, and salt in a medium bowl; set aside.

WHISK together the soy milk and vinegar; set aside until curdled, 5 minutes. Whisk in the oil and vanilla extract. Gradually whisk the soy milk mixture into the flour mixture; mix to combine.

BAKE in 2 lined 12-cup muffin tins at 350°F, 15 to 18 minutes. Let cool.

HEAT the soy milk in a small saucepan over medium heat. Pour over the chocolate, let sit for 2 minutes, then whisk until smooth. Let cool for 5 minutes. Frost the cupcakes and top each with a raspberry.

8

Almond Thumbprint Cupcakes (Gluten-Free)

HANDS-ON: **20 MINUTES** TOTAL: **25 MINUTES** MAKES **12**

 2 **cups (7.5 ounces) almond flour or whole blanched almonds, finely ground in a food processor**
 ⅓ **cup (1.8 ounces) all-purpose gluten-free flour blend, spooned and leveled**
 1¼ **cups granulated sugar**
 ½ **teaspoon baking powder**
 ½ **teaspoon salt**
 ¼ **cup (½ stick) butter, melted and cooled slightly**
 2 **eggs, lightly beaten**
 ¼ **cup whole milk**
 ¼ **cup raspberry jam (or other fruit preserves), for topping**
 Confectioners' sugar, for dusting

WHISK together the flours, sugar, baking powder, and salt. Add the butter, eggs, and milk; stir well with a wooden spoon or rubber spatula to combine.

BAKE in 2 lined 12-cup muffin tins at 350°F for 20 to 25 minutes. While the cupcakes are warm, press down on the center of each with the back of a tablespoon to create a shallow indentation. Fill with about 1 teaspoon of jam, then let cool. Once cool, dust the edges with confectioners' sugar.

9
Peanut Butter Cupcakes

HANDS-ON: **30 MINUTES** TOTAL: **1 HOUR** MAKES **12**

CUPCAKES

1½ cups cake flour, spooned and leveled

1½ teaspoons baking powder

½ teaspoon salt

½ cup (1 stick) unsalted butter, at room temperature

¾ cup granulated sugar

2 teaspoons pure vanilla extract

2 large eggs, at room temperature

¾ cup buttermilk, at room temperature

FROSTING

½ cup (1 stick) unsalted butter, at room temperature

1 cup creamy peanut butter

2 cups confectioners' sugar

⅛ teaspoon salt

WHISK together the flour, baking powder, and salt; set aside.

BEAT the butter and sugar with an electric mixer until fluffy, 2 to 3 minutes. Beat in the vanilla, then the eggs, one at a time. Add in the flour mixture, alternating with the buttermilk; mix to combine.

BAKE in a lined 12-cup muffin tin at 350°F for 15 to 20 minutes. Let cool.

BEAT the butter and peanut butter with an electric mixer until smooth. Add the sugar and salt and beat until fluffy. Frost or pipe frosting onto the cupcakes.

10
Carrot Cake Cupcakes

HANDS-ON: **25 MINUTES** TOTAL: **1 HOUR, 25 MINUTES**
MAKES **12**

CUPCAKES

1½ cups all-purpose flour, spooned and leveled

1 teaspoon ground cinnamon

¼ teaspoon salt

½ teaspoon baking powder

¼ teaspoon baking soda

¼ teaspoon ground nutmeg

1 cup packed dark brown sugar

½ cup canola oil

1 large egg, at room temperature

¾ pound carrots, coarsely grated (about 2 cups)

1 cup pecans, toasted and roughly chopped

FROSTING

1 8-ounce bar cream cheese, at room temperature

¼ cup (½ stick) unsalted butter, at room temperature

½ teaspoon pure vanilla extract

⅛ teaspoon salt

1½ cups confectioners' sugar

WHISK together the flour, cinnamon, salt, baking powder, baking soda, and nutmeg. Whisk together the brown sugar, oil, and egg; fold in the carrots and ½ cup of the pecans. Add to the flour mixture; mix to combine.

BAKE in a lined 12-cup muffin tin at 350°F for 20 to 25 minutes. Let cool.

BEAT the cream cheese, butter, vanilla, and salt with an electric mixer until smooth. Beat in the sugar. Chill for 5 minutes. Frost cupcakes; top with remaining pecans.

TIP
Parbaking keeps a soft custard filling from turning the crust limp. Bake the crust until it smells toasty and looks golden brown on the sides and the bottom. Cool completely before filling.

**CHOCOLATE
CREAM PIE**
PAGE 323

Pies

These desserts work perfectly well with a store-bought crust. But if you prefer an entirely-from-scratch version, get rolling with the simple recipe on page 324.

1
Gingery Pumpkin Pie

HANDS-ON: 25 MINUTES (INCLUDES PIECRUST) TOTAL: 3 HOURS (INCLUDES CHILLING)

SERVES **8**

1 15-ounce can pure
  pumpkin puree

¾ cup granulated sugar

¾ cup heavy cream

2 large eggs

1 tablespoon grated
  fresh ginger

½ teaspoon ground cinnamon

¼ teaspoon salt
  Pinch of ground cloves
  9-inch Basic Flaky Piecrust,
  parbaked (see page 324)

1 tablespoon pepitas
  (hulled pumpkin seeds)

WHISK together the pumpkin puree,
sugar, heavy cream, eggs, ginger,
cinnamon, ¼ teaspoon salt, and
ground cloves.

POUR into the piecrust and bake
at 350°F until the center is set
but still slightly wobbly, 40 to 50
minutes. Let cool completely,
at least 1 hour. Top with pepitas
before serving.

2
Cranberry-Apple Pie

HANDS-ON: 30 MINUTES (INCLUDES PIECRUST) TOTAL: 6 HOURS (INCLUDES CHILLING)
SERVES 8

2 pounds Granny Smith apples, peeled and thinly sliced

2 cups fresh cranberries

¾ cup granulated sugar

3 tablespoons cornstarch

1 teaspoon grated lemon zest

½ teaspoon cinnamon

¼ teaspoon salt

   9-inch Basic Flaky Piecrust, unbaked (see page 324)

½ cup granola

4 tablespoons (½ stick) unsalted butter

TOSS together the apples, cranberries, sugar, cornstarch, lemon zest, cinnamon, and salt.

TRANSFER to the piecrust, top with the granola, and dot with the butter. Bake at 375°F until the apples are tender, 50 to 60 minutes. (If the top darkens too quickly, tent loosely with foil.) Let cool completely.

3

Chocolate-Whiskey Pecan Pie

HANDS-ON: **35 MINUTES (INCLUDES PIECRUST)**

TOTAL: **3 HOURS (INCLUDES CHILLING)** SERVES **8**

- 1 **cup light corn syrup**
- ¾ **cup light brown sugar**
- 4 **tablespoons (½ stick) unsalted butter, melted**
- 3 **large eggs**
- 2 **tablespoons whiskey**
- ¼ **teaspoon salt**
- 2 **cups pecan halves**
- ½ **cup semisweet chocolate chips**
  9-inch Basic Flaky Piecrust, unbaked (see page 324)

WHISK together the corn syrup, brown sugar, melted butter, eggs, whiskey, and salt; fold in the pecans and chocolate chips.

POUR into the piecrust and bake at 350°F until the center is set but still slightly wobbly, 40 to 50 minutes. Let cool completely.

4

Raspberry Buttermilk Pie

HANDS-ON: **30 MINUTES (INCLUDES PIECRUST)**

TOTAL: **7 HOURS (INCLUDES CHILLING)** SERVES **8**

- 1½ **cups buttermilk**
- ¾ **cup granulated sugar**
- ½ **cup (1 stick) unsalted butter, melted**
- ¼ **cup all-purpose flour**
- 5 **large egg yolks**
- 1 **teaspoon pure vanilla extract**
- ¼ **teaspoon salt**
  9-inch Basic Flaky Piecrust, parbaked (see page 324)
- ⅓ **cup raspberry jam**
- ¼ **cup toasted sliced almonds**

WHISK together the buttermilk, sugar, melted butter, flour, egg yolks, vanilla extract, and salt.

POUR into the piecrust and bake at 325°F until the center is set but slightly wobbly, 40 to 50 minutes. Let cool, then chill until firm, 4 to 5 hours. Top with the jam and almonds.

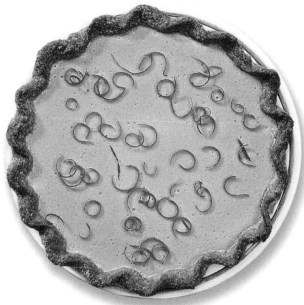

5

Shoofly Pie

HANDS-ON: **35 MINUTES (INCLUDES PIECRUST)**

TOTAL: **3 HOURS (INCLUDES CHILLING)** SERVES **8**

- 1 cup all-purpose flour
- ¾ cup light brown sugar
- 4 tablespoons (½ stick) cold unsalted butter, cubed
- ¼ teaspoon salt
- 1 cup molasses
- ¾ cup boiling water
- 1 large egg
- 1 teaspoon baking soda
  9-inch Basic Flaky Piecrust, unbaked (see page 324)

PULSE the flour, brown sugar, butter, and ¼ teaspoon salt in a food processor until crumbly; set aside.

WHISK together the molasses and boiling water; whisk in the egg and baking soda. Pour into the piecrust, top with the flour mixture, and bake at 350°F until the center is set, 40 to 50 minutes. Let cool completely.

6

Lemon Cheesecake Pie

HANDS-ON: **35 MINUTES (INCLUDES PIECRUST)**

TOTAL: **7 HOURS (INCLUDES CHILLING)** SERVES **8**

- 2 8-ounce bars cream cheese, at room temperature
- 1 cup granulated sugar
- 1 cup sour cream
- 2 large eggs
- ⅓ cup lemon juice
- 1 teaspoon pure vanilla extract
- ¼ teaspoon salt
  9-inch Basic Flaky Piecrust, parbaked (see page 324)
- 2 teaspoons thinly sliced lemon zest

COMBINE the cream cheese, sugar, sour cream, eggs, lemon juice, vanilla, and salt in a food processor until smooth.

POUR into the piecrust and bake at 325°F until the center is set but still slightly wobbly, 40 to 50 minutes. Let cool, then chill until firm, 4 to 5 hours. Top with the lemon zest before serving.

7
Peanut Butter Pie

HANDS ON: 35 MINUTES (INCLUDES PIECRUST)
TOTAL: 6 HOURS (INCLUDES CHILLING) SERVES 8

1½ cups heavy cream
1 cup marshmallow cream
1 cup creamy peanut butter
9-inch Basic Flaky Piecrust, prebaked (see page 324)
¼ cup chopped salted roasted peanuts
¼ cup crumbled chocolate cookies

BEAT the heavy cream until soft peaks form. Beat in the marshmallow cream and peanut butter.

SPREAD the mixture into the piecrust and chill until firm, 4 to 5 hours. Top with peanuts and chocolate cookies before serving.

8
Sweet Potato Pie

HANDS-ON: 20 MINUTES (INCLUDES PIECRUST)
TOTAL: 3 HOURS (INCLUDES CHILLING) SERVES 8

1 pound sweet potatoes, peeled and cut into pieces
1 cup heavy cream
½ cup granulated sugar
4 tablespoons (½ stick) unsalted butter, melted
2 large eggs
½ teaspoon cinnamon
¼ teaspoon salt
9-inch Basic Flaky Piecrust, parbaked (see page 324)
Confectioners' sugar, for dusting

STEAM the potatoes until tender, 15 to 20 minutes. In a food processor, puree potatoes with the heavy cream, granulated sugar, butter, eggs, cinnamon, and salt until smooth.

POUR into the piecrust and bake at 350°F until the center is set but still slightly wobbly, 40 to 50 minutes. Let cool completely, at least 1 hour. Dust with confectioners' sugar before serving.

9

Coconut Custard Pie

HANDS-ON: 35 MINUTES (INCLUDES PIECRUST)

TOTAL: 7 HOURS (INCLUDES CHILLING) SERVES **8**

1 14-ounce can sweetened condensed milk
1 13-ounce can coconut milk
3 large egg yolks
¼ teaspoon salt
  9-inch Basic Flaky Piecrust, parbaked (see page 324)
¼ cup flaked or shredded coconut, toasted

WHISK together the condensed milk, coconut milk, egg yolks, and salt.

POUR into the piecrust and bake at 325°F until the center is set but still slightly wobbly, 50 to 60 minutes. Let cool, then chill until firm, 4 to 5 hours. Top with the toasted coconut before serving.

10

Chocolate Cream Pie

HANDS-ON: 80 MINUTES (INCLUDES PIECRUST)

TOTAL: 5 HOURS, 30 MINUTES (INCLUDES CHILLING) SERVES **8**

2½ cups whole milk
½ cup granulated sugar
¼ cup cornstarch
3 large egg yolks
¼ teaspoon salt
8 ounces semisweet chocolate, chopped
4 tablespoons (½ stick) unsalted butter, cubed
  9-inch Basic Flaky Piecrust, prebaked (see page 324)
1 cup heavy cream
¼ cup shaved chocolate

WHISK together the milk, sugar, cornstarch, egg yolks, and salt in a large saucepan over medium heat. Continue to cook, whisking until thickened, 7 to 8 minutes. Whisk in the chopped chocolate and butter.

POUR into the piecrust. Chill until firm, 4 to 5 hours. Whip the cream until soft peaks form. Top the pie with the whipped cream and shaved chocolate before serving.

Basic Flaky Piecrust

HANDS-ON: 20 MINUTES

TOTAL: 1 HOUR, 40 MINUTES MAKES **ONE 9-INCH PIECRUST**

1¼ **cups all-purpose flour,
spooned and leveled, plus
more for rolling the dough**

½ **cup (1 stick) cold unsalted
butter, cut into small pieces**

1 **tablespoon granulated sugar**

½ **teaspoon salt**

2 **to 4 tablespoons ice water**

PULSE the flour, butter, sugar, and salt in a food processor until it resembles coarse meal, with a few pea-size clumps of butter remaining (1). Add 2 tablespoons of the ice water. Pulse until the mixture just holds together when squeezed (2). Add more water as necessary; do not overprocess.

PLACE the mixture on a sheet of plastic wrap. Shape it into a 1-inch-thick disk, wrap tightly, and chill until firm, at least 1 hour and up to 3 days (3).

ROLL out the dough on a floured work surface to a 12-inch circle (4). Carefully transfer it to a 9-inch pie plate. Fit the dough into the plate (avoid stretching). Trim the edge to a 1-inch overhang and tuck it under itself to form a thick rim (5). Crimp the rim as desired (6). Chill, covered, for at least 30 minutes and up to 2 days before using.

TO PARBAKE OR PREBAKE A PIECRUST: Line the chilled crust with a piece of foil, leaving an overhang all around. Fill with dried beans or pie weights and bake at 350°F for 30 minutes. Remove the beans and foil. For a parbaked (partially baked) crust, bake until dry and set, 5 to 8 minutes more. For a prebaked crust, bake until golden, 10 to 12 minutes more. Let the crust cool completely before filling.

IF USING A STORE-BOUGHT CRUST: Follow the package directions for parbaking or prebaking. For a pie with a baked filling, do not fill the crust more than ¾ full before baking. (You may have excess filling.)

Kitchen Cheat Sheets

How many teaspoons are in a tablespoon?
What temperature does chicken need to cook to?
These handy charts have all the answers.
Bookmark them for whenever you're in a pinch.

BAKING-PAN SUBSTITUTIONS

When you don't have the pan a recipe calls for, this chart will help you find a good substitute. Note: The baking time will be shorter if the pan is bigger than the specified pan, since the batter will be shallower. (The metric figures given below are straight conversions of the U.S. figures. Metric pan sizes vary widely; look for the closest size.)

PAN SIZE	CAPACITY	SUBSTITUTIONS
8" x 2" round (20 x 5 cm)	6 cups (1.4 l)	9" x 2" round 8" x 8" x 2" square 11" x 7" x 2" rectangle 12-cupcake tin
9" x 2" round (23 x 5 cm)	8 cups (1.9 l)	8" x 2" round 8" x 8" x 2" square 11" x 7" x 2" rectangle Two 12-cupcake tins
8" x 8" x 2" square (20 x 20 x 5 cm)	8 cups (1.9 l)	9" x 2" round Two 12-cupcake tins
11" x 7" x 2" rectangle (28 x 18 x 5 cm)	8 cups (1.9 l)	9" x 2" round 8" x 8" x 2" square Two 12-cupcake tins
13" x 9" x 2" rectangle (33 x 23 x 5 cm)	12 cups (2.8 l)	Two 9" x 2" rounds Two 8" x 8" x 2" squares Two 12-cupcake tins
8½" x 4½" x 2½" loaf pan (22 x 11½ x 6 cm)	8 cups (1.9 l)	9" x 2" round 8" x 8" x 2" square 11" x 7" x 2" rectangle 12-cupcake tin
12-cupcake tin (½ cup per cupcake)	6 cups (1.4 l)	9" x 2" round 8" x 8" x 2" square 11" x 7" x 2" rectangle

MEASURING CONVERSIONS

Tripling a recipe? Use this handy list of equivalents and you'll never have to scoop out 12 teaspoons (and lose count!) again.

MEASUREMENT		COMPONENT		FLUID OZ		METRIC
½ TABLESPOON	=	1½ teaspoons	=	¼ fl oz	=	7.5 ml
1 TABLESPOON	=	3 teaspoons	=	½ fl oz	=	15 ml
1 JIGGER	=	3 tablespoons	=	1½ fl oz	=	45 ml
¼ CUP	=	4 tablespoons	=	2 fl oz	=	60 ml
⅓ CUP	=	5 tablespoons + 1 teaspoon	=	3 fl oz	=	80 ml
½ CUP	=	8 tablespoons	=	4 fl oz	=	120 ml
⅔ CUP	=	10 tablespoons + 2 teaspoons	=	5½ fl oz	=	160 ml
¾ CUP	=	12 tablespoons	=	6 fl oz	=	180 ml
1 CUP	=	16 tablespoons or ½ pint	=	8 fl oz	=	240 ml
1 PINT	=	2 cups	=	16 fl oz	=	475 ml
1 QUART	=	4 cups or 2 pints	=	32 fl oz	=	945 ml
1 GALLON	=	16 cups or 4 quarts	=	128 fl oz	=	3.8 l

Kitchen Cheat Sheets

CUPS TO GRAMS

Here are approximate equivalents for some kitchen staples that are measured in cups in the United States...but in grams elsewhere.

INGREDIENT	1 CUP
ALMONDS whole	140 g
sliced	105 g
BARLEY, PEARLED	200 g
BEANS, DRIED	190 g
BREAD CRUMBS dried	95 g
panko	110 g
BULGUR	160 g
BUTTER	225 g
CHEESE hard, grated	85 g
soft or semi-soft, grated	110 g
CHOCOLATE CHIPS	165 g
COCOA POWDER	80 g

INGREDIENT	1 CUP
COCONUT, SHREDDED	70 g
COUSCOUS	190 g
FLOUR (SPOONED AND LEVELED) all-purpose	110 g
whole-wheat	130 g
HONEY	330 g
NUTS, MIXED whole	140 g
OATS, OLD-FASHIONED ROLLED	85 g
ORZO	170 g
PEANUTS whole	130 g
chopped	140 g
PECANS halves	105 g
chopped	120 g
QUINOA	170 g
RAISINS	155 g
RICE, BROWN OR WHITE	180 g
SUGAR granulated	210 g
brown (packed)	210 g
confectioners'	120g
WALNUTS halves	105 g
chopped	125 g

MEAT COOKING TEMPERATURES

The safest, most accurate way to tell when meats are done is to use an instant-read thermometer, inserted in the thickest part of the meat. The following are the *Real Simple* test kitchen's preferred cooking temperatures (which are considered safe by many experts) for meats cooked to juicy perfection.*

*For maximum food safety, the U.S. Department of Agriculture recommends 165° F for all poultry; 160° F for ground beef, lamb, and pork; and 145° F, with a 3-minute resting period, for all other types of beef, lamb, and pork.

	°F	°C
BEEF		
Rare	115°	40°
Medium-rare	130°	55°
Medium	140°	60°
Medium-well	150°	65°
Well-done	155°	70°
Ground beef	160°	70°
LAMB		
Medium-rare	130°	55°
Medium	140°	60°
Medium-well	150°	65°
Well-done	155°	70°
Ground lamb	160°	70°
POULTRY		
White meat	160°	70°
Dark meat	165°	75°
Ground	165°	75°
PORK		
Medium	145°	65°
Well-done	160°	70°
Ground	160°	70°

OVEN TEMPERATURES

°F	225°	250°	275°	300°	325°	350°	375°	400°	425°	450°	475°	500°
°C	110°	125°	135°	150°	160°	175°	190°	200°	220°	230°	245°	260°

Nutritional Information

A by-the-numbers guide to what's in every recipe.

APPLES

Sautéed Cauliflower and Apples with Pecans
PER SERVING: 211 calories | 17g fat (5g saturated fat) | 15mg cholesterol | 159mg sodium | 4g protein | 14g carbohydrates | 5g fiber. 🕙🌱⊘

Apple Vichyssoise
PER SERVING: 318 calories | 17g fat (10g saturated fat) | 48mg cholesterol | 931mg sodium | 8g protein | 37g carbohydrates | 5g fiber.

Slow-Cooker Pork Shoulder with Apple Relish
PER SERVING: 770 calories | 28g fat (8g saturated fat) | 250mg cholesterol | 580mg sodium | 58g protein | 71g carbohydrates | 5g fiber. 🍲🍳

Turkey Waldorf Salad
PER SERVING: 179 calories | 11g fat (2g saturated fat) | 43mg cholesterol | 350mg sodium | 12g protein | 9g carbohydrates | 2g fiber. 🕙

Caramelized Onion Tarts with Apples
PER SERVING: 320 calories | 21g fat (6g saturated fat) | 10mg cholesterol | 403mg sodium | 5g protein | 26g carbohydrates | 2g fiber. 🌱

Ravioli with Apples and Walnuts
PER SERVING: 549 calories | 28g fat (9g saturated fat) | 70mg cholesterol | 964mg sodium | 20g protein | 56g carbohydrates | 5g fiber. 🕙🌱

Apple and Cheddar Tartine
PER SERVING: 368 calories | 11g fat (6g saturated fat) | 30mg cholesterol | 640mg sodium | 16g protein | 53g carbohydrates | 3g fiber. 🕙🌱

Roasted Chicken, Apples, and Leeks
PER SERVING: 418 calories | 23g fat (5g saturated fat) | 105mg cholesterol | 591mg sodium | 31g protein | 23g carbohydrates | 4g fiber. 🍎🍳⊘

Apple, Sausage, and Cheddar Monkey Bread
PER SERVING: 240 calories | 14g fat (5g saturated fat) | 20mg cholesterol | 680mg sodium | 8g protein | 21g carbohydrates | 1g fiber. ▬

Crunchy Dinner Salad with Prosciutto, Apple, and Hazelnut
PER SERVING: 322 calories | 26g fat (3g saturated fat) | 17mg cholesterol | 890mg sodium | 11g protein | 15g carbohydrates | 5g fiber. 🕙🍎

AVOCADOS

Glazed Chicken with Citrus Salad
PER SERVING: 592 calories | 36g fat (8g saturated fat) | 133mg cholesterol | 494mg sodium | 40g protein | 29g carbohydrates | 8g fiber. 🕙⊘

Salmon, Green Beans, and Avocado
PER SERVING: 546 calories | 36g fat (5g saturated fat) | 107mg cholesterol | 459mg sodium | 42g protein | 16g carbohydrates | 10g fiber. 🕙🍎🍳⊘

Shrimp and Avocado Nachos
PER SERVING: 681 calories | 45g fat (13g saturated fat) | 174mg cholesterol | 803mg sodium | 33g protein | 38g carbohydrates | 8g fiber. 🕙

Loaded Baked Sweet Potato
PER SERVING: 612 calories | 34g fat (9g saturated fat) | 22mg cholesterol | 695mg sodium | 13g protein | 66g carbohydrates | 14g fiber. 🌱⊘

Chopped Salad with Avocado Dressing
PER SERVING: 352 calories | 17g fat (4g saturated fat) | 67mg cholesterol | 817mg sodium | 31g protein | 20g carbohydrates | 7g fiber. 🕙

Avocado Caprese Burgers
PER SERVING: 624 calories | 33g fat (12g saturated fat) | 110mg cholesterol | 963mg sodium | 40g protein | 42g carbohydrates | 5g fiber. 🕙

Beet, Potato, and Avocado Salad
PER SERVING: 432 calories | 29g fat (4g saturated fat) | 0mg cholesterol | 704mg sodium | 7g protein | 43g carbohydrates | 14g fiber. 🌱

Avocado, Prosciutto, and Egg Open-Faced Sandwich
PER SERVING: 345 calories | 21g fat (4g saturated fat) | 223mg cholesterol | 773mg sodium | 15g protein | 25g carbohydrates | 5g fiber. 🕙

Bacon, Avocado, and Egg Salad
PER SERVING: 438 calories | 37g fat (8g saturated fat) | 435mg cholesterol | 640mg sodium | 16g protein | 10g carbohydrates | 6g fiber. 🕙

Tofu and Avocado Rice Bowl
PER SERVING: 533 calories | 28g fat (2g saturated fat) | 0mg cholesterol | 763mg sodium | 18g protein | 54g carbohydrates | 11g fiber. ❀🌱🍎

BAKED HAM

Ham Sandwich with Fennel Slaw
PER SERVING: 456 calories | 23g fat (5g saturated fat) | 40mg cholesterol | 1,450mg sodium | 19g protein | 44g carbohydrates | 6g fiber. 🕙

Ham and Asparagus Quiche
PER SERVING: 652 calories | 45g fat (19g saturated fat) | 287mg cholesterol | 1,234mg sodium | 27g protein | 36g carbohydrates | 4g fiber.

Tropical Pizza
PER SERVING: 566 calories | 23g fat (10g saturated fat) | 62mg cholesterol | 1,375mg sodium | 29g protein | 59g carbohydrates | 3g fiber. ●

Crispy Ham and Arugula Salad
PER SERVING: 264 calories | 22g fat (4g saturated fat) | 18mg cholesterol | 721mg sodium | 9g protein | 9g carbohydrates | 2g fiber. ●

Asian Ham Salad
PER SERVING: 394 calories | 18g fat (3g saturated fat) | 18mg cholesterol | 509mg sodium | 17g protein | 42g carbohydrates | 6g fiber. 🍱❄🍎

Ham and Corn Turnovers
PER SERVING: 894 calories | 61g fat (14g saturated fat) | 40mg cholesterol | 1,022mg sodium | 17g protein | 71g carbohydrates | 3g fiber.

Pasta with Ham and Green Beans
PER SERVING: 518 calories | 15g fat (7g saturated fat) | 41mg cholesterol | 878mg sodium | 22g protein | 73g carbohydrates | 6g fiber. ●🍱

Split Pea Soup with Ham
PER SERVING: 420 calories | 18g fat (5g saturated fat) | 43mg cholesterol | 1,266mg sodium | 30g protein | 36g carbohydrates | 13g fiber. 🍱

Quesadillas with Ham and Peppers
PER SERVING: 478 calories | 30g fat (13g saturated fat) | 78mg cholesterol | 993mg sodium | 22g protein | 28g carbohydrates | 2g fiber. ●🌿

Cauliflower and Ham Hash
PER SERVING: 375 calories | 28g fat (7g saturated fat) | 247mg cholesterol | 1,130mg sodium | 22g protein | 22g carbohydrates | 5g fiber. 🍱

BASS

Warm Bass Niçoise Salad
PER SERVING: 403 calories | 29g fat (4g saturated fat) | 140mg cholesterol | 870mg sodium | 31g protein | 4g carbohydrates | 0g fiber. ●🍎

Open-Faced Bass Sandwich
PER SERVING: 254 calories | 8g fat (2g saturated fat) | 97mg cholesterol | 848mg sodium | 25g protein | 19g carbohydrates | 2g fiber. ●

Poached Bass over Frisée with Mustard Dressing
PER SERVING: 538 calories | 42g fat (6g saturated fat) | 140mg cholesterol | 390mg sodium | 34g protein | 7g carbohydrates | 5g fiber. ●🍎

Bass Tacos with Grapefruit Salsa
PER SERVING: 465 calories | 22g fat (3g saturated fat) | 140mg cholesterol | 417mg sodium | 35g protein | 32g carbohydrates | 7g fiber. ●🍎⊘

Provençal Bass in Tomato Broth
PER SERVING: 363 calories | 14g fat (2g saturated fat) | 140mg cholesterol | 1,511mg sodium | 36g protein | 18g carbohydrates | 5g fiber. ●🍎🍱

Bass with Potato-Cauliflower Puree
PER SERVING: 454 calories | 23g fat (3g saturated fat) | 140mg cholesterol | 742mg sodium | 36g protein | 27g carbohydrates | 4g fiber. ●🍎⊘

Coconut Bass over Rice Noodles
PER SERVING: 404 calories | 33g fat (21g saturated fat) | 93mg cholesterol | 971mg sodium | 24g protein | 6g carbohydrates | 2g fiber. ●🍱

Roasted Bass and Carrots over Quinoa
PER SERVING: 347 calories | 18g fat (3g saturated fat) | 140mg cholesterol | 440mg sodium | 32g protein | 14g carbohydrates | 4g fiber. ●🍎🍱❄⊘

Bass, Bacon, and Arugula Sandwich
PER SERVING: 506 calories | 31g fat (6g saturated fat) | 91mg cholesterol | 837mg sodium | 26g protein | 32g carbohydrates | 3g fiber. ●

Smoky Bass, Fennel, and Chorizo Soup
PER SERVING: 414 calories | 22g fat (6g saturated fat) | 126mg cholesterol | 1,141mg sodium | 36g protein | 21g carbohydrates | 5g fiber. ●🍱

BEANS

Red Bean Chili
PER SERVING: 571 calories | 22g fat (8g saturated fat) | 137mg cholesterol | 2,132mg sodium | 56g protein | 34g carbohydrates | 12g fiber. 🍱▬⚒

Lemony Shrimp with White Beans and Couscous
PER SERVING: 510 calories | 12g fat (6g saturated fat) | 195mg cholesterol | 810mg sodium | 36g protein | 66g carbohydrates | 6g fiber. ●🍱

Sausage and White Bean Casserole
PER SERVING: 510 calories | 29g fat (9g saturated fat) | 62mg cholesterol | 1,801mg sodium | 26g protein | 36g carbohydrates | 10g fiber. 🍱

Lemon-Spinach Chickpeas
PER SERVING: 423 calories | 17g fat (3g saturated fat) | 0mg cholesterol | 1,289mg sodium | 10g protein | 60g carbohydrates | 7g fiber. ●🍸

Bean Salad with Bacon and Chives
PER SERVING: 138 calories | 7g fat (1g saturated fat) | 5mg cholesterol | 416mg sodium | 5g protein | 13g carbohydrates | 3g fiber. ●▬⊘

White Bean and Escarole Soup with Chicken Sausage
PER SERVING: 250 calories | 12g fat (7g saturated fat) | 30mg cholesterol | 692mg sodium | 7g protein | 32g carbohydrates | 9g fiber. ●🍎🍱

Beef and Bean Enchiladas with Sautéed Zucchini
PER SERVING: 615 calories | 34g fat (15g saturated fat) | 95mg cholesterol | 1,415mg sodium | 33g protein | 45g carbohydrates | 9g fiber. ⚒

Chickpea, Vegetable, and Pesto Soup
PER SERVING: 299 calories | 15g fat (3g saturated fat) | 5mg cholesterol | 789mg sodium | 10g protein | 32g carbohydrates | 10g fiber. 🍎🍱🍸

Mexican Pinto Bean Salad
PER SERVING: 245 calories | 12g fat (4g saturated fat) | 14mg cholesterol | 567mg sodium | 11g protein | 25g carbohydrates | 7g fiber. ●🍸▬⊘

Greens and Bean Salad with Grapes
PER SERVING: 170 calories | 13g fat (1g saturated fat) | 0mg cholesterol | 163mg sodium | 3g protein | 12g carbohydrates | 3g fiber. ●🍸🍎▬⊘

BROCCOLI

Curried Broccoli Couscous
PER SERVING: 285 calories | 8g fat (1g saturated fat) | 0mg cholesterol | 378mg sodium | 9g protein | 47g carbohydrates | 5g fiber. ●●♥

Broccoli and Blue Cheese Salad
PER SERVING: 188 calories | 14g fat (5g saturated fat) | 18mg cholesterol | 485mg sodium | 9g protein | 9g carbohydrates | 4g fiber. ●♥

Broccoli and Pepper Stir-Fry
PER SERVING: 129 calories | 6g fat (0g saturated fat) | 0mg cholesterol | 293mg sodium | 5g protein | 17g carbohydrates | 5g fiber. ●●♥⚜

Parmesan-Roasted Broccoli and Onions
PER SERVING: 157 calories | 11g fat (3g saturated fat) | 10mg cholesterol | 520mg sodium | 9g protein | 7g carbohydrates | 3g fiber. ●●♥⊘⚜

Sautéed Broccoli, Tomatoes, and Bacon
PER SERVING: 91 calories | 5g fat (2g saturated fat) | 9 mg cholesterol | 420 mg sodium | 6g protein | 7g carbohydrates | 4g fiber. ●●♥⊘⚜

Broccoli Gratin with Crispy Onions
PER SERVING: 361 calories | 25g fat (13g saturated fat) | 59mg cholesterol | 624mg sodium | 16g protein | 20g carbohydrates | 3g fiber. ●♥⚜

Mashed Potatoes and Broccoli
PER SERVING: 237 calories | 14g fat (9g saturated fat) | 40mg cholesterol | 266mg sodium | 4g protein | 25g carbohydrates | 4g fiber. ●♥⊘

Grilled Broccoli and Lemons
PER SERVING: 124 calories | 9g fat (1g saturated fat) | 0mg cholesterol | 278mg sodium | 3g protein | 10g carbohydrates | 3g fiber. ●●♥⊘⚜

Creamy Broccoli and Apple Slaw
PER SERVING: 201 calories | 15g fat (2g saturated fat) | 7mg cholesterol | 471mg sodium | 4g protein | 16g carbohydrates | 3g fiber. ●♥

Broccoli, Orange, and Olive Salad
PER SERVING: 127 calories | 9g fat (1g saturated fat) | 0mg cholesterol | 384mg sodium | 4g protein | 11g carbohydrates | 4g fiber. ●♥●⊘

BUTTERNUT SQUASH

Roasted Squash and Eggplant with Crispy Soba Noodles
PER SERVING: 512 calories | 23g fat (2g saturated fat) | 0mg cholesterol | 486mg sodium | 13g protein | 68g carbohydrates | 12g fiber. ●♥

Butternut Squash and Chickpea Stew
PER SERVING: 228 calories | 8g fat (1g saturated fat) | 0mg cholesterol | 647mg sodium | 7g protein | 35g carbohydrates | 9g fiber. ♥●

Seared Pork Chops and Pesto with Mashed Squash
PER SERVING: 452 calories | 24g fat (9g saturated fat) | 130mg cholesterol | 451mg sodium | 44g protein | 15g carbohydrates | 4g fiber. ●

Creamy Butternut Squash and Parsnip Soup
PER SERVING: 219 calories | 8g fat (2g saturated fat) | 5mg cholesterol | 396mg sodium | 7g protein | 35g carbohydrates | 9g fiber. ●●

Bacon-and-Egg Butternut Squash
PER SERVING: 224 calories | 15g fat (3g saturated fat) | 218mg cholesterol | 342mg sodium | 10g protein | 16g carbohydrates | 4g fiber. ⊘

Squash and Ricotta Toasts
PER SERVING: 326 calories | 12g fat (4g saturated fat) | 16mg cholesterol | 480mg sodium | 9g protein | 46g carbohydrates | 6g fiber ●●♥

Butternut Squash Galette
PER SERVING: 435 calories | 27g fat (14g saturated fat) | 43mg cholesterol | 646mg sodium | 7g protein | 44g carbohydrates | 5g fiber. ♥

Butternut Squash and Kale Lasagna
PER SERVING: 704 calories | 39g fat (23g saturated fat) | 114mg cholesterol | 511mg sodium | 28g protein | 63g carbohydrates | 7g fiber. ♥

Butternut Squash and Barley Risotto
PER SERVING: 388 calories | 10g fat (6g saturated fat) | 25mg cholesterol | 713mg sodium | 13g protein | 61g carbohydrates | 13g fiber. ●♥🗎❀

Butternut Squash and Bean Tacos
PER SERVING: 390 calories | 17g fat (7g saturated fat) | 22mg cholesterol | 567mg sodium | 14g protein | 50g carbohydrates | 11g fiber. ●●♥⊘

CARROTS

Spiced Carrot Soup
PER SERVING: 226 calories | 11g fat (2g saturated fat) | 0mg cholesterol | 540mg sodium | 3g protein | 31g carbohydrates | 9g fiber. ●♥

Creamy Carrot Dip with Crudités
PER SERVING: 267 calories | 20g fat (6g saturated fat) | 17mg cholesterol | 707mg sodium | 6g protein | 17g carbohydrates | 5g fiber. ●♥

Mexican Pork Loin and Carrots
PER SERVING: 396 calories | 20g fat (4g saturated fat) | 100mg cholesterol | 518mg sodium | 38g protein | 16g carbohydrates | 6g fiber. ●🗎⊘

Cod and Spinach with Carrot-Almond Dressing
PER SERVING: 358 calories | 26g fat (3g saturated fat) | 65mg cholesterol | 337mg sodium | 29g protein | 3g carbohydrates | 1g fiber. ●●🗎⊘

Roasted Chicken, Carrots, and Shallots
PER SERVING: 561 calories | 34g fat (8g saturated fat) | 140mg cholesterol | 724mg sodium | 41g protein | 24g carbohydrates | 5g fiber. 🗎⊘⚜

Raisin-and-Carrot Chicken Salad
PER SERVING: 403 calories | 30g fat (5g saturated fat) | 79mg cholesterol | 613mg sodium | 22g protein | 11g carbohydrates | 2g fiber. ●

Slow-Cooker Carrot and Beef Stew
PER SERVING: 240 calories | 6g fat (2g saturated fat) | 50mg cholesterol | 981mg sodium | 28g protein | 19g carbohydrates | 5g fiber. 🍲🗎—⚜

Orecchiette with Rosemary Carrots
PER SERVING: 528 calories | 19g fat (11g saturated fat) | 45mg cholesterol | 443mg sodium | 13g protein | 76g carbohydrates | 7g fiber. ●♥

Lamb with Carrot–Red Pepper Puree
PER SERVING: 237 calories | 12g fat (3g saturated fat) | 44mg cholesterol | 579mg sodium | 16g protein | 18g carbohydrates | 5g fiber. 🍎🍏⊘

Carrot, Bean, and Radicchio Salad
PER SERVING: 272 calories | 17g fat (5g saturated fat) | 16mg cholesterol | 945mg sodium | 9g protein | 22g carbohydrates | 6g fiber. 🍎🍏🍗

CHICKEN CUTLETS

Grilled Chicken and Spring Vegetables
PER SERVING: 400 calories | 11g fat (2g saturated fat) | 94mg cholesterol | 551mg sodium | 40g protein | 33g carbohydrates | 3g fiber. 🍎🍏⊘

Chicken and Chorizo Tacos with Slaw
PER SERVING: 419 calories | 21g fat (5g saturated fat) | 68mg cholesterol | 885mg sodium | 27g protein | 32g carbohydrates | 7g fiber. 🍎

Chicken and Ricotta Pizza
PER SERVING: 571 calories | 20g fat (7g saturated fat) | 81mg cholesterol | 1,096mg sodium | 37g protein | 59g carbohydrates | 2g fiber.

Chicken, Cheddar, and Bacon Salad
PER SERVING: 362 calories | 25g fat (9g saturated fat) | 85mg cholesterol | 827mg sodium | 28g protein | 5g carbohydrates | 2g fiber. 🍎⊘

Jerk Chicken with Seared Pineapple
PER SERVING: 384 calories | 15g fat (2g saturated fat) | 94mg cholesterol | 293mg sodium | 36g protein | 25g carbohydrates | 1g fiber. 🍏

Chicken Salad with Celery and Shallot
PER SERVING: 478 calories | 37g fat (5g saturated fat) | 76mg cholesterol | 280mg sodium | 26g protein | 11g carbohydrates | 2g fiber. 🍎

Prosciutto Chicken with Broccolini
PER SERVING: 350 calories | 14g fat (3g saturated fat) | 116mg cholesterol | 1,105mg sodium | 46g protein | 9g carbohydrates | 1g fiber. 🍎🍏🥄

Lemony Chicken and Olive Pasta
PER SERVING: 556 calories | 17g fat (4g saturated fat) | 73mg cholesterol | 591mg sodium | 33g protein | 65g carbohydrates | 3g fiber. 🍎🍏

Crispy Chicken with Corn Salad
PER SERVING: 645 calories | 31g fat (4g saturated fat) | 200mg cholesterol | 681mg sodium | 42g protein | 50g carbohydrates | 2g fiber. 🍎🥄

Spicy Chicken and Ranch Sandwich with Crudités
PER SERVING: 438 calories | 23g fat (4g saturated fat) | 55mg cholesterol | 1,043mg sodium | 23g protein | 33g carbohydrates | 4g fiber. 🍎

CHICKEN THIGHS

Crispy Chicken with Coleslaw
PER SERVING: 772 calories | 48g fat (9g saturated fat) | 231mg cholesterol | 1,116mg sodium | 41mg protein | 40g carbohydrates | 4g fiber. 🍎🥄

Chicken Cobb Salad
PER SERVING: 513 calories | 40g fat (12g saturated fat) | 296mg cholesterol | 1,026mg sodium | 32g protein | 8g carbohydrates | 5g fiber. 🍎

Chicken with Mushroom Sauce
PER SERVING: 419 calories | 20g fat (5g saturated fat) | 112mg cholesterol | 559mg sodium | 35g protein | 22g carbohydrates | 4g fiber. 🥄

Spiced Chicken Kebabs
PER SERVING: 579 calories | 21g fat (5g saturated fat) | 112mg cholesterol | 360mg sodium | 41g protein | 57g carbohydrates | 5g fiber. 🍏

Teriyaki Chicken with Bok Choy
PER SERVING: 594 calories | 24g fat (7g saturated fat) | 140mg cholesterol | 1,210mg sodium | 45g protein | 47g carbohydrates | 2g fiber.

Chicken Philly Cheesesteaks
PER SERVING: 1,057 calories | 59g fat (19g saturated fat) | 151mg cholesterol | 1,915mg sodium | 55g protein | 74g carbohydrates | 6g fiber. 🍎🥄

Lemon and Garlic Grilled Chicken
PER SERVING: 652 calories | 43g fat (11g saturated fat) | 153mg cholesterol | 776mg sodium | 44g protein | 19g carbohydrates | 4g fiber. ⊘

Pesto Chicken Pasta Salad
PER SERVING: 823 calories | 43g fat (12g saturated fat) | 97mg cholesterol | 1,099mg sodium | 38g protein | 71g carbohydrates | 4g fiber. 🍎🍴

Prosciutto-Wrapped Chicken
PER SERVING: 449 calories | 28g fat (9g saturated fat) | 149mg cholesterol | 1,327mg sodium | 40g protein | 9g carbohydrates | 3g fiber. 🍎

Roasted Chicken with Asparagus
PER SERVING: 433 calories | 27g fat (7g saturated fat) | 140mg cholesterol | 373mg sodium | 40g protein | 6g carbohydrates | 2g fiber. 🍎🍴⊘🥄

CORN

Corn Polenta with Shrimp
PER SERVING: 360 calories | 9g fat (1.5g saturated fat) | 110mg cholesterol | 840mg sodium | 20g protein | 49g carbohydrates | 6g fiber. 🍏🍴

Charred-Corn Succotash
PER SERVING: 226 calories | 9g fat (1g saturated fat) | 0mg cholesterol | 614mg sodium | 7g protein | 36g carbohydrates | 6g fiber. 🍎🍏🍗⊘

Smoky Corn Chowder
PER SERVING: 359 calories | 23g fat (9g saturated fat) | 41mg cholesterol | 597mg sodium | 10g protein | 32g carbohydrates | 6g fiber. 🍴🥄

Green Curry with Halibut and Corn
PER SERVING: 469 calories | 27g fat (18g saturated fat) | 84mg cholesterol | 429mg sodium | 37g protein | 19g carbohydrates | 2g fiber. 🍎🍴

Parmesan Corn Pudding
PER SERVING: 260 calories | 14g fat (8g saturated fat) | 125mg cholesterol | 280mg sodium | 13g protein | 22g carbohydrates | 2g fiber. 🍗⊘🥄

Corn Salad with Parmesan and Chilies

PER SERVING: 220 calories | 11g fat (2g saturated fat) | 5mg cholesterol | 389mg sodium | 8g protein | 29g carbohydrates | 4g fiber. ● ▮ ♥ ⊘

Corn and Tomato Salad with Cumin-Lime Dressing

PER SERVING: 197 calories | 11g fat (2g saturated fat) | 0mg cholesterol | 334mg sodium | 4g protein | 23g carbohydrates | 3g fiber. ● ♣ ♥

Grilled Corn with Harissa Yogurt

PER SERVING: 130 calories | 4g fat (1g saturated fat) | 2mg cholesterol | 610mg sodium | 5g protein | 22g carbohydrates | 2g fiber. ● ♥

Nachos with Corn Salsa

PER SERVING: 450 calories | 26g fat (8g saturated fat) | 30mg cholesterol | 690mg sodium | 12g protein | 45g carbohydrates | 5g fiber. ● ♥ ⊘

Sautéed Corn with Coconut Milk, Chili, and Basil

PER SERVING: 180 calories | 13g fat (5g saturated fat) | 0mg cholesterol | 380mg sodium | 3g protein | 17g carbohydrates | 2g fiber. ● ♥ ⊘

EGGS

Frisée with Bacon and Soft-Cooked Eggs

PER SERVING: 227 calories | 16g fat (4g saturated fat) | 430mg cholesterol | 307mg sodium | 16g protein | 4g carbohydrates | 2g fiber. ● ⊘

Spaghetti with Herbs, Chilies, and Eggs

PER SERVING: 558 calories | 23g fat (5g saturated fat) | 217mg cholesterol | 201mg sodium | 22g protein | 66g carbohydrates | 4g fiber. ● ♥

Baked Eggs with Cream and Herbs

PER SERVING: 271 calories | 24g fat (12g saturated fat) | 471mg cholesterol | 392mg sodium | 13g protein | 2g carbohydrates | 0g fiber. ● ♥

Huevos Rancheros

PER SERVING: 401 calories | 25g fat (5g saturated fat) | 221mg cholesterol | 658mg sodium | 17g protein | 32g carbohydrates | 9g fiber. ● ♥ ⊘

Curried Egg Salad Sandwich

PER SERVING: 345 calories | 26g fat (5g saturated fat) | 430mg cholesterol | 655mg sodium | 15g protein | 14g carbohydrates | 2g fiber. ● ♥

Spinach, Feta, and Sun-Dried Tomato Omelet

PER SERVING: 276 calories | 22g fat (10g saturated fat) | 455mg cholesterol | 518mg sodium | 16g protein | 5g carbohydrates | 1g fiber. ● ▮ ♥

Swiss Chard and Cheddar Quiche

PER SERVING: 352 calories | 25g fat (10g saturated fat) | 133mg cholesterol | 813mg sodium | 9g protein | 23g carbohydrates | 1g fiber. ▮ ▬ ♥

Poached Eggs with Grits and Tomatoes

PER SERVING: 405 calories | 20g fat (7g saturated fat) | 438mg cholesterol | 963mg sodium | 18g protein | 40g carbohydrates | 3g fiber. ● ♥ ⊘

Scrambled Eggs with Chorizo and Onions

PER SERVING: 421 calories | 22g fat (6g saturated fat) | 435mg cholesterol | 684mg sodium | 19g protein | 37g carbohydrates | 3g fiber.

Egg-in-a-Hole with Smoked Salmon

PER SERVING: 535 calories | 29g fat (14g saturated fat) | 331mg cholesterol | 1,017mg sodium | 44g protein | 23g carbohydrates | 2g fiber. ● ▮

FLANK STEAK

Steak and Eggs with Seared Tomatoes

PER SERVING: 306 calories | 17g fat (5g saturated fat) | 251mg cholesterol | 427mg sodium | 32g protein | 7g carbohydrates | 2g fiber. ● ♣ ⊘

Grilled Steak, Plums, and Bok Choy

PER SERVING: 335 calories | 15g fat (5g saturated fat) | 60mg cholesterol | 1,327mg sodium | 39g protein | 10g carbohydrates | 2g fiber.

Spinach-Stuffed Steak Roulades

PER SERVING: 215 calories | 15g fat (3g saturated fat) | 20mg cholesterol | 420mg sodium | 14g protein | 7g carbohydrates | 3g fiber. ● ♣

Chopped Steak Salad

PER SERVING: 252 calories | 10g fat (3g saturated fat) | 30mg cholesterol | 731mg sodium | 23g protein | 18g carbohydrates | 4g fiber. ● ♣

Sweet and Spicy Beef Stir-Fry

PER SERVING: 462 calories | 11g fat (3g saturated fat) | 40mg cholesterol | 638mg sodium | 33g protein | 59g carbohydrates | 4g fiber. ● ▮

Steak Sandwiches with Brie

PER SERVING: 552 calories | 24g fat (12g saturated fat) | 77mg cholesterol | 1,176mg sodium | 34g protein | 49g carbohydrates | 2g fiber. ●

Beef Skewers with Blue Cheese Sauce

PER SERVING: 247 calories | 20g fat (5g saturated fat) | 25mg cholesterol | 483mg sodium | 14g protein | 4g carbohydrates | 0g fiber. ●

Cuban Braised Beef

PER SERVING: 545 calories | 11g fat (5g saturated fat) | 117mg cholesterol | 1,152mg sodium | 44g protein | 63g carbohydrates | 5.5g fiber. ▮ ⊘

Grilled Beef and Pepper Fajitas

PER SERVING: 547 calories | 28g fat (9g saturated fat) | 60mg cholesterol | 834mg sodium | 32g protein | 42g carbohydrates | 6g fiber. ●

Steak with Chimichurri Sauce

PER SERVING: 494 calories | 29g fat (7g saturated fat) | 104mg cholesterol | 461mg sodium | 42g protein | 20g carbohydrates | 2g fiber. ● ♣ ⊘

GROUND BEEF

Easy Shepherd's Pie

PER SERVING: 384 calories | 17g fat (8g saturated fat) | 88mg cholesterol | 827mg sodium | 22g protein | 28g carbohydrates | 3g fiber. ● ▮ ♣

Beef and Mushroom Ragù with Pappardelle

PER SERVING: 378 calories | 13g fat (3g saturated fat) | 33mg cholesterol | 540mg sodium | 19g protein | 41g carbohydrates | 3g fiber. ● ♣

Quick Beef Tacos
PER SERVING: 697 calories | 48g fat (13g saturated fat) | 121mg cholesterol | 1,326mg sodium | 38g protein | 7g carbohydrates | 2g fiber. ●📷🏺

Glazed Meatballs
PER SERVING: 517 calories | 19g fat (7.5g saturated fat) | 122mg cholesterol | 912mg sodium | 25g protein | 63g carbohydrates | 1g fiber. ●🏺

Parmesan Meat Loaf
PER SERVING: 528 calories | 32g fat (13g saturated fat) | 175mg cholesterol | 984mg sodium | 42g protein | 17g carbohydrates | 2g fiber. 🏺

Lemony Meatball and Escarole Soup
PER SERVING: 221 calories | 10g fat (4g saturated fat) | 61mg cholesterol | 1221mg sodium | 18g protein | 16g carbohydrates | 4g fiber. 📷

Burger with Cheddar, Avocado, and Sprouts
PER SERVING: 936 calories | 65g fat (18g saturated fat) | 167mg cholesterol | 976mg sodium | 53g protein | 35g carbohydrates | 9g fiber. ●

Burger with Bacon and Egg
PER SERVING: 558 calories | 31g fat (10g saturated fat) | 302mg cholesterol | 940mg sodium | 40g protein | 28g carbohydrates | 2g fiber. ●

Burger with Barbecue Sauce, Pepper Jack, and Jalapeños
PER SERVING: 573 calories | 28g fat (11g saturated fat) | 11mg cholesterol | 1,195mg sodium | 38g protein | 41g carbohydrates | 2g fiber. ●

Burger with Ricotta Salata and Pickled Zucchini
PER SERVING: 591 calories | 31g fat (14g saturated fat) | 162mg cholesterol | 1,242mg sodium | 38g protein | 39g carbohydrates | 2g fiber.

GROUND TURKEY

Turkey Meat Loaf
PER SERVING: 636 calories | 29g fat (12g saturated fat) | 207mg cholesterol | 899mg sodium | 42g protein | 55g carbohydrates | 6g fiber. 🏺

Turkey Empanadas
PER SERVING: 768 calories | 45g fat (15g saturated fat) | 69mg cholesterol | 873mg sodium | 23g protein | 69g carbohydrates | 3g fiber.

Eggs with Turkey Breakfast Sausage
PER SERVING: 364 calories | 23g fat (7g saturated fat) | 496mg cholesterol | 581mg sodium | 35g protein | 5g carbohydrates | 0g fiber. ●🍴⊘🏺

Turkey Sloppy Joes
PER SERVING: 492 calories | 16g fat (5g saturated fat) | 75mg cholesterol | 1,385mg sodium | 30g protein | 59g carbohydrates | 6g fiber. ●📷🏺

Turkey Fried Rice
PER SERVING: 365 calories | 11g fat (2g saturated fat) | 33mg cholesterol | 256mg sodium | 18g protein | 48g carbohydrates | 5g fiber. ●🍴

Turkey-Chorizo Tacos
PER SERVING: 360 calories | 19g fat (6g saturated fat) | 57mg cholesterol | 655mg sodium | 21g protein | 26g carbohydrates | 4g fiber. ●📷

Turkey and Feta Flatbread
PER SERVING: 470 calories | 17g fat (6g saturated fat) | 58mg cholesterol | 1,220mg sodium | 25g protein | 53g carbohydrates | 2g fiber.

Turkey-Barley Vegetable Soup
PER SERVING: 229 calories | 8g fat (2g saturated fat) | 33mg cholesterol | 1,197mg sodium | 16g protein | 27g carbohydrates | 6g fiber. 🍴📷❄

Pasta with Turkey and Broccoli
PER SERVING: 582 calories | 19g fat (4g saturated fat) | 65mg cholesterol | 333mg sodium | 35g protein | 67g carbohydrates | 5g fiber. ●🍴

Thai Turkey Salad
PER SERVING: 41 calories | 20g fat (4g saturated fat) | 65mg cholesterol | 793mg sodium | 28g protein | 17g carbohydrates | 4g fiber. ●🍴📷

ITALIAN SAUSAGE

Sausage with White Beans and Tarragon
PER SERVING: 447 calories | 31g fat (9g saturated fat) | 49mg cholesterol | 1,396mg sodium | 20g protein | 19g carbohydrates | 4g fiber. ●📷

Mediterranean Stuffed Zucchini
PER SERVING: 254 calories | 20g fat (5g saturated fat) | 23mg cholesterol | 473mg sodium | 10g protein | 10g carbohydrates | 3g fiber.

Shrimp with Sausage and Tomatoes
PER SERVING: 572 calories | 24g fat (7g saturated fat) | 79mg cholesterol | 1,469mg sodium | 25g protein | 62g carbohydrates | 5g fiber. ●📷

Cauliflower and Sausage Flatbread
PER SERVING: 639 calories | 31g fat (13g saturated fat) | 76mg cholesterol | 1,312mg sodium | 34g protein | 57g carbohydrates | 4g fiber.

Sautéed Sausage and Swiss Chard over Polenta
PER SERVING: 513 calories | 31g fat (9g saturated fat) | 49mg cholesterol | 1,510mg sodium | 22g protein | 36g carbohydrates | 4g fiber. ●📷

Roasted Sausage and Grapes
PER SERVING: 481 calories | 27g fat (9g saturated fat) | 49mg cholesterol | 1,292mg sodium | 18g protein | 44g carbohydrates | 2g fiber. ●

Fettuccine with Sausage and Cabbage
PER SERVING: 464 calories | 20g fat (5g saturated fat) | 26mg cholesterol | 822mg sodium | 20g protein | 54g carbohydrates | 5g fiber. ●📷

Sausage, Pepper, and Cheddar Omelet
PER SERVING: 525 calories | 45g fat (16g saturated fat) | 480mg cholesterol | 793mg sodium | 25g protein | 4g carbohydrates | 1g fiber. ●

Sausage Heroes
PER SERVING: 530 calories | 32g fat (10g saturated fat) | 46mg cholesterol | 1,319mg sodium | 23g protein | 38g carbohydrates | 3g fiber. ●

Grilled Sausage and Fennel Salad
PER SERVING: 518 calories | 39g fat (15g saturated fat) | 71mg cholesterol | 1,894mg sodium | 25g protein | 18g carbohydrates | 5g fiber. ⬤

KALE

Kale, Lemon, Artichoke, and Caper Fish Packets
PER SERVING: 304 calories | 15g fat (2g saturated fat) | 65mg cholesterol | 859mg sodium | 31g protein | 13g carbohydrates | 3g fiber. ⬤🍴🗑⊘

Kale and Manchego Frittata with Potatoes
PER SERVING: 592 calories | 34g fat (12g saturated fat) | 453mg cholesterol | 612mg sodium | 28g protein | 45g carbohydrates | 5g fiber. 🍴⊘

Herb-Crusted Chicken with Kale and Croutons
PER SERVING: 623 calories | 30g fat (7g saturated fat) | 161mg cholesterol | 733mg sodium | 57g protein | 30g carbohydrates | 5g fiber.

Kale and Pepper Stir-Fry
PER SERVING: 167 calories | 9g fat (1g saturated fat) | 0mg cholesterol | 543mg sodium | 6g protein | 19g carbohydrates | 4g fiber. ⬤🍴

Kale and Mushroom Skillet Pizza
PER SERVING: 570 calories | 31g fat (10g saturated fat) | 45mg cholesterol | 1,080mg sodium | 22g protein | 60g carbohydrates | 7g fiber. 🗑❄🍴

Mustardy Kale and Butternut Squash
PER SERVING: 198 calories | 8g fat (1g saturated fat) | 1mg cholesterol | 521mg sodium | 8g protein | 30g carbohydrates | 7g fiber. ⬤🍴🗑

Sautéed Kale with Apples and Bacon
PER SERVING: 167 calories | 6g fat (2g saturated fat) | 9mg cholesterol | 583mg sodium | 8g protein | 24g carbohydrates | 5g fiber. ⬤🍴🗑⊘

Creamy Baked Pasta with Kale and Parmesan
PER SERVING: 849 calories | 42g fat (19g saturated fat) | 106mg cholesterol | 1,446mg sodium | 40g protein | 81g carbohydrates | 7g fiber. 🗑

Kale Caesar Salad
PER SERVING: 277 calories | 23g fat (4g saturated fat) | 116mg cholesterol | 673mg sodium | 9g protein | 10g carbohydrates | 2g fiber. ⬤

Pan-Roasted Steak with Creamed Kale
PER SERVING: 830 calories | 43g fat (16g saturated fat) | 225mg cholesterol | 970mg sodium | 78g protein | 33g carbohydrates | 8g fiber. ⊘

MOZZARELLA

Sicilian Caprese with Raisins
PER SERVING: 389 calories | 30g fat (10g saturated fat) | 40mg cholesterol | 583mg sodium | 13g protein | 20g carbohydrates | 3g fiber. ⬤🍴⊘

Classic Margherita Pizza
PER SERVING: 571 calories | 29g fat (11g saturated fat) | 45mg cholesterol | 1,110mg sodium | 24g protein | 53g carbohydrates | 3g fiber. 🍴⚒

Chicken and Olive Bread Panzanella
PER SERVING: 682 calories | 45g fat (12g saturated fat) | 100mg cholesterol | 845mg sodium | 34g protein | 32g carbohydrates | 3g fiber. ⬤

Deep-Dish Eggplant Parmesan
PER SERVING: 600 calories | 44g fat (16g saturated fat) | 67mg cholesterol | 1,077mg sodium | 24g protein | 28g carbohydrates | 12g fiber. 🍴⚒

Pasta with Sausage and Mozzarella
PER SERVING: 696 calories | 29g fat (13g saturated fat) | 69mg cholesterol | 641mg sodium | 34g protein | 75g carbohydrates | 4g fiber. ⬤🗑

Mozzarella, Orzo, and Snap Pea Salad
PER SERVING: 452 calories | 23g fat (10g saturated fat) | 44mg cholesterol | 330mg sodium | 18g protein | 43g carbohydrates | 3g fiber. ⬤🗑🍴

Corn and Mozzarella Chef's Salad
PER SERVING: 661 calories | 43g fat (13g saturated fat) | 256mg cholesterol | 538mg sodium | 23g protein | 48g carbohydrates | 7g fiber. ⬤🍴⊘

Steak and Swiss Chard Panini
PER SERVING: 479 calories | 22g fat (7g saturated fat) | 57mg cholesterol | 852mg sodium | 31g protein | 40g carbohydrates | 3g fiber. ⬤

Mozzarella, Salami, and Green Olive Salad
PER SERVING: 384 calories | 33g fat (13g saturated fat) | 69mg cholesterol | 783mg sodium | 15g protein | 3g carbohydrates | 1g fiber. ⬤🗑

Mozzarella, Prosciutto, and Melon Salad with Mint
PER SERVING: 312 calories | 22g fat (10g saturated fat) | 57mg cholesterol | 882mg sodium | 17g protein | 13g carbohydrates | 1g fiber. ⬤

OATMEAL

Oatmeal with Fried Egg and Avocado
PER SERVING: 483 calories | 26g fat (6g saturated fat) | 224mg cholesterol | 614mg sodium | 21g protein | 46g carbohydrates | 7g fiber. ⬤❄🍴

Oatmeal with Pineapple and Mint
PER SERVING: 329 calories | 5g fat (2g saturated fat) | 14mg cholesterol | 122mg sodium | 17g protein | 54g carbohydrates | 5g fiber. ⬤🍴🗑❄🍴

Oatmeal with Banana and Molasses
PER SERVING: 489 calories | 16g fat (3g saturated fat) | 14mg cholesterol | 129mg sodium | 18g protein | 71g carbohydrates | 7g fiber. ⬤🗑❄🍴

Oatmeal with Yogurt and Marmalade
PER SERVING: 381 calories | 5g fat (2g saturated fat) | 14mg cholesterol | 115mg sodium | 18g protein | 66g carbohydrates | 4g fiber. ⬤🍴🗑❄🍴

Oatmeal with Dried Fruit and Pistachios
PER SERVING: 426 calories | 9g fat (2g saturated fat) | 12mg cholesterol | 110mg sodium | 18g protein | 72g carbohydrates | 6g fiber. ⬤🗑❄🍴

Oatmeal with Cheddar and Scallion
PER SERVING: 391 calories | 15g fat (8g saturated fat) | 43mg cholesterol | 532mg sodium | 22g protein | 41g carbohydrates | 5g fiber.

Oatmeal with Peanut Butter and Grapes
PER SERVING: 508 calories | 21g fat (5g saturated fat) | 12mg cholesterol | 259mg sodium | 24g protein | 61g carbohydrates | 7g fiber.

Oatmeal with Bacon and Maple Syrup
PER SERVING: 349 calories | 8g fat (2g saturated fat) | 19mg cholesterol | 255mg sodium | 18g protein | 53g carbohydrates | 4g fiber.

Oatmeal with Mango and Coconut
PER SERVING: 560 calories | 20g fat (10g saturated fat) | 12mg cholesterol | 121mg sodium | 19g protein | 78g carbohydrates | 8g fiber.

Oatmeal with Blueberries, Sunflower Seeds, and Agave
PER SERVING: 411 calories | 9g fat (2g saturated fat) | 12mg cholesterol | 108mg sodium | 17g protein | 68g carbohydrates | 7g fiber.

PIZZA DOUGH

Sausage and Broccoli Calzones
PER SERVING: 872 calories | 53g fat (19g saturated fat) | 99mg cholesterol | 1,587mg sodium | 41g protein | 62g carbohydrates | 3g fiber.

Garlic Butter Rolls
PER SERVING: 119 calories | 6g fat (1.5g saturated fat) | 5mg cholesterol | 287mg sodium | 3g protein | 16g carbohydrates | 1g fiber.

Potato and Rosemary Flatbread
PER SERVING: 493 calories | 19g fat (3g saturated fat) | 0mg cholesterol | 734mg sodium | 13g protein | 73g carbohydrates | 4g fiber.

Salami and Spinach Stromboli
PER SERVING: 730 calories | 41g fat (18g saturated fat) | 77mg cholesterol | 1,333mg sodium | 31g protein | 59g carbohydrates | 3g fiber.

Fried Dough with Chocolate Sauce
PER SERVING: 307 calories | 10g fat (0.5g saturated fat) | 0mg cholesterol | 378mg sodium | 8g protein | 52g carbohydrates | 2g fiber.

Cinnamon Twists
PER SERVING: 241 calories | 7.5g fat (4g saturated fat) | 15mg cholesterol | 411mg sodium | 4g protein | 40g carbohydrates | 1g fiber.

Bell Pepper and Feta Pizza
PER SERVING: 521 calories | 19g fat (9g saturated fat) | 50mg cholesterol | 1,688mg sodium | 20g protein | 66g carbohydrates | 3g fiber.

Spinach and Artichoke Pizza
PER SERVING: 672 calories | 32g fat (15g saturated fat) | 85mg cholesterol | 1,599mg sodium | 34g protein | 85g carbohydrates | 5g fiber.

Mushroom and Pea Pizza
PER SERVING: 462 calories | 14g fat (8g saturated fat) | 47mg cholesterol | 741mg sodium | 22g protein | 60g carbohydrates | 3g fiber.

Pesto, Sausage, and Tomato Pizza
PER SERVING: 721 calories | 39g fat (15g saturated fat) | 70mg cholesterol | 1,310mg sodium | 32g protein | 61g carbohydrates | 4g fiber.

PORK TENDERLOIN

Barbecue Pork Sandwiches
PER SERVING: 319 calories | 5g fat (1g saturated fat) | 92mg cholesterol | 550mg sodium | 34g protein | 32g carbohydrates | 1g fiber.

Crispy Fried Pork Cutlets
PER SERVING: 440 calories | 27g fat (5g saturated fat) | 166mg cholesterol | 448mg sodium | 36g protein | 12g carbohydrates | 1g fiber.

Spicy Pork and Soba Noodles
PER SERVING: 360 calories | 9g fat (2g saturated fat) | 92mg cholesterol | 894mg sodium | 37g protein | 35g carbohydrates | 1g fiber.

Rosemary-Crusted Pork
PER SERVING: 285 calories | 10g fat (2g saturated fat) | 92mg cholesterol | 705mg sodium | 33g protein | 15g carbohydrates | 4g fiber.

Pork Fajitas
PER SERVING: 646 calories | 27g fat (8g saturated fat) | 105mg cholesterol | 1,221mg sodium | 40g protein | 60g carbohydrates | 6g fiber.

Pork Scaloppine
PER SERVING: 530 calories | 18g fat (6g saturated fat) | 155mg cholesterol | 329mg sodium | 38g protein | 44g carbohydrates | 2g fiber.

Caribbean Pork with Mango Salsa
PER SERVING: 248 calories | 8g fat (2g saturated fat) | 92mg cholesterol | 438mg sodium | 31g protein | 14g carbohydrates | 2g fiber.

Thai Pork Salad
PER SERVING: 283 calories | 13g fat (2g saturated fat) | 92mg cholesterol | 549mg sodium | 32g protein | 7g carbohydrates | 2.5g fiber.

Pork with Buttered Apples
PER SERVING: 333 calories | 15g fat (7g saturated fat) | 115mg cholesterol | 318mg sodium | 30g protein | 19g carbohydrates | 3g fiber.

Glazed Pork and Pineapple Kebabs
PER SERVING: 468 calories | 6g fat (2g saturated fat) | 82mg cholesterol | 306mg sodium | 34g protein | 69g carbohydrates | 3g fiber.

POTATOES

Scallion and Potato Soup
PER SERVING: 511 calories | 37g fat (23g saturated fat) | 130mg cholesterol | 671mg sodium | 8g protein | 36g carbohydrates | 5g fiber.

Salmon, Potato, and Arugula Salad with Dill Dressing
PER SERVING: 510 calories | 28g fat (4g saturated fat) | 95mg cholesterol | 930mg sodium | 39g protein | 25g carbohydrates | 4g fiber.

Creamy Dill Potato Salad
PER SERVING: 223 calories | 9g fat (2g saturated fat) | 10mg cholesterol | 306mg sodium | 4g protein | 31g carbohydrates | 4g fiber.

Grilled Potato and Onion Salad
PER SERVING: 256 calories | 14g fat (2g saturated fat) | 10mg cholesterol | 617mg sodium | 4g protein | 31g carbohydrates | 4g fiber.

Crispy Accordion Potatoes

PER SERVING: 196 calories | 9g fat (1g saturated fat) | 0mg cholesterol | 361mg sodium | 2g protein | 28g carbohydrates | 5g fiber.

Classic Latkes

PER SERVING: 53 calories | 2g fat (0g saturated fat) | 16mg cholesterol | 88mg sodium | 1g protein | 9g carbohydrates | 1 g fiber.

Brown Butter Mashed Potatoes

PER SERVING: 291 calories | 19g fat (12g saturated fat) | 50mg cholesterol | 388mg sodium | 5g protein | 28g carbohydrates | 2g fiber.

Bacon and Blue Cheese Mashed Potatoes

PER SERVING: 324 calories | 18g fat (11g saturated fat) | 48mg cholesterol | 567mg sodium | 9g protein | 32g carbohydrates | 2g fiber.

Chipotle and Cheddar Mashed Potatoes

PER SERVING: 270 calories | 10g fat (6g saturated fat) | 32mg cholesterol | 591mg sodium | 12g protein | 32g carbohydrates | 2g fiber.

Mushrooms and Thyme Mashed Potatoes

PER SERVING: 367 calories | 16g fat (9g saturated fat) | 40mg cholesterol | 412mg sodium | 7g protein | 48g carbohydrates | 2g fiber.

QUINOA

Steak with Cauliflower Puree and Crispy Quinoa

PER SERVING: 510 calories | 35g fat (15g saturated fat) | 125mg cholesterol | 820mg sodium | 30g protein | 18g carbohydrates | 3g fiber.

Quinoa Breakfast Bowl

PER SERVING: 492 calories | 25g fat (4g saturated fat) | 271mg cholesterol | 624mg sodium | 37g protein | 34g carbohydrates | 4g fiber.

Quinoa and Oat Porridge

PER SERVING: 190 calories | 2g fat (0.5g saturated fat) | 5mg cholesterol | 35mg sodium | 6g protein | 40g carbohydrates | 3g fiber.

Chickpea and Quinoa Soup

PER SERVING: 490 calories | 2g fat (2g saturated fat) | 0mg cholesterol | 670mg sodium | 17g protein | 71g carbohydrates | 9g fiber.

Clementine, Fennel, and Quinoa Salad

PER SERVING: 270 calories | 15g fat (2g saturated fat) | 0mg cholesterol | 270mg sodium | 5g protein | 33g carbohydrates | 6g fiber.

Salmon with Creamed Spinach and Quinoa

PER SERVING: 533 calories | 32g fat (13g saturated fat) | 150mg cholesterol | 507mg sodium | 38g protein | 23g carbohydrates | 5g fiber.

Zucchini with Quinoa Stuffing

PER SERVING: 452 calories | 28g fat (6g saturated fat) | 15mg cholesterol | 883mg sodium | 20g protein | 34g carbohydrates | 7g fiber.

Quinoa with Mushrooms, Kale, and Sweet Potatoes

PER SERVING: 361 calories | 12g fat (2g saturated fat) | 5mg cholesterol | 560mg sodium | 13g protein | 51g carbohydrates | 6g fiber.

Tomato, Cucumber, and Quinoa Salad

PER SERVING: 194 calories | 12g fat (2g saturated fat) | 0mg cholesterol | 381mg sodium | 5g protein | 20g carbohydrates | 3g fiber.

Quinoa and Vegetable Salad with Tahini Dressing

PER SERVING: 376 calories | 15g fat (2g saturated fat) | 0mg cholesterol | 345mg sodium | 17g protein | 48g carbohydrates | 8g fiber.

RICOTTA

Radishes with Creamy Ricotta

PER SERVING: 141 calories | 11g fat (6g saturated fat) | 32mg cholesterol | 119mg sodium | 7g protein | 3g carbohydrates | 0g fiber.

Chard and Ricotta Frittata

PER SERVING: 330 calories | 24g fat (9g saturated fat) | 405mg cholesterol | 830mg sodium | 21g protein | 8g carbohydrates | 2g fiber.

Ricotta, Olive Oil, and Honey Toasts

PER SERVING: 210 calories | 7g fat (3g saturated fat) | 15mg cholesterol | 300mg sodium | 7g protein | 29g carbohydrates | 1g fiber.

Whipped Ricotta with Pomegranate and Mint

PER SERVING: 62 calories | 5g fat (3g saturated fat) | 16mg cholesterol | 146mg sodium | 4g protein | 2g carbohydrates | 0g fiber.

Orecchiette with Red Onions, Almonds, and Green Olives

PER SERVING: 730 calories | 35g fat (10g saturated fat) | 45mg cholesterol | 870mg sodium | 29g protein | 78g carbohydrates | 7g fiber.

Baked Ricotta with Parmesan and Herbs

PER SERVING: 210 calories | 18g fat (8g saturated fat) | 85mg cholesterol | 290mg sodium | 11g protein | 2g carbohydrates | 0g fiber.

Watermelon-Ricotta Bites

PER SERVING: 74 calories | 5g fat (2g saturated fat) | 10mg cholesterol | 316mg sodium | 2g protein | 7g carbohydrates | 0g fiber.

Ricotta Cheesecake

PER SERVING: 380 calories | 25g fat (15g saturated fat) | 130mg cholesterol | 250mg sodium | 16g protein | 23g carbohydrates | 0g fiber.

Wine-Poached Pears with Whipped Ricotta

PER SERVING: 210 calories | 7g fat (3g saturated fat) | 15mg cholesterol | 300mg sodium | 7g protein | 29g carbohydrates | 1g fiber.

Spaghetti with Ricotta and Tomatoes

PER SERVING: 492 calories | 12g fat (6g saturated fat) | 32mg cholesterol | 427mg sodium | 21g protein | 73g carbohydrates | 5g fiber.

ROTISSERIE CHICKEN

Gingery Peanut Noodles with Chicken

PER SERVING: 441 calories | 23g fat (4g saturated fat) | 47mg cholesterol | 1,189mg sodium | 29g protein | 34g carbohydrates | 4g fiber.

Chicken and Gruyère Turnovers
PER SERVING: 806 calories | 51g fat (18g saturated fat) | 131mg cholesterol | 931mg sodium | 38g protein | 45g carbohydrates | 3g fiber.

Chicken, Pesto, and Fried Egg Pizza
PER SERVING: 824 calories | 48g fat (15g saturated fat) | 299mg cholesterol | 1,135mg sodium | 44g protein | 59g carbohydrates | 3g fiber. ☕

Cajun Chicken and Rice
PER SERVING: 439 calories | 12g fat (2g saturated fat) | 47mg cholesterol | 539mg sodium | 23g protein | 59g carbohydrates | 5g fiber. ♠🍎🗑❋

Greek Lemon Soup with Chicken
PER SERVING: 274 calories | 11g fat (4g saturated fat) | 361mg cholesterol | 508mg sodium | 27g protein | 14g carbohydrates | 1g fiber. ☕🗑

Chicken and Tortellini Soup
PER SERVING: 328 calories | 8g fat (4g saturated fat) | 74mg cholesterol | 640mg sodium | 29g protein | 34g carbohydrates | 3g fiber. ☕🗑

Buffalo Chicken Sandwiches
PER SERVING: 574 calories | 26g fat (12g saturated fat) | 134mg cholesterol | 1,789mg sodium | 45g protein | 39g carbohydrates | 2g fiber. ☕🗑

Chicken and Quinoa Burritos
PER SERVING: 697 calories | 24g fat (9g saturated fat) | 58mg cholesterol | 1,377mg sodium | 38g protein | 85g carbohydrates | 15g fiber. ☕❋

Buttermilk Chicken and Tomato Salad
PER SERVING: 390 calories | 22g fat (4g saturated fat) | 129mg cholesterol | 336mg sodium | 42g protein | 5g carbohydrates | 1g fiber. ☕

Chicken Niçoise Salad
PER SERVING: 299 calories | 12g fat (3g saturated fat) | 254mg cholesterol | 460mg sodium | 25g protein | 22g carbohydrates | 5g fiber. ☕

SALAD GREENS

Herb Salad Mix with Tomatoes, Pepper, and Feta
PER SERVING: 276 calories | 22g fat (4g saturated fat) | 13mg cholesterol | 569mg sodium | 4g protein | 16g carbohydrates | 2g fiber. ☕🍎🍗

Endive and Radicchio with Grapes
PER SERVING: 218 calories | 19g fat (3g saturated fat) | 0mg cholesterol | 289mg sodium | 2g protein | 11g carbohydrates | 5g fiber. ☕🍎🍗⊘

Watercress with Beets and Fennel
PER SERVING: 208 calories | 16g fat (2.5g saturated fat) | 5mg cholesterol | 646mg sodium | 4g protein | 13g carbohydrates | 4g fiber. ☕🍗

Green Leaf with Chorizo and Apples
PER SERVING: 377 calories | 34g fat (10g saturated fat) | 40mg cholesterol | 579mg sodium | 12g protein | 7g carbohydrates | 2g fiber. ☕

Arugula with Peaches and Cheddar
PER SERVING: 273 calories | 27g fat (6g saturated fat) | 15mg cholesterol | 235mg sodium | 5g protein | 6g carbohydrates | 2g fiber. ☕🍗⊘

Romaine with Pickled Vegetables
PER SERVING: 222 calories | 17g fat (2g saturated fat) | 0mg cholesterol | 894mg sodium | 3g protein | 13g carbohydrates | 4g fiber. ☕🍗

Bibb with Radishes and Pine Nuts
PER SERVING: 129 calories | 12g fat (1.5g saturated fat) | 5mg cholesterol | 179mg sodium | 3g protein | 4g carbohydrates | 1g fiber. ☕🍗

Red Leaf with Roasted Red Peppers and Pecorino
PER SERVING: 229 calories | 21g fat (5g saturated fat) | 9mg cholesterol | 616mg sodium | 5g protein | 4g carbohydrates | 1g fiber. ☕🍗⊘

Frisée with Avocado and Blue Cheese
PER SERVING: 332 calories | 31g fat (6g saturated fat) | 11mg cholesterol | 365mg sodium | 7g protein | 10g carbohydrates | 8g fiber. ☕🍗

Spinach with Bacon and Croutons
PER SERVING: 150 calories | 9g fat (2g saturated fat) | 12mg cholesterol | 563mg sodium | 5g protein | 13g carbohydrates | 2g fiber. ☕

SALMON FILLETS

Roasted Salmon with Fennel and Carrots
PER SERVING: 320 calories | 13g fat (2g saturated fat) | 107mg cholesterol | 497mg sodium | 40g protein | 10g carbohydrates | 3g fiber. 🍎🗑⊘

Spiced Salmon Tacos with Cabbage Slaw
PER SERVING: 473 calories | 27g fat (4g saturated fat) | 72mg cholesterol | 451mg sodium | 30g protein | 30g carbohydrates | 7g fiber. ☕🍎⊘

Horseradish Salmon Burgers
PER SERVING: 656 calories | 43g fat (7g saturated fat) | 187mg cholesterol | 931mg sodium | 36g protein | 31g carbohydrates | 2g fiber. ☕

Mustard-Glazed Salmon with Peas
PER SERVING: 402 calories | 18g fat (4g saturated fat) | 116mg cholesterol | 614mg sodium | 45g protein | 11g carbohydrates | 3g fiber. ☕🍎⊘

Salmon, Radicchio, and Farro Salad
PER SERVING: 533 calories | 29g fat (4g saturated fat) | 54mg cholesterol | 421mg sodium | 27g protein | 46g carbohydrates | 5g fiber. ☕🍎🗑❋

Roasted Salmon with Pesto Vegetables
PER SERVING: 502 calories | 27g fat (5g saturated fat) | 112mg cholesterol | 701mg sodium | 44g protein | 20g carbohydrates | 2g fiber. ☕🍎🗑

Salmon and Arugula Salad
PER SERVING: 321 calories | 17g fat (2g saturated fat) | 54mg cholesterol | 585mg sodium | 25g protein | 17g carbohydrates | 4g fiber. ☕🍎🗑

Buttery Pasta with Salmon and Leeks
PER SERVING: 640 calories | 22g fat (9g saturated fat) | 102mg cholesterol | 429mg sodium | 39g protein | 71g carbohydrates | 5g fiber. ☕🗑

Spicy Salmon with Bok Choy and Rice

PER SERVING: 509 calories | 13g fat (2g saturated fat) | 107mg cholesterol | 363mg sodium | 44g protein | 52g carbohydrates | 2g fiber. ● ●

Salmon with Warm Tomatoes and Dill

PER SERVING: 526 calories | 20g fat (3g saturated fat) | 107mg cholesterol | 457mg sodium | 45g protein | 40g carbohydrates | 4g fiber. ● ●

SHRIMP

Spiced Shrimp with Beans

PER SERVING: 366 calories | 5g fat (1g saturated fat) | 143mg cholesterol | 1,024mg sodium | 28g protein | 52g carbohydrates | 7g fiber. ● 🍴

Shrimp and Hummus Sandwiches

PER SERVING: 360 calories | 12.5g fat (2g saturated fat) | 129mg cholesterol | 809mg sodium | 27g protein | 36g carbohydrates | 7g fiber. ●

Shrimp and Broccoli Tempura

PER SERVING: 562 calories | 9g fat (1g saturated fat) | 107mg cholesterol | 1,500mg sodium | 27g protein | 90g carbohydrates | 6g fiber. ●

Crispy Shrimp Cakes

PER SERVING: 473 calories | 35g fat (5g saturated fat) | 232mg cholesterol | 1,104mg sodium | 27g protein | 12g carbohydrates | 3g fiber.

Shrimp and Sausage with Polenta

PER SERVING: 573 calories | 34g fat (13g saturated fat) | 234mg cholesterol | 1,085mg sodium | 35g protein | 30g carbohydrates | 3g fiber. ● 🍴

Tandoori Shrimp with Rice and Peas

PER SERVING: 364 calories | 4.5g fat (2g saturated fat) | 180mg cholesterol | 469mg sodium | 30g protein | 48g carbohydrates | 2g fiber. ⊘

Shrimp and Mango Lettuce Wraps

PER SERVING: 277 calories | 14g fat (2g saturated fat) | 172mg cholesterol | 403mg sodium | 26g protein | 13g carbohydrates | 2g fiber. ● 🍴

Pasta with Shrimp and Spinach

PER SERVING: 524 calories | 14g fat (4g saturated fat) | 142mg cholesterol | 543mg sodium | 31g protein | 67g carbohydrates | 3g fiber. ● 🍴

Baked Risotto with Shrimp and Watercress

PER SERVING: 375 calories | 8g fat (4g saturated fat) | 187mg cholesterol | 813mg sodium | 30g protein | 43g carbohydrates | 3g fiber. 🍴

Shrimp and Vegetable Soup

PER SERVING: 248 calories | 9g fat (1g saturated fat) | 176mg cholesterol | 945mg sodium | 26g protein | 15g carbohydrates | 4g fiber. ● 🍴

SIRLOIN

Steak with Mozzarella and Tomatoes

PER SERVING: 294 calories | 14g fat (5g saturated fat) | 75mg cholesterol | 336mg sodium | 37g protein | 4g carbohydrates | 1g fiber. ● 🍴

Beef and Broccoli Stir-Fry

PER SERVING: 490 calories | 17g fat (3g saturated fat) | 42mg cholesterol | 181mg sodium | 33g protein | 53g carbohydrates | 5g fiber. ● 🍴

Steak Salad with Avocado and Onion

PER SERVING: 384 calories | 26g fat (6g saturated fat) | 52mg cholesterol | 663mg sodium | 29g protein | 10g carbohydrates | 5g fiber.

Thai Red Curry and Beef Soup

PER SERVING: 693 calories | 36g fat (23g saturated fat) | 47mg cholesterol | 1,197mg sodium | 32g protein | 62g carbohydrates | 4g fiber. ● 🍴

Steak with Mustard-Shallot Sauce

PER SERVING: 272 calories | 9g fat (3g saturated fat) | 63mg cholesterol | 617mg sodium | 36g protein | 11g carbohydrates | 4g fiber. ● ● ⊘

Herb-Crusted Steak with Fries

PER SERVING: 438 calories | 19g fat (9g saturated fat) | 134mg cholesterol | 710mg sodium | 40g protein | 23g carbohydrates | 2g fiber. ● ♣

Beef Paprikash with Egg Noodles

PER SERVING: 606 calories | 23g fat (9g saturated fat) | 131mg cholesterol | 384mg sodium | 36g protein | 61g carbohydrates | 5g fiber. 🍴

Open-Faced Steak Reubens

PER SERVING: 517 calories | 28g fat (10g saturated fat) | 82mg cholesterol | 1,235mg sodium | 38g protein | 27g carbohydrates | 5g fiber. ●

Chicken-Fried Steak with Carrot Slaw

PER SERVING: 607 calories | 34g fat (6g saturated fat) | 76mg cholesterol | 487mg sodium | 40g protein | 34g carbohydrates | 3g fiber. ● ♣

Spiced Beef Kebabs with Yogurt

PER SERVING: 443 calories | 11g fat (3g saturated fat) | 64mg cholesterol | 776mg sodium | 41g protein | 42g carbohydrates | 3g fiber. ● ●

SMOKED SALMON

Smoked Salmon on Crispy Crushed Potatoes with Dill

PER SERVING: 260 calories | 16g fat (5g saturated fat) | 25mg cholesterol | 230mg sodium | 8g protein | 19g carbohydrates | 3g fiber. ●

Deviled Eggs with Smoked Salmon and Fried Capers

PER SERVING: 270 calories | 23g fat (5g saturated fat) | 290mg cholesterol | 740mg sodium | 12g protein | 2g carbohydrates | 0g fiber. ●

Smoked Salmon and Horseradish Cream

PER SERVING: 295 calories | 23g fat (11g saturated fat) | 74mg cholesterol | 592mg sodium | 17g protein | 11g carbohydrates | 1g fiber. ● ▬

Smoked Salmon Pizzettes

PER SERVING: 512 calories | 18g fat (6g saturated fat) | 60mg cholesterol | 772mg sodium | 28g protein | 63g carbohydrates | 2g fiber.

Salmon "Tartare" and Avocado with Sesame Dressing

PER SERVING: 120 calories | 9g fat (1.5g saturated fat) | 5mg cholesterol | 550mg sodium | 7g protein | 5g carbohydrates | 4g fiber. ● ●

Smoked Salmon, Yogurt, and Radish Tartine with Chives
PER SERVING: 140 calories | 3.5g fat (1.5g saturated fat) | 10mg cholesterol | 440mg sodium | 9g protein | 16g carbohydrates | 2g fiber. ●

Creamy Smoked Salmon Dip
PER SERVING: 120 calories | 10g fat (6g saturated fat) | 35mg cholesterol | 330mg sodium | 4g protein | 2g carbohydrates | 0g fiber. ●

Smoked Salmon and Pickled Vegetable Salad
PER SERVING: 60 calories | 1.5g fat (1g saturated fat) | 5mg cholesterol | 720mg sodium | 6g protein | 7g carbohydrates | 2g fiber. ● ●

Smoked Salmon Potato Bites
PER SERVING: 151 calories | 8g fat (2g saturated fat) | 22mg cholesterol | 268mg sodium | 10g protein | 10g carbohydrates | 1g fiber. ● ▬

Smoked Salmon with Creamy Cucumber Salad
PER SERVING: 156 calories | 7g fat (3g saturated fat) | 31mg cholesterol | 871mg sodium | 15g protein | 6g carbohydrates | 1g fiber. ● ● ▬

SPAGHETTI

Cauliflower and Ricotta Spaghetti
PER SERVING: 607 calories | 20g fat (5g saturated fat) | 21mg cholesterol | 1,123mg sodium | 23g protein | 80g carbohydrates | 9g fiber.

Kimchi Chicken Noodle Soup
PER SERVING: 505 calories | 18g fat (4g saturated fat) | 82mg cholesterol | 861mg sodium | 36g protein | 48g carbohydrates | 4g fiber. ▮

Creamy Brussels Sprouts Spaghetti
PER SERVING: 519 calories | 19g fat (11g saturated fat) | 50mg cholesterol | 271mg sodium | 15g protein | 73g carbohydrates | 7g fiber. ● ▮ ☂

Cold Sesame Noodles
PER SERVING: 550 calories | 24g fat (4g saturated fat) | 0mg cholesterol | 543mg sodium | 16g protein | 69g carbohydrates | 5g fiber. ● ▮ ☂

Mushroom and Radicchio Spaghetti
PER SERVING: 561 calories | 21g fat (7g saturated fat) | 33mg cholesterol | 785mg sodium | 21g protein | 71g carbohydrates | 4g fiber. ● ▮ ☂

Shrimp and Tarragon Spaghetti
PER SERVING: 581 calories | 19g fat (8g saturated fat) | 202mg cholesterol | 415mg sodium | 35g protein | 66g carbohydrates | 4g fiber. ● ▮

Mexican Taco-Bowl Spaghetti
PER SERVING: 474 calories | 15g fat (4g saturated fat) | 33mg cholesterol | 650mg sodium | 22g protein | 64g carbohydrates | 6g fiber. ● ● ▮ ♣

Bacon and Escarole Spaghetti
PER SERVING: 540 calories | 16g fat (5g saturated fat) | 16mg cholesterol | 875mg sodium | 18g protein | 78g carbohydrates | 10g fiber. ● ▮

Crispy Chickpea and Caper Spaghetti
PER SERVING: 541 calories | 16g fat (2g saturated fat) | 0mg cholesterol | 641mg sodium | 16g protein | 82g carbohydrates | 7g fiber. ▮ ☂

Artichoke and Sardine Spaghetti
PER SERVING: 727 calories | 35g fat (7g saturated fat) | 54mg cholesterol | 742mg sodium | 30g protein | 73g carbohydrates | 8g fiber. ● ▮

TILAPIA

Blackened Tilapia with Buttered Carrots
PER SERVING: 686 calories | 27g fat (9g saturated fat) | 172mg cholesterol | 1,165mg sodium | 43g protein | 70g carbohydrates | 6g fiber. ● ● ♣

Fish Tacos with Cucumber Relish
PER SERVING: 363 calories | 12g fat (4g saturated fat) | 83mg cholesterol | 466mg sodium | 38g protein | 28g carbohydrates | 4g fiber. ● ● ♣ ⊘

Teriyaki Tilapia with Herb Salad
PER SERVING: 400 calories | 5g fat (2g saturated fat) | 73mg cholesterol | 773mg sodium | 40g protein | 49g carbohydrates | 4g fiber. ● ❄

Garlicky Grilled Tilapia with Couscous
PER SERVING: 337 calories | 7g fat (2g saturated fat) | 64mg cholesterol | 331mg sodium | 32g protein | 38g carbohydrates | 2g fiber. ● ● ♣

Dijon Fish Cakes with Greens
PER SERVING: 633 calories | 49g fat (7g saturated fat) | 188mg cholesterol | 804mg sodium | 38g protein | 11g carbohydrates | 1g fiber.

Crispy Fish Sticks with Coleslaw
PER SERVING: 552 calories | 27g fat (6g saturated fat) | 193mg cholesterol | 1,142mg sodium | 41g protein | 38g carbohydrates | 2g fiber. ● ♣

Tilapia Salad with Apples and Almonds
PER SERVING: 395 calories | 21g fat (3g saturated fat) | 73mg cholesterol | 517mg sodium | 39g protein | 18g carbohydrates | 10g fiber. ● ● ▮ ⊘

Tilapia Po'boys
PER SERVING: 821 calories | 39g fat (7g saturated fat) | 60mg cholesterol | 1,567mg sodium | 39g protein | 80g carbohydrates | 4g fiber. ● ♣

Prosciutto-Wrapped Tilapia
PER SERVING: 305 calories | 15g fat (3g saturated fat) | 84mg cholesterol | 694mg sodium | 38g protein | 5g carbohydrates | 2g fiber. ● ●

Tilapia with Caper-Parsley Sauce
PER SERVING: 444 calories | 18g fat (9g saturated fat) | 103mg cholesterol | 488mg sodium | 37g protein | 30g carbohydrates | 3g fiber. ⊘

TOMATOES

Tomato Soup with Parmesan and Croutons
PER SERVING: 260 calories | 13g fat (4g saturated fat) | 16mg cholesterol | 1,150mg sodium | 13g protein | 20g carbohydrates | 3g fiber. ● ▮ ♣

Tomato, Cantaloupe, and Mint Salad
PER SERVING: 181 calories | 7g fat (1g saturated fat) | 0mg cholesterol | 152mg sodium | 2g protein | 26g carbohydrates | 2g fiber. ● ☂ ⊘

Baked Tomatoes Provençal
PER SERVING: 180 calories | 11g fat (3g saturated fat) | 10mg cholesterol | 628mg sodium | 8g protein | 13g carbohydrates | 3g fiber. ● ☂

Tomato, Corn, and Red Cabbage Salad

PER SERVING: 228 calories | 15g fat (2g saturated fat) | 0mg cholesterol | 274mg sodium | 5g protein | 26g carbohydrates | 7g fiber.

Mediterranean Pasta Salad

PER SERVING: 305 calories | 13g fat (2g saturated fat) | 19mg cholesterol | 1,135mg sodium | 13g protein | 35g carbohydrates | 2g fiber.

Roasted Tomatoes and Fennel

PER SERVING: 145 calories | 11g fat (1g saturated fat) | 0mg cholesterol | 186mg sodium | 2g protein | 13g carbohydrates | 5g fiber.

Tomatoes with Ranch Dressing

PER SERVING: 182 calories | 15g fat (4g saturated fat) | 19mg cholesterol | 404mg sodium | 3g protein | 7g carbohydrates | 2g fiber.

Tomato and Rye Panzanella

PER SERVING: 325 calories | 26g fat (7g saturated fat) | 13mg cholesterol | 627mg sodium | 6g protein | 16g carbohydrates | 8g fiber.

Curried Tomatoes and Chickpeas

PER SERVING: 158 calories | 8g fat (1g saturated fat) | 0mg cholesterol | 386mg sodium | 6g protein | 18g carbohydrates | 5g fiber.

Sautéed Tomatoes, Sausage, and Okra

PER SERVING: 195 calories | 15g fat (4g saturated fat) | 24mg cholesterol | 697mg sodium | 9g protein | 9g carbohydrates | 3g fiber.

TORTILLAS

Beef and Pineapple Tacos

PER SERVING: 352 calories | 13g fat (4g saturated fat) | 71mg cholesterol | 578mg sodium | 28g protein | 33g carbohydrates | 4g fiber.

Spiced Tortilla Crisps with Hummus

PER SERVING: 215 calories | 11g fat (2.5g saturated fat) | 0mg cholesterol | 681mg sodium | 4g protein | 26g carbohydrates | 1g fiber.

Shrimp and Avocado Tostadas

PER SERVING: 556 calories | 28g fat (3.5g saturated fat) | 344mg cholesterol | 876mg sodium | 47g protein | 32g carbohydrates | 10g fiber.

Margherita Tortilla Pizzas

PER SERVING: 360 calories | 21g fat (8g saturated fat) | 24mg cholesterol | 885mg sodium | 16g protein | 29g carbohydrates | 4g fiber.

Salami and Roasted Red Pepper Wraps

PER SERVING: 476 calories | 35g fat (14g saturated fat) | 58mg cholesterol | 1,129mg sodium | 14g protein | 28g carbohydrates | 7g fiber.

Quesadillas Rancheros

PER SERVING: 744 calories | 48g fat (23g saturated fat) | 260mg cholesterol | 1,282mg sodium | 32g protein | 47g carbohydrates | 6g fiber.

Chicken Salad with Crispy Tortillas

PER SERVING: 361 calories | 14g fat (2.5g saturated fat) | 92mg cholesterol | 510mg sodium | 35g protein | 24g carbohydrates | 6g fiber.

Bean and Cheese Taquitos

PER SERVING: 284 calories | 13g fat (5.5g saturated fat) | 23mg cholesterol | 320mg sodium | 10g protein | 32g carbohydrates | 6g fiber.

Cinnamon Tortilla Sundaes

PER SERVING: 215 calories | 9g fat (5g saturated fat) | 15mg cholesterol | 486mg sodium | 4g protein | 29g carbohydrates | 1g fiber.

Chilaquiles

PER SERVING: 140 calories | 5g fat (2g saturated fat) | 8mg cholesterol | 493mg sodium | 4g protein | 21g carbohydrates | 3g fiber.

ZUCCHINI

Pan-Fried Chicken Cutlets with Zucchini Salad

PER SERVING: 527 calories | 27g fat (5g saturated fat) | 200mg cholesterol | 525mg sodium | 42g protein | 29g carbohydrates | 2g fiber.

Zucchini and Corn Pizzas

PER SERVING: 491 calories | 20g fat (6g saturated fat) | 32mg cholesterol | 943mg sodium | 19g protein | 61g carbohydrates | 4g fiber.

Zucchini Gazpacho with Basil and Yogurt

PER SERVING: 439 calories | 42g fat (6g saturated fat) | 4mg cholesterol | 512mg sodium | 4g protein | 16g carbohydrates | 3g fiber.

Gnocchi with Zucchini, Red Chilies, and Parmesan

PER SERVING: 352 calories | 12g fat (3g saturated fat) | 10mg cholesterol | 891mg sodium | 14g protein | 51g carbohydrates | 7g fiber.

Zucchini and Sausage Frittata

PER SERVING: 383 calories | 29g fat (10g saturated fat) | 454mg cholesterol | 948mg sodium | 23g protein | 7g carbohydrates | 2g fiber.

Turkey, Cheddar, and Grilled Zucchini Sandwich

PER SERVING: 542 calories | 28g fat (8g saturated fat) | 51mg cholesterol | 1,491mg sodium | 25g protein | 48g carbohydrates | 5g fiber.

Fried Zucchini with Chive Mayo

PER SERVING: 555 calories | 38g fat (6g saturated fat) | 74mg cholesterol | 853mg sodium | 11g protein | 44g carbohydrates | 2g fiber.

Seared Snapper with Sautéed Zucchini and Tomatoes

PER SERVING: 439 calories | 42g fat (6g saturated fat) | 4mg cholesterol | 512mg sodium | 4g protein | 16g carbohydrates | 3g fiber.

Steak and Zucchini with Greek Beans

PER SERVING: 437 calories | 24g fat (8g saturated fat) | 91mg cholesterol | 894mg sodium | 43g protein | 16g carbohydrates | 5g fiber.

Roasted Zucchini, Potato, and Burrata Salad

PER SERVING: 518 calories | 33g fat (10g saturated fat) | 40mg cholesterol | 581mg sodium | 19g protein | 39g carbohydrates | 5g fiber.

COOKIES, BARS, AND BEYOND

Tangy Lemon Bars
PER SERVING: 117 calories | 5g fat (3g saturated fat) | 47mg cholesterol | 40mg sodium | 2g protein | 16g carbohydrates | 0g fiber.

Jam and Pistachio Icebox Cookies
PER SERVING: 73 calories | 4g fat (2g saturated fat) | 9mg cholesterol | 16mg sodium | 1g protein | 8g carbohydrates | 0g fiber.

Double Chocolate Chip Cookies
PER SERVING: 91 calories | 4g fat (2g saturated fat) | 13mg cholesterol | 62mg sodium | 1mg protein | 13g carbohydrates | 1g fiber.

Black and White Cookies
PER SERVING: 344 calories | 10g fat (6g saturated fat) | 52mg cholesterol | 133mg sodium | 4g protein | 60g carbohydrates | 1g fiber.

Buckeyes
PER SERVING: 134 calories | 9g fat (4g saturated fat) | 8mg cholesterol | 47mg sodium | 2g protein | 13g carbohydrates | 1g fiber.

Salted Oatmeal Cookies with Dark Chocolate
PER SERVING: 163 calories | 9g fat (4g saturated fat) | 18mg cholesterol | 228mg sodium | 2g protein | 20g carbohydrates | 1g fiber.

Chocolate-Dipped Marshmallows
PER SERVING: 57 calories | 2g fat (1g saturated fat) | 0mg cholesterol | 6mg sodium | 1g protein | 9g carbohydrates | 0g fiber.

Pecan Bars
PER SERVING: 199 calories | 13g fat (5g saturated fat) | 17mg cholesterol | 24mg sodium | 2g protein | 20g carbohydrates | 1g fiber.

Sugared Pecan Balls
PER SERVING: 120 calories | 9g fat (4g saturated fat) | 13mg cholesterol | 54mg sodium | 1g protein | 8g carbohydrates | 1g fiber.

Cacao Nib and Pumpkin Seed Toffee
PER SERVING: 443 calories | 32g fat (16g saturated fat) | 46mg cholesterol | 133mg sodium | 5g protein | 40g carbohydrates | 5g fiber.

CUPCAKES

Gingerbread Cupcakes with Lemon Cream Cheese Frosting
PER SERVING: 330 calories | 16g fat (10g saturated fat) | 65mg cholesterol | 170mg sodium | 3g protein | 44g carbohydrates | 0g fiber.

Hot Chocolate Cupcakes with Marshmallow Frosting
PER SERVING: 270 calories | 5g fat (1g saturated fat) | 20mg cholesterol | 120mg sodium | 4g protein | 55g carbohydrates | 1g fiber.

Snickerdoodle Cupcakes
PER SERVING: 390 calories | 24g fat (15g saturated fat) | 85mg cholesterol | 115mg sodium | 3g protein | 42g carbohydrates | 0g fiber.

Salted Caramel Cupcakes
PER SERVING: 300 calories | 12g fat (8g saturated fat) | 45mg cholesterol | 230mg sodium | 3g protein | 46g carbohydrates | 0g fiber.

Lemon Cupcakes
PER SERVING: 318 calories | 16g fat (10g saturated fat) | 76mg cholesterol | 167mg sodium | 3g protein | 40g carbohydrates | 1g fiber.

Maple-Pumpkin Cupcakes
PER SERVING: 259 calories | 12g fat (3.5g saturated fat) | 31mg cholesterol | 216mg sodium | 3g protein | 37g carbohydrates | 1g fiber.

Double Chocolate Cupcakes (Vegan)
PER SERVING: 187 calories | 8g fat (2g saturated fat) | 0mg cholesterol | 202mg sodium | 3g protein | 29g carbohydrates | 3g fiber.

Almond Thumbprint Cupcakes (Gluten-Free)
PER SERVING: 270 calories | 14g fat (3.5g saturated fat) | 40mg cholesterol | 115mg sodium | 6g protein | 31g carbohydrates | 2g fiber.

Peanut Butter Cupcakes
PER SERVING: 444 calories | 22g fat (8g saturated fat) | 53mg cholesterol | 288mg sodium | 9g protein | 55g carbohydrates | 2g fiber.

Carrot Cake Cupcakes
PER SERVING: 449 calories | 27g fat (8g saturated fat) | 48mg cholesterol | 253mg sodium | 5g protein | 50g carbohydrates | 2g fiber.

PIES

Gingery Pumpkin Pie
PER SERVING: 370 calories | 22g fat (13g saturated fat) | 114mg cholesterol | 211mg sodium | 5g protein | 40g carbohydrates | 3g fiber.

Cranberry-Apple Pie
PER SERVING: 379 calories | 18g fat (11g saturated fat) | 45mg cholesterol | 186mg sodium | 4g protein | 58g carbohydrates | 4g fiber.

Chocolate-Whiskey Pecan Pie
PER SERVING: 717 calories | 43g fat (16g saturated fat) | 124mg cholesterol | 252mg sodium | 8g protein | 81g carbohydrates | 4g fiber.

Raspberry Buttermilk Pie
PER SERVING: 480 calories | 29g fat (16g saturated fat) | 195mg cholesterol | 234mg sodium | 7g protein | 51g carbohydrates | 1g fiber.

Shoofly Pie
PER SERVING: 488 calories | 18g fat (11g saturated fat) | 72mg cholesterol | 372mg sodium | 5g protein | 78g carbohydrates | 1g fiber.

Lemon Cheesecake Pie
PER SERVING: 556 calories | 38g fat (23g saturated fat) | 163mg cholesterol | 390mg sodium | 9g protein | 46g carbohydrates | 1g fiber.

Peanut Butter Pie
PER SERVING: 602 calories | 47g fat (21g saturated fat) | 92mg cholesterol | 359mg sodium | 12g protein | 38g carbohydrates | 3g fiber.

Sweet Potato Pie
PER SERVING: 431 calories | 30g fat (18g saturated fat) | 139mg cholesterol | 223mg sodium | 5g protein | 38g carbohydrates | 2g fiber.

Coconut Custard Pie
PER SERVING: 471 calories | 30g fat (21g saturated fat) | 124mg cholesterol | 255mg sodium | 8g protein | 46g carbohydrates | 1g fiber.

Chocolate Cream Pie
PER SERVING: 610 calories | 41g fat (25g saturated fat) | 170mg cholesterol | 228mg sodium | 8g protein | 56g carbohydrates | 1g fiber.

Basic Flaky Piecrust
PER SERVING: 178 calories | 12g fat (7g saturated fat) | 30mg cholesterol | 122mg sodium | 2g protein | 16g carbohydrates | 1g fiber.

Credits

REAL SIMPLE

EDITOR Kristin van Ogtrop

EXECUTIVE EDITOR Sarah Collins

DEPUTY MANAGING EDITOR
Jacklyn Monk

EDITOR, REALSIMPLE.COM
Lori Leibovich

DESIGN DIRECTOR
Abbey Kuster-Prokell

PHOTO DIRECTOR Casey Stenger

GROUP PUBLISHER
Charles R. Kammerer

PUBLISHER Cece Ryan

ASSOCIATE PUBLISHER Julie DeGarmo

EXECUTIVE DIRECTOR DIGITAL
Meg Power

VICE PRESIDENT, MARKETING Kim Tan

**VICE PRESIDENT, CONSUMER
MARKETING** Amy Buckley

GENERAL MANAGER, REALSIMPLE.COM
Lindsay Jerutis

**EXECUTIVE DIRECTOR, BRAND
LICENSING** Tanya Isler

SPECIAL THANKS

RECIPE DEVELOPERS AND TESTERS:
Stacy Adimando, Kay Chun, Sarah
Copeland, Kristen Evans Dittami,
Gina Marie Miraglia Eriquez, Heath
Goldman, Katherine Greenwald,
Lindsay Hunt, Diana Hyle, Jane Kirby,
Genevieve Ko, Sue Li, Charlyne
Mattox, Emily McKenna, Kate
Merker, Ben Mims, Chris Morocco,
Nancy Myers, Cynthia Nicholson,
Greg Patent, Rebekah Peppler, Dawn
Perry, Sara Quessenberry, Samantha
Seneviratne, Anna Stockwell, Susie
Theodorou

FOOD STYLISTS: Christine Albano,
Michelle Gatton, Victoria Granof,
Rebecca Jurkevich, Ana Kelly, Chris
Lanier, Cyd McDowell, Chris Morocco,
Dawn Perry, Brian Preston-Campbell,
Sara Quessenberry, Maggie Ruggiero,
Susan Spungen, Catherine Steele,
Susan Sugarman

PROP STYLISTS: Liz Adler, Tiziana
Agnello, Angharad Bailey, Jessica Baude,
Linden Elstran, Carla Gonzalez-Hart,
Jeffrey W. Miller, Olivia Sammons, Loren
Simons, Deborah Williams, Amy Wilson

PHOTO CREDITS

COVER: Raymond Hom, Danny Kim,
Charles Masters, David Prince,
Paul Sirisalee

BACK COVER: Iain Bagwell, Christopher
Baker, Raymond Hom, Danny Kim,
Charles Masters, Paul Sirisalee

SANG AN: 197, 304 (left)

IAIN BAGWELL: 20-21, 23 (left), 24
(right), 52-53, 54 (right), 101, 102 (left),
124, 127 (left), 148, 150, 151 (right),
152, 153 (left), 172-174, 175 (right),
186, 188, 190 (right), 191 (right), 192
(right), 193-194, 198 (right), 200, 201
(right), 250, 254, 257 (right), 314
(right), 315 (left)

CHRISTOPHER BAKER: 18, 25 (right),
149, 204

ROLAND BELLO: 305 (right)

LEVI BROWN: 25 (left), 98, 100, 103
(left), 104-105, 205, 206 (left), 207
(right), 208, 209 (left), 307

GRANT CORNETT: 178, 180-185

JOSEPH DE LEO: 313 (right),314 (left)

PHILIP FRIEDMAN: 300, 303, 304
(right), 307 (right)

RAYMOND HOM: 130, 132-137, 226,
228-233

KAN KANBAYASHI: 306

JOHN KERNICK: 324

DANNY KIM: 42, 44-50, 57, 162, 164-169,
191 (left), 192 (left), 199, 206 (right),
252-253, 255-256, 257 (left), 258,
260-265, 290, 292-297

EMILY KINNI: 310-312

JOHN LAWTON: 305 (left)

CHARLES MASTERS: 24 (left), 34, 36-41,
106, 108-114, 116-121, 196, 198 (left),
266, 268-273, 282, 284-289, 313

KATE MATHIS: 207 (left)

JOHNNY MILLER: 1-10, 16-17, 102 (right),
298-299, 352

MARCUS NILSSON: 128 (right)

KANA OKADA: 138, 140-145

JOSÉ PICAYO: 23 (right), 54 (left), 56
(left), 125, 126 (left), 308, 315

DAVID PRINCE: 22 (right), 58, 60-65,
174, 175 (left)

TOM SCHIERLITZ: 122, 128 (left), 129,
202, 209 (right)

VICTOR SCHRAGER: 302, 306

PAUL SIRISALEE: 22 (left), 26, 28-33,
55, 56 (right), 66, 68-74, 76-82, 84-90,
92-97, 103 (right), 126 (right), 127
(right), 154, 156-161, 170, 176-177, 190
(left), 201 (left), 218, 220-225, 234,
236-242, 244-249, 274, 276-281, 316,
318-323

CHRISTOPHER TESTANI: 146,151 (left),
153 (right),189

JOHNNY VALIANT: 199

ROMULO YANES: 210, 212-217

Index

Delicious work! Now leave the dishes to someone else.